THE LEADERSHIP BRAIN

THE LEADERSHIP BRAIN

PETER SHEPHARD

PARTRIDGE
A Penguin Random House Company

To order additional copies of this book, contact
Toll Free 800 101 2657 (Singapore)
Toll Free 1 800 81 7340 (Malaysia)
orders.singapore@partridgepublishing.com

www.partridgepublishing.com/singapore

THE LEADERSHIP BRAIN

TABLE OF CONTENTS

ACKNOWLEDGEMENTS

The writing of a book – let alone – a series of books, would rarely, if ever, be achieved as a solo effort. This series of books, based on the 'Whole Brain' model is very much of a team effort and that it is the various members of the team that I owe a great debt to and acknowledge my gratitude to them.

First, I want to acknowledge the persistence, patience and tireless help of my associates at the CREDO Trust. They all, either directly or indirectly, facilitated this project, sometimes with the inevitable stress that comes from sharing the scarce resources of space, time and computers.

A special thanks goes to Esther Appadurai who did most of the production and typesetting of text and graphics. Thanks also to Christine Keong for her help with some of editing of text.

Further acknowledgements go to our team of typesetters, Nurul Hidaya, Owen Munkombwe and Christinna Vanathyar, co-ordinated by Esther Appadurai. Also, thanks to the book cover design team, Owen Munkombwe, and Michelo Hambayi who's ideas contributed to the final design.

To those, too many to name here, who over the recent years have recommended or provided various resources for the book content and design, I also wish to thank.

Additionally, I thank the CREDO Trust for providing library facilities for my research. Also, not forgetting the support from the publisher and printer, who gently reminded me of upcoming deadlines.

Finally, a great big thank you to my wife, Asma, who having completed her Ph.D. in the area of culture and management, has shared valuable insights on many cultural 'puzzles'.

FOREWORD

This is the best book I have read on leadership, the brain and diversity for a long time. It is overflowing with concepts, ideas and insights. It also includes many how to's, tools and techniques to use in becoming a more effective leader.

What makes this book so rich is the context in which Peter deals with leadership and **Neuro Science**. He looks at the key issues of diversity and the effect it has on leadership. He also deals with diversity from two different yet related perspectives, mental diversity and cultural diversity, as well as gender and personality.

Peter is an expert in diversity, as he has worked with Whole Brain Technology for over 20 years. He is practiced in its application to both business and education, and this work has been done in many of the most culturally diverse parts of the world – Asia, Africa and in the Middle East. His experience, knowledge and insights are evident throughout the book.

Peter's seventh book in a range of Whole Brain Behaviour and Learning, looks at the way our effects the way we lead. This book builds on that understanding as he examines the issues of leadership, motivation and team work – across mentally and culturally diverse work groups.

I congratulate Peter in taking many new and sometimes controversial pieces of the jigsaw puzzle, such as behaviourial genetics, gender or cultural differences in leading and helping us get a more complete picture. Of course there are still many unknown pieces to put together. And this may always be the case, because people and cultures are dynamic, changing and rarely static.

Michael Morgan
CEO
Herrmann International Asia

PREFACE

Leadership is usually thought of as an interaction between a leader and follower, which gives rise to the concept of followership. But can we also lead ourselves (self leadership)? After all an entrepreneur, a father or mother with the children, even the chairman of the board have no one to lead them, so they must be able to lead themselves, before leading others. Effective self leadership should precede the leading of others.

This book aims to cater for all types of individuals who aspire to lead themselves or others, more effectively. The book therefore logically starts with each of us as an individual personality, with our unique inherited traits (Nature) and the culture, upbringing or environment that stimulates or shapes us (Nurture). Thus our learning, thinking or behaviour is influenced by our genetically predisposed strong personality traits, and the culture into which we are born – or find ourselves moving in and out of, call it experience of you will. Yet still modified by our learning and thinking styles and skills – including perceptions, motivation and values. So we address the perennial debate of whether leaders are born or developed.

Modern evolution has seen eras of history that has shaped our views of leadership, from Heroes and 'great' people, to the 'humble' small business entrepreneurial leader. If you ask yourself who are these heroes, we can go back thousands of years and names like Gengis Khan, Alexander the Great, Caesar, Jesus, Prophet Muhammad and Napolean, to contemporary times, like Churchill, Hitler, JFK, The Pope, Chairman Mao, Gandhi, Mother Theresa, Mandela, Margaret Thatcher, Jack Welch, Warren Buffet, Bill Gates and Richard Branson. Thus leaders can be in the Military, Politics, Economics, Science, Academia or Business. They can lead Religious, Terrorist, Mafia, Multinational or government organisations.

Historically we've gone from an era of control to empowerment. From where a few elite, well educated, aristocratic leaders directed the masses who were uneducated and largely illiterate manual workers, to an era where the masses are better educated, well informed and technologically literate.

Leadership has moved from being merely an art or skill to being more scientific. It now requires a strategic as well as an innovative and global mindset. It is all about change in an increasingly complex, unstable, unpredictable and fast moving technological world. We now need thought leaders who can interact with people from all levels, and motivate and inspire a diverse mix of people, as well as themselves.

Considerable research has been published in this quest, mostly in the West, with European and North American theories and models emerging. Unfortunately, less research has been done on, or within, the African, Asian, Middle Eastern and Oriental cultures, except perhaps on the Japanese culture. This book attempts to contrast some of these cultural paradigms of leadership.

Why I have included cognitive and behavioural neuroscience as a factor is based on the fact that leadership is all about behaviour, and our behaviour is directed by our brain. I have also selected the 'Whole Brain' model, as a well accepted way for behaviour to be more easily understood.

While we are a coalition of both brain hemispheres, each representing a cluster of mental and emotional preferences, some are preferred more naturally and strongly than others. This is what we call 'Brain Dominance', where each of us can differ slightly or significantly in our behaviourial preferences. This is the result of both nature (genetic) and nurture (environmental) influences. Such influences do affect our styles of leadership.

This Whole Brain Model combines the concepts that we not only have a left and right hemisphere of our brain, but 'thinking' or cerebral modes, as well as 'emotional' or limbic modes. Thus, we can say we have left and right thinking selves, as well left and right emotional selves. In addition, some of us are more balanced and are more comfortable integrating these parts of our brain so fast, that there doesn't seem like a 'dominance' of any one.

The focus of the book is also on Personality, Gender and Culture. Due to the growing impact of globalization, especially in business leadership and management, many of us find our selves working with people of diverse cultural and ethnic backgrounds. Working in or leading teams – sometimes in virtual teams that are global – we may experience increasing diversity of personality, gender, ethnicity or age among our co-workers. However, all behaviour is influenced first by how our brains work, and continue to develop.

One philosophy of this book is that leadership, motivation and teambuilding each overlap and are inter-dependent. We cannot separate them. Another philosophy is that due to such diversity, there may be no credence to a 'one best' style or 'fit' in terms of leadership or motivation theory. While the book attempts to contrast certain African, Asian, Eastern and 'Western' models, it realises that it can be unwise to generalize or stereotype such behaviours of leaders as 'either-or'. It takes the position that our preferred styles in using power, communication or enhancing employee performance, may equally be influenced by our personality, by our brain dominance, or by our ethno-cultural self.

Just as leadership at CEO or front-line level would differ in demands. Yet assuming we could isolate certain qualities, what would be the ones more common to all types and all levels? This book attempts to identify these within the WholeBrain model.

Peter C. Shephard, Ph.d., D.Litt.

INTRODUCTION

Many theories of leadership have been developed in the west, especially the classic ones from Ohio and Michigan University studies, McGregor's Theory X and Y, Grid Leadership (Blake & Mouton, 1980) or from Love or Servant Leadership (Autry,1991 & Greenleaf, 1998) to Quantum leadership (Wheatley,1999) and Eastern theories from Tzun Zhu 's Art of War, The Tao of Leadership (Heider 1985). Intuition, Ethics and Ecology (Parikh, 1994), Spiritual leadership, (Hawley,1993). Finally, Global Leadership models like TQM, Knowledge Management, Learning Organizations, Balanced Score Card, Blue Ocean Strategy, Whole Brain Leadership, Behavioural Genetics and Gender and Generational Differences have all contributed to the enormously wide range of leadership theories

THE MANY TYPES OF LEADER

And you can be more than one or these

1. Academic   -   Chancellor, Vice Chancellor, Dean and Professor
2. Business   -   Chairman, Director, Manager
3. Economic   -   Chief Economist, Economic Advisor
4. Entrepreneurial   -   Founder, Owner, Inventor
5. Global   -   UN, IMF, Chairman/CEO of an MNC
6. Government   -   Minister, Deputy Minister etc.
7. Local   -   Mayor, CEO of a National/State Company
8. Military   -   Field Marshal, General – Most Officers
9. Musical   -   Conductor, Band Leader
10. Parental   -   Mother, Father, Guardian
11. Political   -   Prime Minister, Deputy, President, MP
12. Religious-Spiritual -   Imam, Dalai Lama, Pope, Bishop, Guru
13. School   -   Principal, Assistant Headmaster/Mistress
14. Social   -   NGO, Charity, Social Entrepreneur
15. Youth   -   Youth Association Leader (eg Scouts/Girls Guides etc)

And many more

There are leaders of global, transnational, multinational or regional organisations.
There are non-government organizational (NGO's) commercial (profit centred) enterprises (firms) and Not-for-Profit or Charitable associations/trusts/foundations. Also professional associations (Professional/Trade) government owned or linked corporations, councils, committees, teams and task forces.

THE COMMON FACTORS ARE PEOPLE AND
All Require Effective Leadership!!

The Octagon of 8 modes in the
WHOLE BRAIN MODEL

Our Cerebral or Thinking Modes

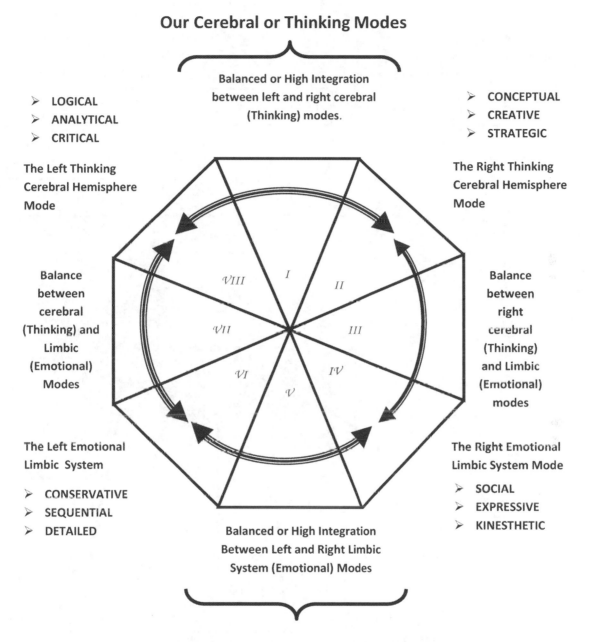

Balanced or High Integration between left and right cerebral (Thinking) modes.

> LOGICAL
> ANALYTICAL
> CRITICAL

The Left Thinking Cerebral Hemisphere Mode

> CONCEPTUAL
> CREATIVE
> STRATEGIC

The Right Thinking Cerebral Hemisphere Mode

Balance between cerebral (Thinking) and Limbic (Emotional) Modes

Balance between right cerebral (Thinking) and Limbic (Emotional) modes

The Left Emotional Limbic System

> CONSERVATIVE
> SEQUENTIAL
> DETAILED

The Right Emotional Limbic System Mode

> SOCIAL
> EXPRESSIVE
> KINESTHETIC

Balanced or High Integration Between Left and Right Limbic System (Emotional) Modes

Our Limbic System Or Emotional Modes

Most people are a coalition of all 8 segments but usually have a natural inclination to use some more than others

THE MANY INFLUENCES ON LEADERSHIP STYLE

MORE NATURE (GENETIC)

MORE NURTURE (CULTURE)

CHAPTER ONE

LEADING THE WHOLEBRAIN WAY
(Transformational Leadership)

LEARNING OBJECTIVES FOR THIS CHAPTER

By the end of this chapter, you will be able to:

- Identify the core concepts of the science and art of leadership.

- Differentiate between Leading and Managing and discover that leading is more 'right brained'.

- Interpret more about the age old debate on whether leaders are born or made and on leadership, personality traits, charisma and emotional intelligence.

- Distinguish the concept that a leader's charisma, personality and natural style are more nature than nurture.

- Contrast some aspects of leading and leadership style that differs in Eastern and Western cultures.

- Identify the role of culture and personality on humour.

- Recognize how differences in gender, influence leadership style preferences.

- Assess the role the brain plays in behaviour and gender differences in talent and thinking and its influence on leadership.

TABLE OF CONTENTS

LEADERSHIP: AN OVERVIEW

INTRODUCTION

More has probably been written on the subject of leadership - at least in the management, business or political literature - than any other subject. To do justice to the subject, even one Ph.D thesis of a hundred thousand words would not be enough. So, for this book in general and this chapter in particular, we will focus more on **the whole brain model of leadership.**

While there are many levels of leadership and many types - we will treat leadership here as a general concept. We will try to identify the key **concepts, styles, values and competencies** common to most leadership types and levels. **Leadership can be said to possess both a rational and emotional aspect. This fits into our whole brain model of cerebral and limbic.**

There is also an assumption that for someone to exert leadership there must be 'followership'. There is a concept that suggests we can 'lead ourselves' (self-leadership). More commonly this is referred to as 'Self-Management'. However this leads to another key concept, that **there is a difference between 'managing' and 'leading' (Bennis, 1989).**

LEADERSHIP DEFINED

Here are a few short definitions, which may help to give us some balanced perspectives.

• **"Aligning people towards common goals and empowering them to take action needed to achieve these goals" (Fortune).**
• **"The capacity to translate vision into reality (Ibid).**
• **" Influencing others so they are motivated to achieve a set of shared values and a common vision."**

LEADERSHIP, MOTIVATION AND COMMUNICATION

From this last definition, we can see that leadership and motivation are interdependent; they are inseparable. Thus, whatever a leader does, their effectiveness can we measured by the degree which others are motivated. We can perhaps conclude from these definitions that **goals, vision and values must be articulated in a way that make sense and are meaningful** to the employee or team member. Effectiveness in leading means, being a competent communicator. As Peter Ducker says, "Communication is a leader's number one priority, without which he cannot lead".

Leadership: Science or Art

Lets first look at whether leadership is a science or an art before defining leadership. The science element suggests the subject can lend itself to scholarly research, where theories and models can be developed. Where hypotheses, can be proven or disproven. The 'Art' aspect of leading is in its application and style, which can differ for each leader. Work done by Bass & Stogdill (1990) reflects their claim of over 8000 employees, that leadership is a blend of both science and art.

"A leader is best when people barely know he exists. Not so good when people obey and acclaim him, Worst of all when they despise him, But, of a good leader, who talks when his work is done, his aim fulfilled, they will say, We did this ourselves".   *Lao Tzu*

LEADING VERSUS MANAGING

THE WHOLE BRAIN MODEL

Leading has to do with vision, values mission and goals - and aligning individual, team and organizational perspectives - it is whole brained. Yet, it has become a popular paradigm to **differentiate leading from managing**. We can safely say - that not all leaders make good managers - and not all managers make great leaders. So, how do these two concepts differ?

Leading is more right brained in its 'spirit' and managing is more 'left' in 'task'. Put them together and we could call this 'Managerial Leadership'. This is 'Whole Brained'.

LEADING VERSUS MANAGING

The left-brain components of leading would include the rational, logical, factual and analytical mode of thinking. The facts-based approach often leads to a style that is authoritarian and directive. The interesting phenomena here, is that due to this critical and logical analysis, the 'authoritarian' leader is invariably correct. They have done their homework', as when being directive, few people can argue, and a consultative or participative style may seem unnecessary. Left brain managing also includes the function of operationalizing and implementing plans. Administration, structure, detail and sequence are all components of the left limbic brain. This same part of the brain is the conservative, stable and traditional part that acts as a check, control or balance to the **more 'entrepreneurial right'**.

RIGHT BRAINED LEADERSHIP

Much of contemporary leadership - that focuses on values, vision and inspiration is right brained. **Our cerebral right is the more open, flexible, conceptual and intuitive thinking self.** It is our entrepreneurial, ideational, innovative and strategic self. Here is where a holistic, synergistic vision can be highly inspirational. This part of our brain nurtures the stereotype of the visionary and inspirational leader.

The right limbic and emotional self is where leadership values find their strength. It is here that our humanistic and caring self gives us the inter-personal and responsive leadership drive. Here is where we may use our intuitive 'gut feel' when making decisions - especially about people - and when we don't have the facts to help us. Whereas idea based intuition is more right cerebral (Pink, 2005).

LEADING AND MANANGING FUNCTIONS
Sharing Vision – Values and Goals - Planning and Goal Setting
- Engaging Employees Continuously - Organising and Designing Structure
- Ensuring Fairness and Justice Prevails - Staffing : Ensuring all Jobs Filled
- Developing Individuals - Clarifying Leader Direction
- Building Team Morale - Monitoring and Controlling Results

"He, who would be a leader, must be a bridge."

A Welsh Proverb

LEADERS: BORN OR MADE

NATURE VERSUS NURTURE
The science aspect of leadership is where we apply **behavioural science, biology and physiology** to the theoretical concepts of leading. It is people who lead, but how do they find themselves in a leadership position? Are there more qualities that are innate or inborn (nature) or more that are learned and developed? As we observed earlier, **not all people seem to be equally successful or effective as a leader**. As some don't want to lead!

If leadership is something that can be learnt and developed, then anyone could become an effective leader. Of course we know that is not the case. **Countless people have attended leadership training programs, with very mixed results**. Equally, we find people who emerge as so called leaders, from very young, without any formal training. We can see signs of 'natural' leadership appearing in some children at kindergarten and more strongly by secondary school. **It has more to do with personality and innate qualities, than learned skills.**

CAN LEADERSHIP BE LEARNT?
If the qualities of a leader are more inborn, then why spend money and effort in leadership training and development? I like Henry Ford's quotation at the bottom of this page!

What we need to assess, before or early in an adults career, is their potentiality to be developed. If the 'raw material' has the basic ingredients, then the investment of time, can give us a return. So what might be these ingredients - the qualities possessed by a potential leader - which can be nurtured to give us a better pay-off? A return on our development investment!

LEADERSHIP QUALITIES
The qualities of effective leadership would of course differ for different types of leader. Leadership in Academia, Science, and Politics, the Military or a commercial private sector enterprise could differ in terms of external demands. Just as leadership at CEO or front-line level would differ in demands. Yet, assuming if we could isolate certain qualities, what would be the ones more common to all types and all levels.

Considerable research has been published in this quest - mostly in the west - with European and North American theories and models emerging. Unfortunately, not so much has been done on or within the African, Eastern, Asian and Oriental cultures.

A CITIBANK-IMD STUDY
The International Management Development (IMD) Centre researchers identified 750 leadership practices among fast track high potentials. They then reduced these to 59, based mainly on semantics, and further distilled them down to 5 behavioural practices:
1) Obtaining commitment. 2) Coaching & Appraising. 3) Rewarding. 4) Managing group processes.

EUROPEAN FOUNDATION OF MANAGEMENT DEVELOPMENT (EFMD)
Another major study done on managers at United Technologies, found these four factors to be the key to leadership effectiveness:
1) Shared vision 2) Empowerment 3) People development 4) Recognising merit 5) One can see there is considerable overlap from these two independent European studies.

"The question, 'who ought to be boss?' is like asking, 'Who ought to be the tenor in a choir?' Obviously the man who can best sing tenor".
Henry Ford

LEADERSHIP AND PERSONALITY

LEADERSHIP AND INTELLIGENCE

Having a high IQ would be less important than a high EQ. (Emotional Intelligence Quotient). In fact one survey found that having a very high IQ may even be a disadvantage. If the majority of employees are only of average to moderately high IQ, it may be less easy to establish rapport, and bond easily with team members. However if one is a leader of intellectuals or high IQ scientists, such as in academia, then a high IQ can help. So, **some traits may only be useful situationally.**

There does not seem to be a correlation between a very high IQ and success in business leadership, whereas there are studies that show **EQ correlates with success**. Also, there is a low correlation between imaginativeness or creativity and IQ. And some research points to **imagination, creativity and innovativeness** as being **important characteristics for leadership.**

LEADERSHIP AND CHARISMA

Much has been written about charismatic leaders. From the earlier views that only a few great people like Ghandi, Martin Luther King, Winston Churchill or Gorbachov had charisma. But these are great figures in history or politics. What about the everyday business or sports or military leaders of today. In order for us to assess their charisma - it may help to elaborate more on the phenomenon.

From the observations of Weber, Nietzsche, McClelland and Bass, the following seem to be the characteristics of charismatic leaders: **emotional expressiveness, self-confidence, self-determination and freedom from internal conflict.** They often display **a strong conviction of the own beliefs, are visionary, entrepreneurial and risk taking.** Some of these are the personality traits of a high achievement motivated individual (McClelland, 1985).

Charismatic leaders have an **insight into the needs, values, and hopes of their followers**. They have the **ability to conceive and articulate goals** that lift people beyond their ordinary pre-occupations. **They project a more dynamic or magnetic presence. They speak with an engaging tone of voice**, reinforced by a more **animated facial expression**, yet remain **calm, relaxed and confident, even under stress and pressure.** Perhaps leaders are after-all, more born than made, which also is the view of a recent major survey among 5000 leaders in the Asian region (Shephard, 2000).

PERSONALITY TRAITS
Based on one definition of personality, which includes innate drives, temperament and talent; we can conclude that many leadership qualities are personality traits. Certainly this is so with several characteristics of charismatic leaders. Such traits as : conscientiousness and self discipline, emotional stability and calmness, cooperativeness and warmth or caring, sociableness and assertiveness and openness to experience, which embodies curiosity, creativity, flexibility and imaginativeness, are more strongly inborn than learnt

"IQ will get you hired, but EQ will get you promoted"   *Daniel Goleman*

PERSONALITY AND CULTURE

EARLY NURTURING INFLUENCES

Nurture can start even before we are born. Whether a mother has an extroverted, bubbly, musical, rhythmic disposition - or is depressed, smokes and drinks alcohol. **These dispositions can already influence the temperament of the unborn. That's the beginning of nurture!**

At birth, we have many innate or genetic predispositions (nature), yet we are not born a completed human, we are responsive to development. **Our parents, teachers and the culture into which we are born contribute to that completion. The context and locale provides much of this.** For example, we all speak a language, but our accent, dialect or rhythm varies with the region we grow up in and how our parents and siblings speak. Early schooling further shapes this (Wright, 1998).

NURTURING OUR NATURE

We are born into a world that shapes our individuality and collective patterns of behaviour (culture), **yet this culture can only nurture that which we inherited.**

We are like a plant, grown from a seed, but we can only reach our full potential, given the right amount of water, sunlight or type of soil and perhaps also a good gardener. But even the best gardener cannot change our DNA, **so our genes are still the main architecture of our destiny.**

CULTURAL INFLUENCES

Culture influences our values, beliefs and types of behaviour that are acceptable (norms) or unacceptable (taboos). While our personality strongly determines our natural behavioural tendencies, culture also influences how it is tolerated or respected.

EARLY NURTURING IS CRITICAL

As culture is learned, it can have a powerful influence early in our life, while we are more susceptible to unconscious programming. This is why early religious programming, or character building works. We are more susceptible in the formative years, especially before we start to think conceptually or argue rationally.

Children exposed to cultural diversity develop a more open and flexible personality, which shows how nature also influences behaviour.

CULTURAL PROGRAMMING

Geert Hofstede (1991), a well known cultural anthropologist, defines culture as 'the collective mental programming of the mind, which distinguishes the members of one group (nation, company or ethnic group) or a category of people, from another group". He and other notable anthropologists, like Brown and Hall have provided some useful descriptions or 'laws' that explain broad, yet definitive patterns of cultural behaviours.

"We are captives of our own culture, and the values we internalize in the process of growing up, have a significant influence on our lives."
Edward Hall in 'Beyond Culture' (Hall, 1976)

EASTERN VERSUS WESTERN LEADERSHIP

LEADERSHIP AND CULTURE

We know that African and Eastern cultures **are more collectivist**, where hierarchy, relationships, face and harmony are key values. Contrastingly, the western cultures of Australia, North America, Northern Europe and the UK **are more Individualist**. In each culture, the role and expectations of a leader would differ. Even within Europe, there are differences between the British, French or German styles of leadership.

Culture therefore **is certainly a major factor in understanding which leadership qualities and styles are acceptable**. The most popular models or theories taught widely in MBA or Management development programs, originated in western business schools or in large U.S. based multinational companies. While these models may fit western organizational cultures, they may not be so appropriate for global - or Eastern organizations (See Chapter 3: The GLOBE Studies, House, 2007).

TRADITIONAL EASTERN MODELS

In traditional African and Eastern societies, values emphasize respect for the elder, for wisdom, for a more paternalistic type of leader, often in highly hierarchical structures. Respect for people in authority or for long service, may be higher than respect for competency or results. We can say that **these models put long term relationships, trust and 'who you know'** (Cronyism and Nepotism) **ahead of 'know-how'**, especially when it comes to hiring or promotion. It helps to have a 'sponsor', a contact or a relative to put in a good word'.

Now we are not saying this applies to all leaders or organizations in Africa and the East. This is more common in the larger bureaucracies, the older established dynasties or in government. Even in the west, most government agencies are still very bureaucratic. But the leadership styles do differ - because of the local or national culture - regardless of the size and structure of the organization. Styles of communicating and motivating within a hierarchy still differ.

WESTERN MODELS

Most western models would put competency, task achievement and results ahead of relationship, face saving, seniority or loyal service. Western theories of leadership show that more egalitarian, consultative, or even participative styles are valued. Values of openness, directness and frankness are promulgated more in the western leadership models.

EAST MEETS WEST

A type of 'glocal' (Think Global and Act Local) culture is emerging. MNC's now respect local cultural values and norms and realise that what is 'best in the west', may not always work in the east. Employees who are acculturated and socialized to respect elders, for harmonious relationships and face saving, are not about to change so suddenly. Granted the younger generation employee is acquiring a new more western set of values; today's 'generation Y, who have had a diet of MTV or open internet chatrooms, may not yet be the leaders of today. So westernization of leadership values and styles may take another generation.

"Leadership is figuring out which way your people are going and to run fast enough to get in front of them"   Gandhi

GLOBAL VS GLOCAL LEADERSHIP

SEARCHING FOR THE GLOBAL LEADER

In a Harvard Business Review classic (2003) five top global Leaders were asked to give their perspectives on global leadership. The first was Stephen Green, then Group CE0, HSBC. Next was Fred Hassan, Chairman and CEO of Schering-Plough, and Jeffery Immelt, Chairman and CEO of G.E. followed by Michael Marks, CEO of Flextronics, and lastly Daniel Meiland, Executive Chairman of the Global Executive Search Firm, Egon Zehnder.

HONG KONG AND SHANGHAI BANKING CORPORATION (HSBC).

HSBC, famous for their tagline "The Worlds Local Bank", hire international managers with the expectations that they will spend their careers being highly mobile and given exposure to international situations. They recruit from 68 universities in 38 countries globally and these managers interact multi culturally on a continuous basis. HSBC prizes themselves on the diversity of teams and the richness that it can bring to clients needs around the world.

SCHERING PLOUGH*

Fred Hassan of Schering-Plough after two difficult mergers with another American Giant, UpJohn and the Swedish company, Pharmacia, and before they merged yet again, looked for people who have a global attitude, showing openness and respect for ethnic differences. When large companies merge with other foreign companies, there will always be some corporate and cultural clashes, and some can be successful like Novartis (Ciba Geigy and Sandoz) of Smith, Kline and Glaxo** or Exxon-Mobil. But some may not overcome these cultural differences, like the Chrysler and Daimler Benz merger, that only lasted a few years. Fred Hassan focused on openmindedness, shared accountability and transparency, as well as collaboration across geographic boundaries. He also believed in the CEO being the chief developer of talent. The essence of a global culture, is having managers who are well tuned into the local culture, yet able to absorb best practices from anywhere in the world.

GENERAL ELECTRIC (GE)

Jeffrey Immelt, who had to fit into the shoes of the iconic former CEO of GE, Jack Welch, maintains a good global company does three things: Being customer centric with customers from all over the world. It operates with factories, technologies and products made for the world. The second thing is that it's a global people company. That means H.R takes on a truly global role. Jeffery maintains he spends around 40% of his time on people issues. This means spending a lot of time in the global field. Again, networking with employees from around the world, and ensuring talent is both recognised and rewarded. He says "you can't be alone ranger and also be a global manager". The third thing is that the company must have a culture that is performance oriented. This again comes back to not only the talent it attracts globally, but how they are developed with a global mindset.

*Schering-Plough later merged with Merck, yet another giant, western multinational company
** At time of print, Smith, Kline and Glaxo were in merger talks.

FLEXTRONICS

Other views from these Global CEO's, reinforce the need to hire and develop people who are able to travel extensively and gain a multicultural experience. Today, with instant communication through a global internet and telecommunication network, cultural sensitivity has become an imperative. It is essential to respect that people work and sleep in different time zones, they behave according to differing local or regional cultural norms and values. Michael Marks of Flextronics had manufacturing operations in over 28 countries, and had a truly global top team. For example the CFO could be from New Zealand, the CTO from Grenada or the CLO from Brazil. He says " Strong leaders will be just that – a strong leader – whether Brazilian or Malaysian". The global aspects of leadership have now become increasingly more critical.

EGON ZEHNDER

Daniel Meiland says that "With the world getting smaller and global brands and markets getting bigger, the search for leaders with a global mindset is a challenge." Learning about other cultures now becomes important, not just from the TV or Textbook, but living and working in other cultures, on a rotational basis. However, not all people want to be uprooted and be replanted in foreign soil, which can take its toll on the spouse, children's education and their network of relatives and friends.

Companies like GE or Shell do seem to manage these career job rotations. They track people throughout their career, assessing their potential for global assignments. Shell rewards people when they return from an overseas assignment with opportunities for promotion and career advancement. They also provide cultural orientation training, both before and after departure, for the working manager or professional as well as for their spouse and children. Cultural sensitivity doesn't always occur naturally, so such training helps employees see and understand the ethnic or cultural biases from multiple perspectives. Daniel also conclude that leaders who truly respect their employees and peers, as human beings, will always be more successful.

"We don't look so much at what or where people have studied but rather at their drive, initiative, cultural sensitivity and readiness to see the world as their oyster"

Stephen Green

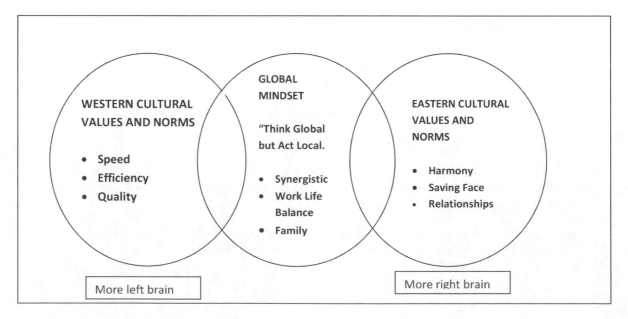

CULTURE, PERSONALITY AND HUMOUR

SENSE OF HUMOUR

While having a strong sense of humour is more a personality trait, the type of humour and what we respond to can be shaped by cultural programming. Types of humour are not universal, and can be embedded in our culture. In every culture, some personalities are more inclined to enjoy humour and laugh more easily than others (Nisbett, 2003).

For example, a person with a strong 'right' cerebral brain preference, will be more open to unusual or subtle forms of humour. They may respond well to humour that uses metaphorical or abstract language. People more strong in the Left Emotional Brain, may find some humour offensive or distasteful. Strong left brained people may not even find this humour easy to relate to. Ability to laugh helps reduce stress. This helps leaders and their building of relationships.

PERSONALITY OR CULTURE

We can see that identifying the causes of behaviour, and whether it is more personality based (nature) or more culturally influenced (nurture) is a very complex equation. There are many judgements made about behaviour; being typically American, British or Japanese, etc. Yet that same behaviour may stem from an individualistic or collectivist culture rather than from a personality trait. So, should leaders have a sense of humour? And what type of humour?

INDIVIDUALISM VS COLLECTIVISM

In the more 'eastern' collective cultures, elder people in senior or political positions are often given more respect. **Respect may be attributed to them based on age, position or status.** Prominent people are less likely to be the centre of fun or ridicule. In the Western or individualistic cultures, however, **respect may come more from competence and has to be earned.** Age, position or status may not be the nexus of respect. Humour can differ between individualistic and collectivistic cultures.

HOW CONGRUENT ARE WE?

In individualistic cultures, people can poke fun at their leaders, caricature them and also laugh at their own idiosyncrasies. A western leader can see the funny side of their own behaviour which may not be the same in the East. Remember the Danish Cartoons on Prophet Mohammad.

If our personality profile matches more closely to some cultural grouping, we can conclude that this culture is more congruent with our personality type. Alternatively, if our strong traits conflict with certain cultural norms, we may find that this culture is less accepting of certain behaviours. We may feel less comfortable or more inhibited in that culture. That culture is less congruent with our personality (Pink, 2005).

CULTURE, PERSONALITY AND HUMOUR
A controversial example might include those highly individualistic cultures, like Australia or North America and much more of Western Europe and Scandinavia . Here, the freedom of speech, religious secularity or individual rights is valued more highly than in collectivist or higher context cultures. Moreover, in individualistic cultures, people also do differ in the type of humour they prefer.

"We are captives of our own culture, and the values we internalize in the process of growing up, have a significant influence on our lives."
Edward Hall in 'Beyond Culture'

THE BRAIN, GENDER & THINKING

How often have you pondered over sex and gender issues, wondering why men and women or boys and girls are different? Not so much **what** the differences are - be they intellectual, emotional or more obviously physical - but **why they are what they are.**

STRUCTURAL DIFFERENCES IN BRAIN

In total, differences can be attributed to anatomy, physiology, biology and socio-cultural influences. Here, we cover the least mysterious of these factors - anatomy, physiology or structural differences. On the next page we will look at hormonal differences in the male and female brain. We also can consider 'transgender' individuals and how they differ.

THE CORPUS CALLOSUM

The first - and perhaps most significant structural difference - concerns the body of tissue that connects the left and right hemispheres of our brain. Called the 'corpus callosum', it enables the left and right brain hemispheres to communicate with each other.

The **corpus callosum matures 2-3 years earlier in girls than in boys**. In the female brain, this **connective tissue is 10-12%** denser, containing more nerve fibres and brain cells (Neurons).

GREATER BRAIN HEMISPHERIC INTEGRATION

What is actually happening is that the female brain hemispheres are 'iterating' more and faster, i.e. **there is greater integration between the two hemispheres**. Due to this, women may take longer to make a decision, but the decision is usually more holistic, and more whole brained, **combining facts and feelings**.

LIMBIC AND CEREBRAL LINKAGES

Another key brain structure difference is the link between a part of the **limbic system, called the Amygdala and the frontal lobes of the cerebral cortex.** The frontal lobes which are the 'judgement' or 'executive' centres of the brain, control the emotions. This linkage is stronger in women, compared with males, whose control over violent emotion is weaker. **The amygdala interprets the emotional context of experience,** affecting what we remember. It amplifies memories that are pleasant or frightening. It 'tells' the hippocampus, another part of the limbic system, where memories are formed and to be stored. **Men and women have different processes to create enhanced memories** more strongly. They also form different strengths about certain types of memories.

SKILLS DIFFERENCES

Women on average, also have superior language skills - both in vocabulary - as well as in grammar and spelling. However, due to the faster or greater connections with the emotional right brain, this language is often more influenced by feeling. This may be the reason why women seem able to be more empathetic than men. Men on the other hand, tend to be more aggressive, due to higher levels of testosterone. This hormone enhances gross motor skills, visual spatial skills - like manoeuvring a car - although women excel more in the fine motor skill areas, like needlework. From the perspective of brain dominance, this is reflected in the vast worldwide research on brain intelligence.

"If 'NATURE' is left to its own ways, it will seek out an environment that is 'NURTURING'"

Matt Ridley

TALENTS/PREFERENCES AND GENDER

WHY WE DIFFER IN EXCELLENCE

While we say talent or talent potential is more nature (genetic) than nurture, we know that genes are merely 'switches' that turn on/off hormones. It is the hormones that produce behaviour and talent, which is **excellence in action** or potential. This is one key to why it differs in gender. On the next page we can see some of these differing talents, which naturally coincide with occupational preferences.

HORMONES, TALENTS & PREFERENCES

As we already mentioned, the male sex hormone, testosterone, influences visual spatial ability. **The right amygdala is more active in the male brain** and is tuned to the visual cortex which controls vision of the larger external environment. **In women, the left amygdala focuses more on the 'inner self',** producing emotionally relevant content from the senses.

Other hormones, 'wire-up' the female and male brain differently, during early development and even later in life. This is especially so with the balance between androgen, estrogen and testosterone, in the female brain, after puberty.

A newly discovered hormone called kisspeptin has been found to be the stimulus for the production and balance of the sex hormones in women. A type of growth hormone, produced in the hippocampus, is twice as high in females. And together **with the Amygdala, influence emotions differently in men and women.** For example, this results in women being **more empathetic and nurturing,** but they are also more susceptible to depression, than men.

OXYTOCIN: THE LOVE HORMONE

When we give or receive love, emotional circuits in the brain produce a hormone called oxytocin. This has been found to occur **in higher amounts when people fall in love.** It is also critical for mothers and new born babies for **bonding.** Oxytocin is a neurotransmitter that acts as an opiate and helps prevent sadness and anger. That's why people in love seem happier!

It is produced in the same brain areas critical for **intuition, mood, empathy and decision making**. When we feel good, such as being in love, we tend to be more optimistic. The positive feeling when we make a good decision is also produced by oxytocin.

THE FEMALE BRAIN
A female brain that has been masculinised by testosterone in the womb is more likely to have unusual intellectual gifts in the right-hemisphere areas, like map reading, mathematics, mechanical technology and athletics. Of course, development doesn't stop in the womb. It continues to be shaped throughout our life by education, parenting, mentoring, nutrition, social status and trauma. The 'raw material' of the exceptionally feminized or masculinised brain that begins to develop in a mother's body can either be 'normalized' post-natally or become even further polarized.

Mona Lisa Schulz

"Success is discovering your own natural talents and finding work that fully capitalizes on them."

Conyngham, 2014

GENDER & OCCUPATIONAL PREFERENCE DIFFERENCES

HORMONAL INFLUENCES

Let's look at the more complex and less well understood influences – hormones. E.g., the male hormone, testosterone influences both physical and emotional aspects of behaviour, producing more muscle density and strength, as well as a predisposition towards more aggressiveness and competitiveness. However, it has been found that testosterone influences some specific left and right brain hemisphere abilities, like the visual-spatial.

Another hormone, found in greater amounts in women, is oestrogen. It promotes brain cell activity, enabling parts of the brain to become more alert and receptive to increased information. Whereas progesterone, another hormone also produced in a greater quantity in women, has an opposite or inhibitory effect. It reduces blood flow to the brain resulting in lower oxygen and glucose. This effect produces more fatigue or feelings of depression, anxiety and lower libido, all of which have potential for influencing behaviour.

SIGNIFICANCE OF DIFFERENCES

It must be stressed that the cognitive differences between men and women are still very small on average. It is only when we look at the extremes – such as among genius mathematicians, music composers, great architects, or multi-lingual simultaneous translator – do we see significant differences in such brain related talents. Women tend to have the patience to do more detail work and are often regarded as more 'reliable'. The reliability is in the patience, making fewer errors and completing the task at hand. Men are equally reliable to complete some projects but they prefer larger projects like constructing bridges, highways or skyscrapers.

BIOLOGY vs. CULTURE

These differences are caused by biological (genetic and hormonal) factors as well as physical and anatomical differences in actual brain structure. But also socio-cultural, where the differences are emphasised more when it comes to upbringing, social values and pressures, or on role models of what men and women should do or be better at?

This study of gender differences in the brain, does throw some light on why men and women think differently. In summary the differences include anatomy, physiology and biology as well a cultural stereotyping. It also helps explain preferences in leadership styles.

Function	Brain location	Summary	
Mechanics of language (Speech, grammar)	Men: LH, F& B.	More diffuse	
	Women: LH, F.	More specific	
Vocab. Defining words	Men: LH, F & B.	More diffuse	
	Women: L& RH, F & B.	More specific	
Visio-spatial perception	Men: RH.	More diffuse	LH = Left hemisphere
	Women: R & LH.	More specific	RH = Right hemisphere
			F = Front B = Back
Emotion	Men: RH.	More diffuse	
	Women: R & LH.	More specific	

"An ideology that does not confront this basic issue (gender differences) is an exercise in wishful thinking, and a social science that does not confront it, is sterile."   *Alice Rossi, Sociologist*

GENDER DIFFERENCE IN LEADERSHIP

LEADERSHIP AND GENDER

We know from whole brain profiles of most women, that their right limbic system is stronger and more responsive. This means **women are more inclined to empathize with, and be sensitive to, the feelings of others**. Could these make women leaders more nurturing and caring? In studies on female leadership style, women seem more effective than men in transformational and relational leadership.

A major study done on managers influence styles, in a fortune 100 company, found **females showed greater concern for others**. Females were more likely to act with the organization's broad interests in mind and consider how others felt about their influence style. They involve others more in planning, and focus on both task and interpersonal aspects. Males on the other hand, were more likely to act out of self-interest and show less consideration for how others might feel about their influence style. They tend to work alone in developing their strategy, and working on tasks. But perhaps more in individualistic cultures!

LEADERSHIP DIFFERENCES

A recent study by Bass and Avolio (1994) showed same traits and styles where women leaders were rated out of '5' more favourably by their subordinates. These were: Extra Effort (4.2), Intellectual Stimulation (4.1) Idealized Influence (3.9) and Employee Satisfaction (3.3). In another study on Emotional Intelligence (EI) Shephard, (2008) it was noted that out of six clusters of EI, woman tended to score higher on three of them. Here we can see the natural, empathetic and nurturing traits of women play a role. The same study showed that African and Asian women overall, scored higher than among their European counterparts. It was concluded that women in traditionally male dominated societies, have to 'fight' harder to win over the emotions of others. However, this augers well for leadership's styles, like, coaching, coalitional, relational or **transformational** which all rest comfortably with female leaders, who may be naturally more inclined towards such styles.

FEMALE VALUES

Female leadership aspirations are higher when linked to social responsibility. Women seem to place a higher value on 'doing the right thing', or on what are morally and ethically right. They place a higher value on what feels - intuitively - right.

Major gender differences in thinking, feeling and behaving are rooted as much in anatomical and physiological differences of male and female brains, as in socio-cultural conditioning. The corpus callosum of the female brain- that web of nerve fibres that connect the two halves of the brain, is some 10 to 12% more dense in speed and frequency with which the two halves of the brain communicate. This enables women to connect 'facts' and 'feelings' more easily than men, and make more holistic responses

"Power in an organisation is the capacity generated by relationships"

Margaret Wheatley
Leadership and the
New Science

THE GLASS CEILING

Leaders should ideally be neutral and free from bias or prejudice, especially when it comes to gender. In some Western countries this is addressed by legislation, such as the Equal Employment Opportunities (EEO) act. Female gender bias, mainly negative among male managers, gave the concept of the glass ceiling – a type of invisible barrier that prevents women moving up into senior leadership positions.

Historically we have seen great women leaders in politics, Catherine the Great, Queen Elizabeth I and II, Indira Ghandi, Bandaranaike (Sri Lanka) to the modern days to Margaret Thatcher, Hilary Clinton, Angela Merkel, or Park Geun of South Korea. Women in the cooperate world find a different set a male prejudices, and often, in order to succeed they need to think or behave more like men. Sometimes the glass ceiling is only at Board Level, however legislation has now come into a few countries (notably Scandinavian), where a quota has been introduced, as for example, 30% of board or even senior management should comprise women. This is now a 'guideline' in others countries like Malaysia.

WORK-LIFE BALANCE

Due to the stereotypic roles of woman needing to leave the work place to have children, this debate has opened up a whole world of issues around, flexi- hours, paternity as well as maternity leave, telecommuting. Workaholics may no longer be the heroes. Some corporations have responded to this call. Among them are United Airlines, Xerox, Amex, DuPont, W.L Gore, PepsiCo and KPMG, but these are large well known US based multi-nationals. In Europe there are also several, like Unilever, Shell and BP, to name a few. There are cultural biases, such as in many Middle Eastern countries, some African and Asian countries, like Japan – but in the words of a well known Ballard "for the times they are a changing". Women in some countries now outnumber men as business graduates. Also in some professions, like Human Resources. So times are changing, yet slowly! So would the French still say 'Viv la difference?

KEY STYLE DIFERENCES

We have already shown that hormonal differences in the brain - especially higher oestrogen levels in the female - give some advantages in some situations. **Women are more collaborative and less aggressive or confrontational than men**. Their achievement motivation emphasizes getting results through **cooperation and relationship building**, rather than mens' more competitive nature. Women are also generally superior in tasks requiring **rapid and fine motor skills**. They have **a better eye for detail** and tend to be **more reliable in completing tasks**. One strong motivation for greater affiliation is acceptance or popularity. This certainly helps in their networking and building of influence coalitions. When asked to achieve a tough goal, **women leaders are far more likely than men to consult others or seek group cooperation**. In women, the speed and frequency and intuition are superior, contributing to a more caring leadership style.

"People want to go along with people they get along with"   *John Maxwell*

SUMMARY OF KEY POINTS

- Leadership includes the articulation of shared values, vision and goals which are all aligned, yet meaningful and inspirational.
- Leadership comprises a set of practices which are applied situationally by using appropriate behavioural skills and styles. These should result in followers feeling empowered and motivated.
- With the whole brain model, we can classify most administrative managerial functions as left brained, and leading as more right brained.
- Leading effectively requires a range of behaviours and skills, many of which are strongly influenced by the leader's basic personality, as well as training.
- Some personality traits are believed to be as much as eighty percent genetic in predisposition, so strong leadership style preferences are more inborn (nature) than learned (nurture).
- Personality includes temperament, like introversion/extraversion, natural talent, intelligences, motivational drives, and the traits of charisma.
- Of equal and significant importance are the cultural influences in leadership. While many practises don't differ, their style of application may differ much more.
- As some Asian, African and Western values and norms differ, styles that work in the west, may not all work in the East. They may even be counterproductive.
- Gender also influences a leader's preferred style or approach. Male and female brains differ in structure and physiology. Cultural values and norms also influence expected gender roles and style.
- Competence of leaders, comprise knowledge, skill, talent and attitudes. These can be assessed more easily when they are thus classified.
- The concept of a 'glass ceiling presents an invisible barrier to many women rising to senior leadership positions. However many organisations are metarialising this bias.
- g a work-life style of balance is shown.
- Some key motivational difference in gender are also highlighted and include women being naturally more collaborative and relational than their more competitive male counterparts. Differences in detail mindedness; reliability and integrity between gender are also discussed.

LEADERSHIP DEVELOPMENT

We first need to select a person who has the desired personality traits, including general as well as emotional intelligence. In addition, a basic drive to lead and influence others must be strong. To succeed as a leader in today's competitive world requires a certain type of drive and range of specific talents. Once we have this 'right stuff' (the raw material) we can then invest effort, money and time in developing a range of competencies. This will result in a positive return on investment. G.E. uses a development model that is divided into 'Skills', Time applications and Work values. These differ for each level of leadership.

"The heart of development lies within a person's ability to learn from experience.
High Flyers: Developing the next generation of leaders "
Morgan W.McCall

References

Bass and Stogdill. (1990). *The Handbook of Leadership.* New York: Free Press.

Bass, B.M. and Avolio,B.J. (1994). *Shelter The Glass Ceiling: Women May Make Better Managers. Penguin*: UK.

Bennis, W. (1989). *Why Leaders Can't Lead.* San Francisco : Jossey-Bass.

Browning, G. (2006). *Emergenetics: New Science of Success.* New York: Harper Collins Publishers.

Drucker, P. (1954). *The Practice of Management.* New York: HarperCollins.

Goleman, D. (1996). *The New Leaders.* London: Time-Warner Books.

Hall, E. (1976). *Beyond Culture.* New York : Double Day Pub.

Herrmann, N. (1996). *The Whole Brain Business Book.* New York: McGraw-Hill.

Hofstede, G. (1991). *Culture and Organisation.* New York: McGraw Hill.

House, R. (2007). *Culture, Leadership and Organisations.* London: Sage Publications.

McClelland, D. (1985). *The Achievement Motive.* New York: A Century Crofts.

Nietzsche, F. (1883). *Thus spoke Zahrathustra .* USA: Cosmo Inc.

Nisbett, R. (2004). *The Geography of Thought.* USA: First Press.

Pink, D. (2005). *A Whole New Mind: Why Right-Brainers will rule the world.* NY: Riverhead .

Pinker, S. (2007). *The Stuff of Thought.* London : Penguin Group.

Ridley, M. (1994). *Nature via Nurture.* USA: Library of Congress.

Schultz, M. (2005). *The New Feminine Brain.* New York: Free Press.

Schulz, M. L. (2005). *The New Feminine Brain .* New York: Free Press.

Shephard, P. C. (2014). *A collection of quotations: unpublished paper.* Cardiff: Wales.

Shephard, P. C. (2001). Asian Strategic Leadership Institute Research Paper. Kuala Lumpur.

Shephard, P. C. (2008). *Personality Matters.* Kuala Lumpur: BrainWorks Media.

Wheatley, M. (1992). *Leadership and the New Science.* San Francisco : Berrett-Koehlar.

Wright, W. (1998). *Born That Way .* New York: Alfred Knopt.

CHAPTER TWO

THE LEADERS PERSONALITY: NATURE AND NURTURE

LEARNING OBJECTIVES FOR THIS CHAPTER

By the end of this chapter, you will be able to:

- Contrast the nature of personality and the relationships between genetic and cultural influences on personality traits.

- Describe your own behavioural style preferences and their relationship to your personality type.

- Distinguish how and why personalities differ.

- Identify some ways to capitalize on the unique strengths of our personality.

- Differentiate between personality traits, clusters of traits and how they include Temperament, Talents and Drives.

- Discover if you are more introverted, extroverted or in between and how this affects your leadership behavior.

- Describe the brain's evolution and composition and its functions and relationship to left and right brain personalities.

- Identify how the brain's plasticity and forming of new neuronal connections can help us learn, adapt or change.

- Clarify why peoples' talent, character and drives contribute to different learning styles.

TABLE OF CONTENTS

THE NATURE OF PERSONALITY

WHAT IS PERSONALITY?
Personality can be defined as: **"The sum total of our mental, emotional, social and physical characteristics that distinguishes us from others, the core of which is those traits generally remain stable for life between the ages of 25 to 30. They are what make us the unique person we are"** (Wright, 1998).

What are Traits?
Personality traits are long-term predispositions for behaviour.
In the study of personality, **traits are any enduring and relatively consistent characteristics of our feelings, thoughts and behaviour.** They comprise aptitudes (talents/intelligences), some motivational **drives** (or needs) and **temperament.**

APTITUDES
They include our talents and intelligences. They are natural or inborn.
Sometimes if they are very strong they are called gifts. Intelligence is more than just intellectual (IQ) or emotional (EQ). In later pages, we identity more than a dozen intelligences. And each type encompasses many talents.

There are physical talents such as body-kinesthetic intelligence and our ability to coordinate and move the body gracefully or gymnastically (Gardner, 1999). More **talents which are also intelligences are shown on page 17.**

TEMPERAMENT
This can be called the core of personality and includes the 'Master Traits' of **Introversion or Extroversion, and Deliberation or Liberation. It is how active or reactive we are, and includes our emotional moods that we tend to feel or display.**

DRIVES
These are another key component of personality. Not the instinctual survival drives for food, shelter or oxygen, but the **social drives to achieve, to be with people (affiliation or gregariousness) or to dominate and influence others (power).**

Drives are really an extension of our temperament, which are strongly chemical and rooted in the limbic system of our brain. They probably can be nurtured more than temperament. There are, however strong cultural influences on how we should use power to persuade or lead others (McClelland,1988).

THE EMERGENCE OF PERSONALITY TRAITS
Traits tend to be strongly influenced by our inherited endowment, some perhaps as high as 80%. While culture, upbringing and nurture can stimulate or reward such behaviour, the root causes are more genetic. This is why they tend to endure for life and become a visible predictor or patterns of behaviour. They are often noticed as a consistent or repetitive pattern of behaviour. They are thus, a good indicator for the type of job or work that motivates and satisfies each of us differently, based on the degree of their intensity/strength.

"You cannot be anything you want to be, but, it is possible to be all you can be."
Hammer & Copeland..

"Living With Our Genes"

TEMPERAMENT AND TRAITS

TEMPERAMENT IS MORE INBORN

Nature still requires the stimuli of nurture, but the genetic predisposition towards those stimuli is inborn. Genes also play a role in what experiences we seek, pushing us to select environmental stimuli that is not only satisfying or rewarding, but shapes our behaviour.

Temperament is like a natural response or 'memory', which is what we call a habit. In order to determine the type and strength of temperamental traits, **all we need to do is map out the frequency and intensity of the behaviours.** We look for consistent patterns of behaviour under similar environmental conditions. (Shouts when angry).

TRAIT STRENGTHS OR WEAKNESSES

Traits can be measured as very strong, medium and weak or placed in a continuum of opposites. Traits do not exist in isolation. They interact with each other. They also interact with, and are stimulated by the environment. (Nature via Nurture). Traits can be intensified, modified or weakened, but will rarely disappear or completely change. Some drives, values and behaviours may change, when needs change, but strong basic traits are unlikely to. (Wright, 1998).

All traits can be measured on a continuum. One end will be extreme strength and the other, extreme weakness or an almost absence of the trait. However, this absence or opposite may actually be called another trait. **E.g: Shyness (Opposite to Boldness).**

One helpful way of seeing temperament is how much or how little a person 'deliberates' as a reaction to stimuli. We can each position ourselves on this continuum on a point scale of how well and how often and in what detail we 'deliberate' about and then control our daily actions. Examples of 'deliberation' and its opposite, 'liberation' (Ornstein 1993)

TRAITS UNDER TEMPERAMENT

- Activity and Energy Level
- Curiousness or Inquisitiveness
- Seeking Novelty or Variety
- Risk Taking, Venturesomeness
- Violence, Aggressiveness
- Calmness or Short Temperedness
- Talkativeness or Quietness (Passivity)
- Boldness, Shyness, Cautiousness

- Sadness or Brightness/Cheerful
- Spontaneity of Behavior
- Optimism or Pessimism
- Stress Absorption/Tolerance
- Introversion or Extroversion
- Patience or Impatience
- Easy going or tough
- Resilience

INTERACTION OF TRAITS
Deeply held religious values may make a friendly person become dogmatic and judgmental and intolerant of others. Musical-Rhythmic or Kinesthetic people may increase their openness to explore and experiment. A trait must exist for a competence or several traits can equal a competency, but not all competencies are traits.
Example: An analytic, creative or strategic thinker. Each is a different 'thinking' trait and style. Each can be a talent and competency on their own, or interact together.

COMPONENTS OF PERSONALITY

PERSONALITY THEORIES
Over the past century, there have been many theories of personality, from the early pioneers such as Freud, Adler, Catell, Allport and Jung, to the **more recent behavioral geneticists** like Pinker, Ridley, Wright, Hammer and Neuro-scientists LeDoux, Gazzaniga and Ornstein.

One study found about 2000 personality tests. Another found over 1800 words to describe personality traits and even after combining those words with a similar meaning, there were still 200 personality traits remaining.

Further reduction analysis enabled psychologists to generally agree on several clusters of around 100 traits. So, with hundreds of tests available, how might we select a tool that suits our needs.

For this book there is one profiling tool that has been selected. **The CREDO PERSONALITY PROFILE (CPP)™. It is a result of over 30 years of research.** It has held up well in many analyses over the past three decades, especially across many cultures. It is based more on biology, brain physiology and genetic make-up. (CREDO, 2013) You can discover your profile on-line (www.credotrust.org)

TEMPERAMENT:'FROM CRADLE TO GRAVE'
Temperament can be described in three measurable aspects:

 1. Activity 2. Reactivity 3. Mood

TEMPERAMENT IS NOT LEARNED
These aspects are not learned or copied or picked up. Nor can they be easily controlled by will power. **A small child is not active, noisy, inquisitive or quiet because it wants to be, it's born that way.** A toddler doesn't feel sad just because it fails to get its mother's attention. **This sadness or 'mood', such as brightness, bubblyness, shyness or calmness is more biological than psychological (Hammer and Copeland. 1998).**

Temperament exists at the level of instinct. It is a natural and inherent disposition or inclination to act or react in a particular way. While our traits may be 'tempered' from life's experience, the tendency of predisposition for them to be a part of us, will always be there. They are more genetically 'hard-wired' into us.

CAN TEMPERAMENT CHANGE?
Temperament is not easy to change; it tends to endure as we mature. A shy baby will become a shy adult. An adventurous child is curious, enjoys exploring and doing new things which continues throughout life.
We are born with the same genes as we die with, but genes themselves do not make us cry or giggle, want to be social and gregarious or more alone. What genes do is control certain aspects of brain chemistry, which influence how we perceive and react to our environment, this initially occurs in the emotional part of our brain, called the Limbic System.
"Where there is a will, there is a way". Ancient Saying

INTROVERSION AND EXTROVERSION

OUR SUPER TRAITS

The 'super' traits of temperament - indeed of personality as a whole - are usually called **'Introversion' or 'Extroversion'.** These are also on a continuum of opposites or anywhere in between the extremes.

Introverts tend to process information internally and reflect a moment longer before responding. And the response is usually more deliberated, cautious, quieter and often slower. But compared with whom? (Jung, 2006).

Well **extroverts**, are the opposite! They tend to prefer **external stimulation and process information by expressing themselves.** They appear to speak as they think or even speak seemingly without thinking - appearing more spontaneously expressive.

WHICH ARE YOU?

There can be two extreme opposites in traits. However, we can be more in the middle of some, making it difficult for people to label us as either.
What we need to assess is - how we are at a non conscious level - overall more introverted or more extroverted.

When we think of charismatic, optimistic and assertive leaders, they are often more extroverted. When we behave without thinking or being aware of it, we call this non conscious behavior, which is often emotionally spontaneous or impulsive.

OUR FRAMES OF REFERENCE

Let's look at examples. A naturally extroverted, social, outgoing and expressive person will prefer interacting with people when learning. They process information better when sharing ideas and expressing themselves.

Extroverts need an external frame of reference, so they get their stimuli from the learning environment. People, who are naturally more cautious, conservative, introverted and shy, however, process information from an **internal frame of reference**. They are more reflective and may be less comfortable learning in a group. They may be more passive and quiet in a group, preferring to listen rather than talk.

This shyness or boldness is due to the genetic switching on or off, of the arousal hormone called norepinephrine. Shy children produce more of this chemical when stimulated.

ARE YOU EASILY AROUSED?
Dr Robert Ornstein makes some interesting conclusions on the differing reactions of Introverts and Extroverts. Since everyone seeks an optimal level of excitement in daily life, introverts, being more aroused to begin with, need less stimulation than extroverts. An introvert's cortex inhibits the lower brain centres more than an extrovert's does. Extroverts have a better short-term memory but also forget things more quickly, while introverts remember things better under stress, e.g. during exams. Extroverts are more rebellious because they don't form conditioned reflexes easily; making them more difficult to train. They also talk and make eye contact more and feel good more often during the day than introverts do.

"If NATURE is left to its own ways, it will seek out an
environment that is NURTURING ."   *Matt Ridley*

BIOLOGICAL BASES OF PERSONALITY

NATURE VIA NURTURE

A trait (more nature) that is exhibited by behaviour (trait manifestation), first requires a stimulus or trigger from the external environment (more nurture).

Traits tend to reflect the physiological activity of our brain's neurological (chemical) arousal systems (nature/biology/genes). **It is not Nature versus Nurture, but Nature via Nurture.** A trait can equally exert influences on our behaviour. **Traits like intelligence, calmness, flexibility and openness can strongly influence our behaviour (Ridley, 1994).**

"For example, external stressors can produce a brain chemical called Cortisol, yet still requires genes to switch it on; to release it into our brain. If we are genetically built to be calm and with a high tolerance to stress, less cortisol will be released and we are less prone to react to stress".

BEHAVIOUR AND GENES

Deviant behaviour can be due to a stronger genetic influence than environment. Examples like **aggressiveness, violence, bullying or criminal behavior** have strong genetic influences - mainly in males - from genes controlling the flow of testosterone.

VIOLENCE AND PERSONALITY

A person of lower IQ, unattractive, greedy, impulsive, alcoholic and emotionally unstable, is more likely to be predisposed to violence but **still requires an environment that stimulates violent behaviour.** For example, in a gang, poor neighbourhood, deprived of education or love or a fulfilling interest, and provoked by another's threatening behaviour.

A NURTURING ENVIRONMENT

Place that same person into a caring or loving and enriched environment - **while the negative traits still exist - they may not be stimulated or triggered into violence. But introduce negative stimuli, and the violence gene can quickly switch on.**

When people are aggressive or violent, the agreeableness traits may be low or lacking. Harm avoidance (temperament) and low co-cooperativeness (character) traits may be implicated. Aggression is the acting out of hostile feelings, yet an environmental stimulus is still required. Subject to how we are wired-up, we each respond differently to the same stimuli.

HOSTILITY AND YOUR HEART
One theory for hostility's role in heart disease is that certain people are "hot reactors." As a response to everyday stress, hot reactors exhibit extreme increases in heart rate and blood pressure. According to this theory, these surges may gradually damage the coronary arteries and the heart itself. Many cardiovascular rehabilitation programs help us learn how to reduce stress and, in so doing, become less impatient or hostile.

"The human brain is hardwired to be capable of anger .... genetically and biologically speaking, we are all close to the edge." Hammer & Copeland

DEGREES OF GENETIC INFLUENCE

WHAT WE INHERIT
On average, genetic influence on behaviour is probably around 50%
And 25% is due to unique environmental influences and 25% to chance or random factors. **Less than 10% is due to a shared environment. Inherited potential can be from a high of 100% from each parent**, but on average, we inherit around 50% from each parent. (Wright, 1998)

MUTATION OR RECESSIVENESS
However, **some genes may mutate (change), some become dormant or recessive -** skipping one or more generations; some become **dominant** (eg: hair colour) and Some weak.

INHERITENCE OF INTELLIGENCE
Intelligence (a talent) may overall range from 50 to 80% inherited, but specific Types of intelligences or aptitudes that are close to genius or giftedness (Mozart, Einstein, Picasso, etc.) are **more likely to be due to a genetic mutation** in a small part of the brain responsible for that behaviour. While IQ maybe as high as 70 - 80%, EQ is closer to 50%, and can be strengthened as we age.(Einstein's brilliance 'was a mutation')

TRAITS MORE STRONGLY GENETICALLY DISPOSED

	%		%
• Hair and Skin Colour	99.9	• Most Other Intelligences	70
• Tallness/Shortness and Obesity	99.9	• Achievement Needs	50
• Extroversion/Introversion	90	• Work-a-holism	50
• Intellectual Intelligence	60	• Power/Influence Needs	30-50
• Venturesomeness/Thrill Seeking	80	• Affection/Affiliation Needs	30-50
• Energy Level/Exuberance	70	• Caffeine-Alcohol Tolerance	30-50
• Imaginativeness/Curiosity	70	• Religiosity/Religiousness	30-50
• Stress Tolerance	70	• Sexual Orientation/Drive	30-50
• Most Other Intelligences	70	• Anxiety/Panic Attacks	30-50

Check yourself against these traits! Rate yourself high or strong on some, medium in some and low or weak in others! The more strong or weak ratings are more likely to be genetic.

Depression and potentially over 4000 diseases have a genetic predisposition.
The actual percentage risks differ from disease to disease, and from parent to parent or even previous generations.

GENDER DIFFERENCES
A recent study, published in the journal named 'Nature'; found a small 14.5 points or 2% difference in IQ between men and women. Up to age 16 - 18 there was no difference. Only upon maturation did the average show up. This is probably due more to nurture than nature where roles and expectations of men vs. women are more culturally determined. In other areas of intelligences, there are several differences, as male-female brain physiology and biology is different

"Intellectuals solve problems; geniuses prevent them.."
Albert Einstein

PERSONALITY AND BEHAVIOUR

BEHAVIOURAL INFLUENCES

We can say that our traits, especially of temperament **and drive, are predispositions to how we behave. Cultural programming also influences how we behave.** Both of these are influences at the non-conscious level and determine how we may naturally behave when not consciously deciding how to behave. But we know **some behaviour is rewarded and some punished, so society may it.**

We can each choose to behave in a certain way as the context or situations change. We often see behaviour changes when the boss or a relative is present, which is usually conscious. When there is no external pressure, we revert to our natural patterns of behaviour - be they internally driven - or culturally programmed.

CHEMICAL INFLUENCES

What actually determines these patterns genetically, are the mix of two major hormones (brain chemicals). Each of them is controlled by genes that activate their release and mix through receptors or transporters. The **first is called Serotonin, which influences the excitation or calmness of a person.** The second called **Dopamine causes impulsiveness and risk taking**.

Depending upon the balance of the two hormones, we can behave one way or the other. **In summary, genes produce chemicals which influence traits, traits influence our natural behaviour, and culture further nurtures it.**

PERSONALITY TYPES AND LEARNING

Personality traits can strongly influence behaviour. **Learning is part of our behaviour where we experience some new stimuli and try to make sense of it (perception).** This involves both our emotional and cognitive brain where we feel and/or think about the new experiences. It is useful or important to understand and remember this.

Here, our personality type influences how we prefer to process new information and make meaning out of it. **We call these preferred processes, Learning and Thinking Styles.**

Whether we are more visual, auditory or bodily kinesthetic, more introverted or extroverted, more cognitive or emotional, these traits will each influence how we naturally prefer to think and learn. **Some of our learning requires us to think, so how we think influences how we learn and vice versa.**

THIS CHEMISTRY OF HORMONES
Some hormones increase our positive attitude and optimism. Conversely, if we find our behaviour has not satisfied our needs, other hormones can cause tension, stress or even depression. We can then conclude, we feel 'demotivated'.

The positive hormones are called endorphins and negative ones are endocrines
, like cortisol. So, the feelings of motivation have a chemical basis. Emotions produce chemicals which in turn stimulates behaviour. The secret of motivation then is to ensure we produce the right mix and as much of the time as possible.

"Emotions produce chemicals and chemicals produce emotions."Conyngham

THE TRIUNE BRAIN

Dr. Paul MacLean, (1990) former Chief of the Laboratory of Brain Evolution and Behaviour at the National Institute of Mental Health in Washington, D.C. divides the brain into three distinct systems each of which represents a different stage of our evolution.

1. 'REPTILIAN' OR HIND BRAIN

This first part of our brain is the oldest and lowest part of the brain. It consists of the brain stem and allied organs such as the basal ganglia and the reticular activating system. It is ruled by all of the primitive functions and concerns of our reptilian ancestors. These include **physical space, basic survival, possessions, and urges of self-defense.**

The reptilian brain is a slave to ritual and precedent. If you want to see someone's reptilian brain in action, steal their coffee cup, chair or morning newspaper.

Alternatively, if you wish to test the power of your own reptilian brain, stand in front of an oncoming bus and attempt to calculate its oncoming speed. The 'survival' instinct kicks in, activating our reptilian brain!

2. 'MAMMALIAN' OR LIMBIC SYSTEM

A group of cell structures in the brain's centre, that is just above the brain stem or reptilian brain. It evolved some two to three hundred million years ago. It equates to the reptilian forebrain, being the highest order brain in reptiles.

In evolutionary terms the limbic system performs the function vital to mammalian **survival, including memory, learning, emotions, social and family interaction**. In motivational theory, it is where we respond to rewards and punishments. We share this part of the brain with lower mammals such as cats, dogs, rabbits, goats and horses.

In higher mammals such as apes and humans, it is also known as the visceral or emotional brain, and is connected with behavioural and emotional expression. It appears to include within its functions most of those strategies necessary for our preservation, such as feeding behaviour, as well as those vital to the continuance of the species such as mating, reproduction and care of the young. In addition; it is centrally involved in enabling us to relate to our environment, both in the immediate sense and long term.

In the human, it plays a key role in the storing and direction of memory and the processing of emotions, especially those of survival; **the four F's (Feeding, Fighting, Fleeing and Feeling)**

The limbic system, while only occupying about 10% of the mass of the human brain, is like the turbo charger of an engine. Dr. Paul Maclean describes it as playing the central role in generating affective feelings, including those important for a sense of reality, and a belief of what is true and important. It plays a vital role in memory.

"Emotion has taught mankind to reason."   Marquis de Vauvenargues

It houses the key chemical producing glands, like the hypothalamus which, directs the brain's master gland called the pituitary gland that regulates hormone production. It also comprises the hippocampus and amygdala two other critical parts of the limbic system.

The limbic system **is also a "paired" organ, with left and right parts** that are almost symmetrical. The linkage between these two halves is through the hippocampus commissural, a mass of connective fibres that facilitates communication between the two halves of the limbic system, similar to the interactive function of the corpus callosum in the cerebral hemispheres.

3. HUMAN BRAIN (CEREBRAL CORTEX, NEOCORTEX/FOREBRAIN)

This cerebral cortex is the last of our brain systems to evolve. It consists of the cortex and the cerebellum. **It performs the basis of our being able to reason things out and try different solutions – it could be thought of as the "thinking cap".**
We share the cerebral cortex with higher mammals such as chimpanzees, dolphins and whales. What distinguishes us from these other animals is that the neocortex of man is so large in relations to both the brain and body.

The Cortex or grey matter is the convoluted outer layer of the brain, and is the thinking branch of the brain, responsible for **higher order conceptual, analytic and abstract thinking. The frontal part contains the executive and judgment functions.**

Just beneath this cortex is a dense layer of fibrous tissue, containing millions of nerve fibres. This is often called the "white matter" and is responsible for the reception and flow of information.

Each of these cortical layers are folded into two hemispheres – left and right brain – and if open and out stretched, would resemble a small thick rubber-like mat. This would be almost 50cm by 75cm and 1/2cm thick (1/4 inch). However the brain comprises 6 layers and if all were to be laid out flat they would be the size of two soccer pitches!

BRAIN FACTS

Dimensions

Width	*20cm*	*Length*	*20cm*
Depth	*15cm*		
Av. Weight Male	*1,300-1,400g*	*Av. Weight Female*	*1,200-1,300g*
Effective weight	*150-200g*	*Weight at birth*	*350g*
Annual rate of shrinkage			
Between 20 and 60 years	*1.3g*	*Over 60 years*	*3.4g*

* effective weight is due to buoyancy and support of surrounding cerebrospinal fluid and membranes. The blood supply to the brain is 20% of the body's total supply (7.9times requirement of most organs) Brain to body weight ratio: Human - 1:50 Dolphin - 1: 100 Chimpanzee - 1: 120
Major parts Cerebellum/Cerebrum, Diencephalon(thalamus), Hypothalamus, Brian stem (pons, medulla) Four ventricles (inner chamber's containing cerebrospinal fluid). Blood supply is 20% of the body's total supply.

"I am better about things than about people. I'm more interested in people, but I'm better at ideas."

THE CORPUS CALLOSUM
The two hemispheres are connected by a "butterfly" shaped web of nerve fibres called the Corpus Callosum. It is also over one hundred million years old, and is the latest parts of the human brain to evolve (MacLean,1990).

This body of tissue, which actually has 10 – 12% more nerve fibres in the female brain, is the critical path that enables the two hemispheres to function as a whole brain. It is responsible for the iteration of signals or messages between the left and right cerebral hemispheric cortices. In girls, it matures 2 to 3 years earlier than in boys.

To enable the various parts of the left and right brain hemisphere to connect and communicate, the brain functions as an integrated whole. There are a number of pathways for this which serve as a 'bridge' and make it whole: The corpus callosum!

These **"pathways" are a collection of some 300 million connective nerve fibres**. The term "corpus colossal" comes from Latin. Corpus means "body" and Callosum is also Latin for colossal or huge. **Within these connective fibres, are billions of nerve cells or neurons**. One appropriate metaphor for this function would be a "super computer link cable", but in speed and capacity, not so much in design.

NEURONS AND AXONS
Maybe there are **over 180 billion neurons** which are located in the cortex. However, **each neuron has a long linkage called an axon**. These axons stretch into the brain below the cortex. This mass of axonic fibers, also known as "white matter", connects other "mirror image" neurons in the opposite hemisphere, through the corpus callosum.

Each neuron can receive signals from up to 200,000 other neurons that are adjacent. **The point of contact is called a synapse,** which is like a gap or space where the signals are transmitted electro-chemically. These chemicals are called **neuro-transmitters**. Each **synapse is enhanced by clusters of micro cells called astrocytes**. Positive neural networks are produced when we start with and build on the familiar or simple. This happens when we are not rushed or panicky, when stress is lower and we are in a relaxed yet alert mode – as in an alpha learning state. Negative neural networks are formed when excessive confusion, or complexity, are introduced too soon or too fast – producing panic and stress and stress produces hormones destructive to memory.

Apart from these longer neuronal linkages called axons, there are other smaller fibres that extend out to connect with the axons of other cells. **These are called dendrites.**

Most neurons can link up with 200,000 others, but the average is 60,000. When any part is functioning actively, millions of neurons may be connecting (firing). This constitutes a neuronal network that is active at any one point. The more senses or intelligences we use, the greater the ratio of connections. While as few as 50 neurons may be active in recall, the connections could be in hundreds of millions.

> *"The more connections that can be made in the brain, the more integrated the experience is with memory."*
> *Conyngham, 2010*

NEUROPLASTICITY AND NEUROGENESIS

NEURONAL GROWTH

Neuroplasticity, as suggested by the word, **is when new neurons can grow**, especially where neurons have been damaged. It used to be thought that we are born with about 100 million neurons and when not used, they die off and that was it. This is now known not to be the case, and new neurons and related gliel cells can grow. This is called neurogenesis, and the related cells called **fibroblasts and astrocytes are more 'plastic'** and can grow or change. Some of this new cell growth is in the hippocampus, which is important for learning and memory.

THE ROLE OF ASTROCYTES

The real magic of the brain is in one type of gliel cell – called astrocytes – which can **migrate to areas of the brain to enhance neuronal activity and connectivity.** This is like a swarm of bees moving from one clump of plants to another to pollinate the flowers. Or, like chemicals being dropped into clouds to 'seed' the rain, what we call cloud seeding. This migration can include movement of astrocytes between the brain hemispheres. While there are the 'dominant' functions that are unique to each "hemisphere", there is a co-dependency, with one side sometimes helping the other.

BRAIN HEMISPHERE CO-DEPENDENCE

The two hemispheres are highly complementary. One example is in spatial reasoning. The right hemisphere deals with a more general sense of space, with the left side processing the more precise location of objects. For example, the right sees a tennis ball travelling, through space, but the left can pin point exactly where it will bounce when it hits the ground. Another example is where both language cortices are co-dependent. The left side processing rules for grammar, spelling and sequence, with the right processing the emotional intonation of words spoken, or even interpreting metaphorical meanings.

THE POWER OF ASTROCYTES

Now back to the **astrocytes, which are abundant and mobile**. They actually out number neurons with about **900 thousand per synapse and make up some 30-50% of the brain**. They surround the synapses where messages are passed between the neuronal fibres (axon and dendrites). Their functions are to **enhance synapse, formation, plasticity, effectiveness and growth**, especially **enhancing blood flow, energy metabolism** (the brain burns up a lot of oxygen and glucose) **strengthening immunity**, **speeding up** neurotransmission and growth or regeneration of cellular material (neurogenesis). They regulate the release of more or less all of these neurotransmitters.

More recent studies of astrocytes mobility in the brain supports this phenomena, as does the idea of brain plasticity. In newer theories of the brain, information is widely distributed, not necessarily limited to specific neuron sites. In mapping areas of the brain to determine those that relate to specific signals (for example, those related to hand movements), neuroscientists have found that these "sites" do not correspond to any particular neuron. Instead of a specific physical place, they observe a more fluid pattern of electrical activity. If information is stored in these networks of relationships among neurons, damage to a particular area of the brain will not result in the loss of that information. Other areas in the network may retain that information in some form. This is the essence of plasticity.

DIFFERENCE IN TYPES OF ASTROCYTES

Learning occurs through neuronal connectivity. By strengthening this, **astrocytes become essential to learning and memory**, and induce long term potentiation. (LTP) which is critical to laying down long term memory (refer to pages on memory later in the book). Different classes of astrocytes play different roles. Some live around the brains white matter or axonic cables that connect each hemisphere. They are domain specific.

THE MOBILITY OF ASTROCYTES

However another class of astrocytes are more mobile, and provide some pathways linking grey and white matter, travelling across the various layers of the cortex. **Astrocytes could also metaphorically be rather like the booster engines of a rocket, helping with speed and thrust.** Except, astrocytes are electrical in nature, can rush to speed up the synaptic connectivity to greatly enhance learning, thinking and memory. Damage to, or decline in their numbers, can lead to short circuitry, as in Dementia or Alzheimers disease. In a way we can thank them for our smartness or quick thinking and are critical, both in supplying more information, thoughts, ideas and connections, as well as speeding up the decision process.

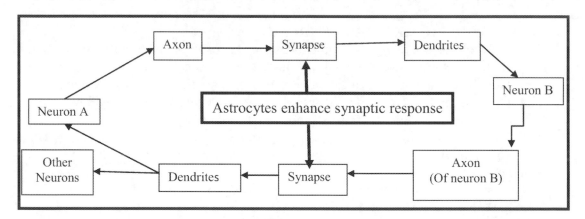

Number Brain cells lost between age 20 and 60 years	10,000-100,000 per day (Potentially)
Number of nerve fibres in Corpus Callosum	300 million
Number of nerve cells (Neurons) in Brain	100 billion approx. (plus millions of supporting cells)
Signals a neuron can receive, via synapses	200,000 (from other neurons)
Number of Astrocytes per synapse	900,000 (average)

WHOLE BRAINED CEO's
"The role of the general manager requires it to be very whole brained. To be a generalist who is multi talented in terms of brain dominance. To be a bridge that links all the specialist functions of management. This whole brained G.M. or CEO may also be viewed as a 'Jack of all Trades, yet Master of None'. While he or she may have once been a specialist, this ceases to become essential. In fact, it may even be a handicap to remain a specialist".

"The brain is like all muscles, use them or lose them"
Conyngham, 2013

LEARNING, TALENT AND CHARACTER

LEARNING STYLE DIFFERENCES

Much of our temperament is influenced by our emotional disposition. The centre for control and direction of emotions is in the **Limbic System** of the brain. Aspects of our personality that are more emotional in turn influence our memory and recall. Our learning style is one of these (Dryden, and Vos, 2010).

TALENT INFLUENCES LEARNING

Talents also have a strong influence on how we prefer to learn. If talent can be defined as a natural ability or aptitude and is genetically predisposed, it is very significant. Talent is any occurring pattern of thinking, feeling and doing where we naturally use our innate abilities. What creates this sustaining pattern of behaviour is that it is 'hard-wired' into the brain. By between 16 to 18 years, as the brain matures, these neuronal connections become well-cemented. As our **personality changes little throughout adult life,** our preferred styles of learning probably do not change much either.

CHARACTER IS PARTIALLY LEARNED

Character, on the other hand, has more to do with our beliefs and our sense of morals. We acquire these from our parents, teachers or role models. We learn what is right from wrong. especially from religious or spiritual teachings. **Sometimes we are punished if we do wrong and these memories are what form our character**. These are mediated by the cerebral cortex, which remembers people, places and things. This allows us to calculate, judge, compare or plan. As much as our behaviour is chemically driven, nurturing character is still limited to a certain extent (Hammer and Copeland, 1998).

GOING AGAINST GOOD CHARACTER

However, character and temperament are intertwined. Character, or certain memories of what is good or bad, right or wrong, can be modified by temperament. **At the heart of character are the concepts of self, shame and guilt**. If we are by nature a risk-taker, venturesome or curious, we may try out new and sometimes 'wrong' things, despite knowing they are so. We take the risk that we won't get caught or be found out. **"While the cat's away the mice will play". Here nature dominates nurture.**

STRONG DRIVE IS NEEDED

We can change our character, with sufficient incentives, or a strong emotional drive. For example, when a person gets into bad company, and desperately wants to conform, or is then offered a big enough incentive.

GOING AGAINST NATURE
If we persist in doing something 'against our nature' and constantly get rewarded with praise, this can boost our confidence and self-esteem. Eventually we start to become more comfortable with this newly modified temperament. We have, in effect, reprogrammed our temperament or 'rewired' our 'soft-wired' self.
We will not, however, re-wire the 'hard-wiring' or genetic self, as this would probably be almost impossible if that is part of our personality. So, given a non-nurturing environment or low will (motivation), we are unlikely to change our nature very much.
"Character in action is habit." Stephen Covey (1989)

WHY PEOPLE LEARN DIFFERENTLY

As we can see from previous pages, those aspects of personality called "temperament" and "talent" are strongly genetic. As such, they probably exert the strongest influence on how we prefer to learn. These include **more dominant intelligences, that we are inclined to want to use these more.**

Motivation and what McClelland (1980) calls the 3 social motives, including the need for **Power, Achievement or Affiliation**, are also believed to be strongly genetic. **These drives will also determine how we like to learn differently.**

People with a higher need for power tend to be dominant or directive in a learning group. Whereas those who have a high affiliation drive may not. They will prefer to work with people, but in a more compliant or even helpful way.

Those with higher achievement needs may be more task-oriented. They may not like working with others who are not equally as achievement-oriented. Often they typify the "lone wolf" who may not be good team players as those with affiliation needs.

Culture, as we have learned, is different. **It is also a strong determinant of style preference,** but more a group or social influence.

In many traditional cultures, especially in Asia, "face and harmony" are strong values. People generally accept the authority of the teacher unquestionably. Acceptance of authority and respect for elders go unchallenged (Asma, 2001).

The external environment plays an important role. Political and economic factors, while not directly influencing learning styles, impacts the education system and philosophy. **School systems and teaching methods definitely influence our learning styles.**

For example, how school classrooms and learning technologies are designed. With IT and "smart schools", and the growing use of Internet and web based learning technology, the concept of E-learning is becoming more popular. However, most schools and homes of the poor don't have such facilities. Equally, not all people like, or are competent enough to use them (Shephard, 2001).

Finally, the physical setting of the learning environment, such as seating, lighting, temperature or even noise are factors influencing learning style preferences (Kline, 1988).

An enriched environment can improve brain function. Dr. Marion Diamond, while at UCLA; found that neural connections and synaptic responses increased by more stimulation from games, variety, exercise and diet. For optimum growth in our brain, it needs stimulation; early, often and throughout life.

"Nature arms each man with some faculty which enables him to do easily some feat impossible to any other."
Ralph Waldo Emerson

FACTORS AFFECTING LEARNING

The chart shows a number of factors that affect learning and we have touched on most of them briefly so far. **One set of factors has to do with external influences** such as physical settings and teaching or training styles. **The other set is internal** (Gardner, 1999).

These include our psychological and physiological states and the inner meaning and significance of the learning. This includes our "spiritual" self and how much the learning experience is aligned with our real self our values and motivational needs. Perhaps whether we are sensing an intrinsic motivation and satisfaction and "inner" reward, rather than the extrinsic or outer meaning or external rewards.

To maximize our learning (understanding and retention), it could help when we know or can do the following:
- **Know our culturally programmed values and norms** and which are:
  - Most productive and helpful
  - Less productive or helpful
- **Consciously** reflect on these and try to optimize a productive balance.
- **Know our strong personality traits** and how they influence our natural or preferred style of learning (or behaving).
- **Use as many senses as possible to strengthen learning. E.g.**

  Seeing, Hearing, Smelling, Expressing, Questioning, Tasting, Moving Doing/Touching, Listening and Writing.

- **Know our natural talents and intelligences and in which we are stronger. E.g.**

  Logical /analytical, Verbal/linguistic, Body kinesthetic, Interpersonal, Moral/ethical, Spiritual, Creative/imaginative, Visual/spatial, Musical/rhythmic, Intrapersonal, Naturalistic, Intuitive.

- Being able to **know and capitalize on other natural talent strengths**, such as:
  - ✓ Adaptability and flexibility
  - ✓ Achievement and activism
  - ✓ Communication and connectedness
  - ✓ Harmony, empathy and fairness
  - ✓ Futuristic, strategic, positivity

Long-term memory is stored and reinforced in many parts of the brain. The more senses or areas of the brain that are used in learning, the bigger and better our memory. This also ensures less of our total memory is lost, when the brain is damaged – e.g. through a stroke or traumatic injury.

"We all have the extraordinary coded within us, waiting to be released." Jean Houston

SUMMARY OF KEY POINTS

- Personality is defined as our mental, social and physical characteristics that remain stable, after age 25, to make us the unique person we are.

- Personality can be conveniently 'typed' by categorizing the many traits that influence our behaviour, in to clusters. These in turn can be divided into aptitudes/talents/intelligences, motivational drives and temperament.

- Personality traits are more the result of genetic influence (nature) than of culture and upbringing (nurture). But the expression of genes, which are like chemical switches, still require stimuli from our environment (nurture).

- Other ways of understanding our temperament and preferences comes from discovering whether we are more a 'deliberation' or 'liberation' type.

- The 'Triune' Brain Model of Cerebral, Limbic and Reptilian is depicted as 3 evolutionary layers.

- The connection between the left and right hemispheres is called the corpus callosum. It can be likened to a superfibre optic cable with millions of nerve fibres that enable signals or messages to iterate at a higher speed between the two brain hemispheres. The female brain has some 10-12% more of these fibres and matures around 2 years earlier at puberty in girls, then boys.

- There are perhaps up to 180 million (nerve cells) in the brain, which in turn each have fibers that enable them to interconnect. The connection points are called synapses, which are further strengthened by clusters of even smaller (gliel) cells, called "astrocytes". Some of which have mobility and can move around to enhance and protect synaptic connectivity.

- People learn differently, due to their own personality types (eg: introverts versus extroverts) and cultural norms in education and teaching.

LEFT BRAIN
- Neurons more densely packed.
- Better suited to intense detailed or analytical work.
- Controls most of right body functions.
- More 'maleness'.

RIGHT BRAIN
- More white matter (axonicfibres).
- More wider or diverse areas are linked.
- More sensory and holistic or integrated.
-Controls most of left body functions.
- More 'femaleness'.

"With a good heredity, nature deals you a fine hand of cards; and with a good environment, you learn to play the hand well ."   *Walter Alvarez*

MULTI - SENSORY / MULTI -TRAIT LEARNING

- Use as many senses as possible

> Seeing
> Hearing
> Smelling
> Expressing
> Questioning

> Tasting
> Moving
> Doing / Touching
> Listening
> Writing

- Know our natural talents and intelligences and which we prefer to use

> Logical / analytical
> Verbal / linguistic
> Bodily kinesthetic
> Interpersonal
> Moral / ethical
> Spiritual

> Creative / imaginative
> Visual / spatial
> Musical / rhythmic
> Intrapersonal
> Naturalistic
> Intuitive

- Being able to know and capitalize on other natural talent strengths, such as:

> Adaptability and flexibility
> Achievement and activism
> Communication and connectedness
> Harmony, empathy and fairness
> Futuristic, strategic, positivity

ARE YOU A DELIBERATE OR LIBERATE LEARNING LEADER?
Check out which styles you favour. More left or right column styles

DELIBERATION (More Left Brain)	LIBERATION (More Right Brain)
1. More routine	1. Free spirit
2. More rational	2. More intuitive
3. Introverted	3. Extroverted
4. Plans ahead	4. Goes with the flow
5. Avoids risks	5. Takes risks
6. Steady and reliable	6. May be less reliable
7. Systematic/punctual	7. Erratic / often late
8. Ignores dreams	8. In touch with dreams
9. More 'cold'	9. More 'warm'
10. Snaps awake	10. Slow to awake
11. Plays by the rules	11. Plays it by ear
12. Can separate 'feeling' from thinking	12. Integrates feelings in expression

Source : Orstein, 1993
The Roots of the self

REFERENCES

Asma, A. (1996). *Going Glocal* . Kuala Lumpur: MIM.

Catell, R. (2013). An Open Letter to the American. *American psychologist.*

Covey, S. (1989). *The 7 Habits of Highly Effective People* . NY : Simon and Schuster.

Dawkins, R. (1989). *The Selfish Gene.* UK: Oxford Press.

Dryden, G and Vos.J. (2010). *Learning Unlimited* . UK: Learning Web.

Freud, S. (1983). *A primer on Freudian Psychology.* Amazon: NY.

Gardner, H. (1999). *Intelligence Reframed.* NY: Basic Books.

Gazzeniaga, M. (1992). *Nature's Mind.* NY: Basic Books.

Hammer, D and Copeland. (1998). *Living with our Genes.* NY: Doubleday Press.

Jacques, E. (1994). *Human Capability.* USA: Cason Hall.

Jung, C. (2006). *The Undiscovered Self.* NY: Signet.

Kline, P. (1988). *The Everyday Genius.* USA: Great Ocean Publications.

Le Doux, J. (2002). *The Synpatic Self.* London: Penguin Books.

McClelland, D. (1988). *Human Motivation.* UK: Simon and Schuster.

McCrae, R.R. and Costa, P.T. . (1990). *Personality in Adulthood.* NY: Guildford.

O'Conner J. Et. al. (1994). *Training with NLP.* NY: Harper Collins.

Ornstein, R. (1993). *The Roots of The Self.* NY: Harper Collins.

Pinker, S. (1997). *How the Mind Works.* London: Penguin Books.

Ridley, M. (1994). *Nature Via Nurture.* UK: Fourth Estate.

Schultz, M. (2005). *The New Feminine Brain.* NY: Free Press.

Shephard, P. (2001). *Whole Brain Thinking and Learning.* Kuala Lumpur: Brain Works Media .

Shephard, P. C. (2014). *A collection of quotations: unpublished paper.* Cardiff: Wales.

Sperry, R. (N.d.). Mid-Brain Interaction. *Neuroscience, 5*(2).

Wright, W. (1998). *Born That Way.* New York: Alfred Knopt.

*Some references are not cited in the chapter text.

CHAPTER THREE

COMPETENCE POTENTIAL AND DEVELOPMENT

LEARNING OBJECTIVES FOR THIS CHAPTER

By the end of this chapter, you will be able to:

- Contrast the roles of thinking and learning and their relationships to brain dominance and competence.

- Identify the difference between Abilities, Aptitudes and Talents.

- Distinguish between competence and competency development.

- Clarify some leadership characteristics and competences that are universal and culturally contingent.

- Recognise how important it is to first know our natural talents, before learning, or developing our competence.

- Differentiate the influences of nature (genetics) and nurture (culture) on competence potential.

TABLE OF CONTENTS

COMPETENCE DEFINED

For academic purposes, we will define competence it here, as: "**The Right Combination of Know-How, Skills and Effort to Produce Desired Results.**" The term comes from the word "compete" and infers that a winning performance or standards of excellence would be implicit in it. These performance standards (inputs) would change - as the results expected (outputs) - change.

Assuming the corporate goals are ones of competitive excellence, high quality and continuous improvement towards zero defects, then the competencies will need to be dynamic and of a higher "degree" (performance standard) due to the outputs of quantity or quality being continuously greater.**Thus the term "competency" assumes a cluster of "micro skills" needed to be well integrated and timed.**

Consider the example of a competent pianist who needs to combine a precise and differing pressure on the piano keys, aligned with the reading of notes from the music score, pressure on the foot pedal and a precise speed (tempo). They may also need to speak to, and smile at the audience. **Within a competent pianist are more than a dozen "competencies" in the cognitive, psychomotor and affective domains.** What often makes the difference between winners and champions is training or coaching from the best, with practice, practice, practice (experience) and a **"winning" attitude**.

Incentives that affect motivation are also to be considered when it comes to effort. (Thus, some competencies are not only cognitive or psycho-motor), but also affective (attitudinal or emotional).

Further Definitions of Job Competencies
1. What a person must know (Knowledge) and/or be able to do (Skill) to perform their work successfully (Performance Standard).

2. An area of Knowledge or Skill that is critical for producing key outputs.

3. Internal capability for a given job, which may be expressed in a broad, even infinite, array of on-the-job behaviours.

We need the right balance between 'skill' and 'will'. Skill without will is like a super trained racing driver with no car to drive. Will is added when the highly motivated driver slides into the cockpit and drives the car to win the race. The will to win alone however, will not make us a winner. We still need the skill to operate the car. The winner's competence is the right balance between skill and will. But which comes first? As we are not born with skill, and need will to learn, it must be will. Yet, increased skill raises our self-worth, and this in turn motivates us, thus fuelling our will.

"Most Americans don't know what their strengths are. When asked, they look at you blankly, or respond that they are subject knowledge. This is the wrong answer."
Peter Drucker

COMPETENCE DEVELOPMENT

Thinking and learning are inseparable. We think in order to learn and while learning. **Effective thinking contributes to effective learning. We also need to learn how to think**. While we are born with the ability to learn and think, their interdependent processes can be improved more easily if we analyze them separately. We can see better their relationship and how they zigzag like lighting in our brain, before being stored as knowledge and skill potential.

Competence therefore, can be developed and enhanced with improved thinking and learning processes. So let's take a look first at thinking.

DIMENSIONS OF THINKING

We need something to think about, a sort of "raw material". This could be anything that we have perceived and stored in our memory; from the moment we are able to recall life's experiences. This is usually around 3 to 4 years of age. (The Past) It could be something we **presently perceive**. As you are reading this text, some thinking is occurring. Even if you daydream or take a mental detour, you are still thinking. **We can also think about the future.**

We can describe this dimension as processing input data that is new, which the brain will normally relate or compare immediately with past or existing memories and experiences. While this may happen at a conscious or deliberate level, it is usually non consious. From this we may formulate new concepts, ideas and relationships or associations.

New thought processes will continue until our mind is distracted, redirected or perhaps, "falls asleep". The experience can continue in the form of dreams! Have you ever fallen asleep while reading a book or watching TV? And later recall having a dream that included aspects of your earlier perceptions and experiences? In other words, **the brain is thinking most of the time**, even if we are not conscious of it.

TYPES OF LEARNING PROCESSES

What are these types of learning we need, in order to become a more competent leader? First are natural/instinctive processes, such as learning how to crawl or walk. Further processes could be conscious and deliberate, such as learning a foreign language. To develop competence, these processes that come to us more naturally and at a greater level of competence, may be developed earlier or faster. These are what we refer to as potential competence and include those natural talents with a strong genetic predisposition.

In a study of 1,800 Asian professionals, their No: 1 contributor to job satisfaction was the opportunity to learn, grow and develop. Another similar study in the UK found that the most important aspect of their work was "using knowledge and experience to make decisions"; equal to "having control over what they do". There is a strong correlation between the amount of competence and control given. Paradoxically though, the more control we experience, the more we have an opportunity to learn, grow and develop greater ability.

"Learning is a process of turning experience into knowledge, knowledge into understanding, and understanding into wisdom. Wisdom is more important than thinking, its knowing which initially still comes from learning. Thus we cannot become all knowing - or all wise - without Learning".

Conyngham, 2001

ABILITIES, APTITUDES AND TALENTS

SOME DEFINITIONS

There is often confusion between **Ability, Capability, Aptitude or Talent**. Earlier, we defined "Talent" as a component of personality, and as a naturally recurring pattern of thought, feeling and behaviour. But we won't know it exists until it is applied. Unless one has the opportunity to discover and nurture it, it may remain hidden or "latent". **Talent** is also a potential, so tests may be given to help discover the degree of talent possessed. These are called **"Aptitude" tests**, thus talent is an aptitude. Some call it '**potentiality**'.

Aptitudes can be defined as a capacity or natural talent that someone possesses. They are genetically predisposed, so are often referred to as natural or innate. Intelligence, also largely genetic, is a dimension of talent. But some intelligences are more genetic.

Ability on the other hand, can be differentiated, and is defined as a '**power to perform a physical or mental act**'. It is a capacity to learn and perform, and usually refers to skills. Such skills can be physical or mental. Ability is more easily measured, observed and improved with training.

THINKING ABILITIES VERSUS STYLES

In assessing our level of competence in thinking, or what psychologists call cognitive abilities, we must differentiate them from style. **Ability is how well we think, whereas style is how we like to think**. Style is a natural preference, but we can learn to use a range of styles. E.g., some readers may not be familiar with Mind Mapping® or what I call Idea Mapping and others call "Thought Mapping". It can be learnt, and the more we use it, the better our ability to master it. But **our degree of preference for it determines how long we persevere** to master it. Extreme left-brainers tend not to master it as well as those who are more whole-brained. Why? Because it uses a lot of the right brain, which extreme left-brainers find strange or difficult. It isn't logical or linear; it's too random or spontaneous. But it is 'Whole Brained!'

So ability influences style, and in turn, our preferred style increases our ability. How do we test thinking ability, which is much more difficult than measuring style preference? Experts disagree about the predictive powers of ability testing. They do agree though, that **tests are highly imperfect predictors (Sternberg, 1988)**. As a general consensus, differences in ability from testing students' performances are about 20%. Among adult workers it's probably as low as 10%. The variation is explained by thinking styles. (See for more on learning, see chapter 10).

According to a Gallup poll study of 1.7 million employees, in 101 organizations, from 63 countries, only 20% felt their strengths were being used each day. All people have a unique and wide range of abilities and talents, but if only 20% are being regularly capitalized upon, organizations are allowing an enormous waste of talent. This must contribute to a great amount of human resource inefficiency and ineffectiveness. But beyond this, the lack of employee's self-worth would lead to low job satisfaction and low motivation (Buckingham, and Clifton, 1999).

"No one can manage you if you don't give them permission to do so. But, if you are interested in accomplishing as much as you are capable of, then I believe there are good reasons to grant that permission".   *David Maister, True Professionalism*

NATURE REQUIRES NURTURE

Natural or genetic predisposition alone is not enough. Nature requires nurture for development. Just as we may have a plant seed lying dormant for years, the seed lies dormant until a nurturing environment is provided. Given the right moisture, temperature and light, the seed germinates and flourishes, hopefully to reach its full potential. People are similar.

If we like safe bets, we probably say '50, 50', i.e., half genetic (nature) and half environment (nurture). However, that is too simplistic and general. In a way, from the DNA we inherit, the whole embryo is genetic. There is a form of 'predestiny' and in here is the genetic inheritance of what we become, shaped by perhaps 50 to 100 thousand genes.

What do genes really do? They don't actually produce behaviour; they **control the mix of biochemical's that influence a behavioural response to our environment.** The brain chemicals that turn on and off when we experience sadness, happiness, fear, courage and our emotional and temperamental disposition are controlled by genes. They also act on the neuro-transmitters essential for thinking, learning and memory.

Human experience - and that includes learning continuously - shapes and reshapes our brain. This is the concept of the 're-wiring' of neuronal networks. The environment around us, our culture, hobbies, interests and work all give 'shape' to our brain. While basic **personality and brain dominance remain remarkably stable, our potential to think and learn can grow forever** (Le Doux, 2002).

WE ARE WHAT WE DO

Our brain has immense capacity for reason, forethought, insight, intuition and creativity. To become great, we must constantly exercise and stretch this capacity and, as we do, we continuously 'reprogram' our brain. **Personality characteristics determine the type of job or work we like and the unique talents we discover that we 'naturally' have.**

DEFINING POTENTIAL

Potential can also be equated with the 'talents' that we have latent, dormant or discovered. The better known talents that are physical, such as in most sports are more anatomical in nature and easy to discover and observe. However, the opportunity for discovery must be present. For example, one may have long legs and be tall and could potentially be good at basketball, but the culture and opportunity to play basketball may not provide for that talent to be nurtured, let alone be discovered!

Disease is a generic term that includes mental, psychological, psychiatric and physical. Many personality disorders and diseases that have a genetic predisposition (nature) - occur more readily in adverse environmental circumstances (nurture). But some environmental Circumstances are created. While some circumstances cannot be avoided, some can. It requires awareness and education. E.g., children with a low birth weight (LBW) or underweight pre-term babies may have greater difficulties in reading and learning. They may develop more Behavioural problems and their overall intelligence may also be lower later in life.

"Human beings inherit a basic capacity for learning, from a certain range of experiences, and when these happen, the brain develops normally." Robert Ornstein The Roots of the Self (1993)

A WHOLE BRAINED CHECKLIST

TALENTS AND TEMPERAMENT ARE ANATOMICAL AND BIOLOGICAL

Robert Ornstein (1993), an eminent neuroscientist and writer, classifies talents into anatomical and biological. Anatomical includes body or organ size, shape and structure. These are easily measured in athletes, for example. Biological refers to the biochemical and physiological functioning within the brain and central nervous system.

Of the most biologically similar talents are the 'motivators', which are located in those brain areas that regulate hunger, thirst and various appetites from food to sex. **These are sometimes called 'drives'** and are not mental or cognitive. **They are regulated by hormones,** and each of them still has a controlling or influencing gene. E.g., some people have a high metabolic rate, burning up calories faster, and thus have a greater drive or appetite for food. Some people have a high sex drive and yet others a lower one, just as each differs in terms of our tolerance levels of hot or cold temperatures. Ornstein (1993) lists further talents, to include our natural inclination (aptitude) for such things as sensory acuity, which includes smell, movement, eye-hand coordination, or manual dexterity. We know some people naturally move with grace and fluidity, whereas others are clumsy or awkward, and no matter how hard they try, will not be a great dancer or gymnast.

TALENTS: LEFT vs. RIGHT BRAINED

Ornstein also **classifies many of our talents** as having a special concentration **within** either **the left or right brain hemispheres**. He includes the talents of locating and identifying, such as knowing space and relationships between objects, size, shape and proximity. These are right brained.

TALENT IS INTELLIGENCE (OR INTELLIGENCES ARE TALENTS)

Many of these talents would be what Howard Gardner calls Multiple Intelligences (MI). For example, knowing space and spatial ability is what he calls 'visual-spatial' intelligence. And we know that this differs from person to person and between genders. (Gardner, 1999).

As an example, airline pilots would need to have this talent or capability highly developed. The talent itself is innate or genetic, without which the pilot would not be able to learn and master the skills required. While flying a 787 requires high visual-spatial intelligence, it also requires other talents too.

Temperament is chemical. From even before birth, our brains are awash with a chemical soup mix. Major chemicals are the sex hormones of testosterone (male), estrogens (female), adrenalin (nor epinephrine) and serotonin, ACTH and DHEA, to name a few. Levels of serotonin will influence certain aggressive leadership or dominance behaviour. High levels of adrenalin produce higher arousal needs. It lowers the threshold of shyness or inhibition that we see in introverts, for example. High testosterone levels typically are associated with dominance, aggression, dogmatism & rigidity whereas high estrogens produce increased nurturing, collaborative and flexible thinking. And these chemicals - while turned on or off by genes - still need environmental stimulation.

"I may not be totally perfect, but parts of me are excellent." Brilliant, J.

3 LEVELS OF CAPABILITY POTENTIAL

According to Jacques and Cason (1994) 'Potential Capability' can be divided into three levels: Current, Currently Applied and Future. The first and second levels are not difficult to assess, given an objective system of appraisal and leaders who know how their employees are doing. **But unlocking and developing future potential is a greater challenge.**

POTENTIAL CAPABILITY OVER TIME

Jacques and Cason define this 'future potential capability' as the predicted level that a person will possess at some specific time in the future. They present evidence that **potential capability grows throughout life,** from early childhood to old age, along regular and predictable maturational pathways.

SELF-MANAGING TALENTS

There are also the talents possessed by many leaders of inferring, organizing, planning and controlling. These 'self governing' or self managing talents probably have a strong evolutionary origin late in human evolution, perhaps with the emergence of modern man some four million years ago, when there was a period of rapid cortical growth in the brain.

THE THREE DIMENSIONS OR LEVELS

In their book *Human Capability and Work*, the authors explain that capability has three dimensions, viz: (Jacques and Cason, 1994).

(i)   **Complexity level of mental processing,** an 'information-gathering' and processing function centered in specific areas of the brain;
(ii)   **Level of knowledge and skill possessed.**
(iii)   **Level of interest or commitment**. This would include the level of drive, interests, enthusiasm or strength of values and attitudes possessed about the work or any activity, subject, concept, etc.

Dimensions (ii) and (iii) act on dimension (i), or mental processing.

6 PERSONALITY TRAITS OF SELF-MADE MILLIONAIRES:
1. Excessive energy: Most are workaholics, who can't stop thinking about their work, even while relaxing, who don't take vacations or talk about retiring.
2. Ambition: They're motivated by a need to be active and creative, a compulsive will to succeed.
3. Emotional & cardiovascular stamina: Ability to take risks and the resulting stress.
4. Supreme self-confidence: They stick to an idea, even if ridiculed by others, and make it succeed.
5. Disciplined mind: Not necessarily a brilliant mind, but a basic intelligence, common sense, ability to concentrate and a gift for solving problems.
6. Outer-directed personality: They're not introspective but action-oriented, and many have a 'sales' personality that can generate enthusiasm in others.

Charles Garfield

"There are Dynamos, Cruisers and Losers....Dynamos are always working to learn something new and are continually adding to their knowledge and skills."

David Maister

COMPETENCE IS CONSCIOUS AND NON-CONSCIOUS

Learning is all about perception, recognition and memory, and involves many parts of the brain functioning almost simultaneously. It happens at both the un conscious and non-conscious levels. The conscious level is not so much a level per se, it is a process. It involves the cerebral cortex, often thought of as a "higher" level and is dominated by the left hemisphere.

CONSCIOUSNESS IS AWARENESS

A conscious state is when we are aware of a thought or feeling (including a competence level). It is a state of full alertness or wakefulness, where our brainwaves are operating **at the beta level of between 13 to 30 cycles per second (cps)**. A brainwave is an electro-magnetic impulse emanating from the high activity of a neuronal circuit. **When a thought or idea occurs the neurons around that area in the cortex fire together more rapidly.** Neurotransmitters (chemicals) are mixing, supported by astrocytes, while it moves from short term memory – totally lost – or to a stronger mid-term memory.

CONSCIOUS AND NON-CONSCIOUS MEMORY

Once the idea/thought/feeling is recognized, it can pass into mid or long term memory. That is a part of the learning process which resides now in the right hemisphere. The automatic recognition happens when the incoming information – a stimulus – passes back through the limbic system which registers its emotional connection, such as familiarity or non-familiarity. Mainly a non-conscious process, it only becomes conscious when it passes into the cerebral cortex. Here it takes on an identity, provided the procedure is not disrupted (like during a distraction). Full recognition then fails, as all or some of the information is lost (short-term memory). Thus an emotional connection strengthens memory. The non-conscious mind is when we relax; when daydreaming, fantasizing or when meditating or praying, our brainwaves slow down. Initially we enter a state of between **8 to 12 cps, (cycles per second) called alpha**, and move to a deeper level called **theta, of 4 to 7 cps**. Here we are close to sleep, but may not actually yet be asleep.

BRAINWAVES AND LEARNING

During **alpha and theta** modes, our non conscious brain becomes **highly receptive** to suggestion or information presented to it. This is because the conscious beta state does not compete or distract. In these modes, the absorption of new cognitive learning – like language – is very effective. The key is to maintain this mode without **going up to beta or down further to delta, of 1 to 3 cps**, where we literally have fallen asleep.

Emotions are generated non consciously but we do experience a conscious awareness of the emotion, as a later response, which may seem like it is simultaneous with the feeling. In fact, we have little direct control over our emotions. Although we may have some conscious control, it is at best very weak. While emotions can flood our consciousness and we may be aware of them, we often cannot control them (eg. uncontrollable weeping or laughter). This is so because the wiring of the brain at this point in human evolution, is such that connections from the unconscious emotional limbic systems to the cognitive (cerebral) systems are stronger than their reverse connections.

"The non-conscious mind cannot distinguish between the imagined and the real"
Maxwell Maltz

BRAIN DOMINANCE AND COMPETENCE

While dominance and competence are not the same, they are closely correlated in a causative way. If we are to develop high levels of competence more quickly and easily, interest and motivation are essential. See below. One rationale for looking at brain dominance is to assess the cognitive/thinking and emotional/feeling **preferences** of people. (Herrmann, 1996).

BEHAVIOUR, PERFORMANCE & RESULTS

Because our thinking and feeling selves (or our 'cerebral' and 'limbic' selves) govern our behavioural selves, such assessment can be highly predictive of our behaviour. And it's our **behaviour that produces results**. E.g., when we appraise employees, do we attach more value to – the 'input' performance (behaviour) - or the 'output' performance (results)?

While we may appraise both, there is inevitably a causative relationship. And it's the behavioural component that includes the 'competencies' we have developed and applied. But, it's also the **strength of competencies** that determine the final outcome: the results.

MEASURING THE COMPETENCE

While we probably know the results we want, be it 'bottom line', task achievement, or harmonious and synergistic teamwork – we may not always know which thinking or feeling behaviours or competencies specifically are responsible. Using Brain Dominance profiles, help us assess and measure these behavioural competencies for individuals and teams. Thus, we can also use the profiles to identify learning/training needs or for career counselling. (Herrmann, 1996). **There is therefore a positive causative relationship between preference and competence.** While we are born with a genetic potential for cognitive style, we need our abilities and aptitudes to be nurtured. We can respond to our **nurturing environment** positively and seek to develop our mental abilities. But we may **need incentives and training** once we experience success.

From our learned efforts, we feel more motivated to try harder. We also win praise and other rewards. This tends to reinforce our motivation and strengthen our preference, which in turn leads us to acquire even greater competence. This **feedback loop** can turn a brain hemispheric dominance, into a powerful competence to continue to use that thinking preference even more.

Brain Dominance → leads to Preference →which leads to Interest →which leads to Motivation → which leads to Competence.

Because preference has a strong emotional or limbic association, it promotes greater interest or desire. Desire is also driven from the limbic system which produces brain chemicals and hormones to strengthen behaviour. Habit, which is a form of addiction, is also strengthened by brain chemicals. Receptors for these chemicals gradually form, thus further strengthening the need or desire for that behaviour. Due to this, the competence that we are trying to develop will come faster and easier if it matches our preference. Style is also a preference.

"The performance-praise-preference loop works not only for individuals, but indeed for entire cultures." Ned Herrmann

LEARNING POTENTIAL AND COMPETENCE

If we agree that learning takes place in the brain, the question might be how fast and to what degree. What potential have we to excel at some skill, to become a genius, to achieve mastery? How much of this potential is 'pre-destiny' and locked in our genome and how much can be nurtured and strengthened through learning?

BEHAVIOUR AND NEURONS

Behaviour occurs, due to the billions of our neurons networking and firing. While we are born with more than 100 billion neurons, maybe even 180 billion, it's not the numbers that is important. **From the moment of birth we start losing thousands of neurons each day due to their lack of use**. What's important is how well the remaining ones are stimulated and strengthened. Neurons form connections with thousands of others and these connections are called synapses. (Gazzaniga,1992)

HARDWIRING AND SOFTWIRING

As we exercise our natural talents and learn new skills, the neuronal networks responsible for each task become stronger and faster. Hardwiring remains the mainstay of our potential with these latent or discovered talents waiting to be nurtured. Springing from this mainstay are the abilities and skills that we can develop through our life. This is the **'soft wiring' that can be continuously rewired**. (Le Doux, 2002). This is where the plasticity of the brain enables us to unlearn, relearn and achieve mastery. However, training given in an area where there is no talent, means we are wasting a lot of time, energy or costs. **It's like training chickens to swim**. They **don't have the natural talent**. Whereas with **ducks, swimming comes naturally**. When we refer to learning ability, we must appreciate that **a great deal of learning occurs through language**. If we have not mastered the language in which we wish to learn, we are extremely handicapped. Ability to learn our native tongue seems to be a natural function, 'hardwired' into the human brain. How quickly and how well we master the language is believed to be strongly genetic. However, learning to master a second or third language is more a gift that a few have more than most, and becomes more difficult the older we become.

- *42 days after conception, while still an embryo, our first neurons are formed.*
- *120 days later, we have 100 billion neurons.*
- *At 210 days, axons connect to hundreds of thousands of other neurons. These are called "synapses". Learning produces a synaptic response, which strengthens the connections. Between birth and up to 24 months, learning is mostly right brained.*
- *Synapses, which are electro-chemical connections, probably number around 20 quadrillion.*
- *We are born with over 100 billion neurons and between ages 3 to 15 years we lose billions.*
- *By age 16 to 18, our brain has matured and rewiring become harder and slower. Learning a new language becomes harder and harder.*
- *But due to neurogenesis, we do form new connections as we learn a new language.*

> *"The danger of training, where talent doesn't exist or is weak, is that we burn out before any significant improvement shows. We also waste time, energy and cost, and no matter how good the training, at least we can only achieve mediocrity. If we want mastery, we must train where a natural talent already exists to a strong degree."*
> *Buckingham and Clifton*

CULTURAL INFLUENCES

- Competence is not cultural, as there will be individuals who are competent in the same thing – in all cultures.
- Culture can sanction or strongly nurture types of values and competencies.
- Most of our personality traits are not cultural in their make-up, and family and upbringing seems not to influence them much.

CULTURE DETERMINES ACCEPTANCE

Culture will determine, to some degree, how acceptable they are and of ways the behaviours may be displayed, condoned, reinforced or inhibited. E.g., aggressiveness may be more acceptable, even admired, **in highly individualistic cultures** such as those in America or Australia. And warmth or caring may be seen as too 'feminine' or weak in these, more **'macho' cultures**. In individualistic cultures where individual innovativeness is more valued, individual originality, creativity and imaginativeness will be fostered or encouraged more. But in **collectivist cultures**, these qualities will be valued more as group or team oriented. (Asma, 2001).

COGNITIVE STYLES

Although our cognitive styles and learning preferences are more strongly genetic in predisposition, culture may 'force' the mass of children, due to the educational system and philosophy, to learn in a particular way. But this way may not suit a significant portion of the student population who are genetically programmed to learn in another mode.

EASTERN VERSUS WESTERN INFLUENCE

Take for example 'rote' learning versus 'critical thinking'. **Collectivist cultures**, as in Africa or Asia, would reinforce the more rigid, disciplined and 'class drill' type of learning. These cultures would not value the more **individualistic expression** of self and freedom to experiment or deviate.

Most American education systems permit or encourage this, placing a value on individual self-esteem and self-fulfilment. Much more emphasis is placed on the **individual self**, which values initiative, originality, independence and self-sufficiency, or self- reliance. Such **individualistic cultures, therefore, tolerate or value a higher level of frankness, assertiveness, confrontation** and even challenging openly those who are in authority or who may be elder, e.g. a teacher/trainer or superior.

We are each born into a culture, and cultures differ in terms of structure, values and norms. All these affect our development, as the brain is not matured at birth. While the "hard wiring" (genetic predisposition) is there, the brain needs a range of signals from the environment for it to continue developing. This is "soft wiring" and will be continuously rewired from our cultural programming. We inherit a capacity for learning, and the brain is not complete without this capacity. But it wires up differently from culture to culture, as environments differ. Adaptive flexibility also diminishes after ages 12 to 13, as the brain matures.

"Most of what is unusual about man can be summed up in one word: culture."
Richard Dawkins , The Selfish Gene

CULTURE AND LEADERSHIP

When researching culture and leadership, it often begs the question – is there any one style that can be universally effective across all cultures? Many notable scholars on the subject have been searching, several of which we have shared already in this book and in this chapter. One of the central themes is around similarities and differences and how they have evolved – or are still – evolving. With the internet or jet travel bringing leaders of the world ever closer through education or business and trade, is there a set of values, behavioural norms or competencies that could be globally universal?

THE 'GLOBE' STUDIES

One interesting research project that is longitudinal and ongoing, is called 'GLOBE', which is an acronym formed from: "Global Leadership and Organisational Behaviour Effectiveness". It was conceived in 1991 and after some research funding, **commenced in 1993. 170 social scientists and management scholars from 62 cultures, in all major world regions,** produced a book (Ed. House, et. al 2004). One phase of the project focused on **9 core cultural dimensions**. They became the independent variables for the research, and are: Uncertainty (RISK) Avoidance, Power Distance, Institutionalised Collectivism, In-Group Collectivism (Refer to section on LMX), Gender Egalitarianism, Assertiveness, Future Orientation, Performance Orientation and Humane Orientation. The first six originate from Geert Hofstede's pioneer studies (1980). Gender Egalitarianism and Assertiveness, replace Hofstede's "Masculine Feminine" dimensions. Future Orientation was derived from the dimensions "Past, Present and Future" (Kluckhorn & Strodtbeck, 1961). This is similar to the "Confucian Work Dynamism" dimension, or "long-term orientation" (Hofstede, 2001). "Performance Orientation" is derived from David McClelland's "Achievement Motivation Theory" (1961).

THE RESEARCH SAMPLE

The focus was also more on middle management, where numbers are larger than senior or top executives. There is also greater interaction with more employees from peers to subordinates, as well as pressures from top management. Overall efficacy of the GLOBE study **showed a correlation of .85 or higher on all leadership and cultural variables**, so it is very strong, reliable and valid global research. Also, national borders don't always demarcate cultural boundaries, especially in multi-ethnic societies. Where this existed (eg: Malaysia, USA, UK or Australia), the subculture that was more commercially active, was included in this sample. More than 17,000 middle management responses, from 62 cultures and 951 organizations formed the sample.

CONCLUSIONS

So we can conclude that their study provides our answer to the opening question – "Is there a universal set of Leadership styles and competencies that can be effective across all cultures?" The findings provide a highly practical template for a truly "Glocal" leader, who is also highly acceptable at the local level as well.

"An outstanding leader is exceptionally skilled at motivating influencing or enabling you, others, or groups to contribute to the success of an organisation or task" Hoppe, M.H. 2007

LEADERSHIP CHARACTERISTICS

From this study, 35 leader attributes or behaviours were identified, some of which are contributors and 8 universally viewed as impediments. The researchers finally agreed on 6 clusters of leader behaviours that could be considered 'Global'. These were:

i) **Charismatic/Value-Based Leadership** – the ability to inspire and motivate and achieve high performance. This ability had 6 sub categories:
  a) Visionary
  b) Inspirational
  c) Decisiveness
  d) Self Sacrificial
  e) Integrity
  f) Performance Orientation

ii) **Team Oriented Leadership** – with 5 categories:
  a) Collaborative
  b) Integrative
  c) Diplomatic
  d) Benevolent
  e) Administrative

iii) **Participative Leadership** – Involving others in decision making and implementation with 2 categories:
  a) Participative
  b) Democratic

iv) **Humane Oriented Leadership** – Supportive, Considerate, Compassionate and Generous, with 2 categories:
  a) Modesty
  b) Humane

v) **Autonomous Leadership** – Independent and Individualistic, and self-centric with 1 category – important for self – directed leadership.
  a) Autonomous

vi) **Self Protective Leadership** – Ensuring Safety and Security of individuals and groups through status enhancement and face saving with 5 categories:
  a) Self Centred
  b) Status Conscious
  c) Conflict Inducer
  d) Face Saver
  e) Procedural

This in total actually gives us 21 behavioural competencies. The theoretical model focused on 4 main propositions, viz:
  1) Societal-Cultural Norms and Practices
  2) Organizational Structure, Culture and Practices
  3) Strategic Organizational Contingencies (PESTELIED)
  4) Each having an impact on: Leader Attributes and Behaviour (See Above).

The above VI orientations can also be called "style preferences" and strongly correlate with personality traits. Thus, no (1) can be called a performance oriented style, with such traits as self-sacrificial, visionary, inspirational, decisiveness and action-oriented (performance driven). But integrity is often called a value. The Globe research also looked at other factors, including Leader Acceptance (Followership) and Effectiveness (Economic).

UNIVERSAL AND CULTURAL LEADERS COMPETENCIES

So, back to our conclusion on the "GLOBE" Leadership study,that there is a universal acceptable style, the following core competences were found from their research. (Hoppe,2007).

Contribute to being seen as 'outstanding' leaders

Trustworthy	Decisive	Excellence-oriented
Just/Fair	Dependable	Intelligent
Effective bargainer	Win-win problem solver	Foresight/visionary
Plans ahead	Administrative skilled	Team builder
Coordinator	Motive arouser	Communicative/Informed
Encourager	Positive/Optimistic	Dynamic/charismatic

Behaviours that hold back from becoming an 'outstanding' leader

Being a Loner	Irritable	Anti-Social	Non-cooperative
Indirect/Non-explicit	Ruthless	Egocentric	Dictatorial

Cultural contingent leader characteristics

Traits more acceptable in individualistic cultures.

Anticipatory/Intuitive	Self-effacing	Independent
Ambitious	Logical	Individualistic
Sincere	Orderly/Procedural	Worldly
Intra-group competitor	Risk taker	Enthusiastic
Provocateur	Willful	

Traits that maybe valued lower: in high achieving individualistic or egalitarian cultures and still important in more collective cultures.

Cunning	Indirect	Intra-group conflict avoider
Elitist	Self-sacrificial	Ruler
Sensitive	Formal	Compassionate
Evasive/indirect	Status-consciencous	Cautious Micro-manager
Subdued	Domineering	Class conscious
Habitual/consistent/predictable (ie: inflexible)		

Across all 61 countries in the 2007 study, people want their leaders to be trustworthy, just, honest, decisive, and so forth. However, how these traits are expressed and enacted may noticeably differ from culture to culture. For example, leaders to be described as decisive in the US, are expected to make quick and approximate decisions. In contrast, in France or Germany, being decisive tends to mean a more deliberate and precise approach to decision-making. The same caution applies to the universally undesirable leader traits.

> *"My final conclusion is that we are in a positionto make a major contribution to organisational behaviour and leadership. Which more than 90% reflect US based research(so will now) be able to liberate(it) from the US hegemony"* Hoppe,200

GEOGRAPHIC CLUSTER AND LEADERSHIP STYLE

The Globe studies of culture and leadership effectiveness (House et at, 2004) shows some leadership styles that are culturally favoured see table below.

Performance (charismatic) Value base	Team	Participative Involved in Decision	Humane Supportive compassionate	Autonomous Independent, Self - centric	Self or Group-protective
Anglo Germanic SE Asian	SE Asian Confucian L.American	Germanic Anglo Nordic	SE Asian Anglo African	Mid Eastern Germanic E.European Confucian	Confucian SE Asian L.American E.European
L.European	E.European		Confucian	Nordic	
L.American	African L.European Nordic Anglo Mid Eastern Germanic			SE Asia Anglo African Mid Eastern L.European L.American	
Confucian		L.European	Germanic		African
African E.European		L.American Africa	Mid Eastern E.European		L.European
Mid Eastern		E.European SE Asian Confucian	L.European Nordic		Anglo Germanic Nordic

Source: Adapted from House et al., 2004

You have a filter, a characteristic way of responding to the world around you. We all do. Your filter tells you which stimuli to notice & which to ignore; which to love & which to hate. It creates your innate motivations - are you competitive, altruistic or ego driven? It defines how you think - are you disciplined or laissez-faire, practical or strategic? It forges your prevailing attitudes - are you optimistic or cynical, calm or anxious, empathetic or cold? It "creates in you all your distinct patterns of thought, feeling & behaviour. In effect, your filter is the source of your talents.

Buckingham and Coffman, 1999
(First, Break All The Rules)

"Don't try to put in what was left out. Try to draw out what was left in."Buckingham and Coffman, 1999

SUMMARY OF KEY POINTS

- We do need to think to learn, however we can also learn how to think. Both processes are interdependent.

- Thinking, and especially learning, is essential to the development of competence of leaders

- Competence can be defined as the right combination of know-how, skills and effort, required to produce desired results.

- Skill means (can do) and effort means attitude and energy (will do). Competence therefore, includes both "skill and will". One without the other does not result in a high level of competence.

- Ability is also a form of competence. It is the capacity to perform a physical or mental act. Ability can increase from training and practice.

- Aptitudes or talents are different from learned abilities, as they are inborn and come naturally. They are genetic and form a key component of our personality. So, some potential for competence is genetic.

- Teaching or training given, in an area where no talent exists will mostly be a waste of time, effort and cost, and may damage learners self esteem.

- Talents are both anatomical and biological. Anatomical talents – or physical – could be typified by excellence in specific sports, where the body or parts of it, display a high level of natural strength or coordination.

- Biological talents on the other hand, have more to do with such things as brain chemistry. Examples might include such intelligences as language, maths, art, music and spatial awareness.

- Capability potential can be assessed at 3 levels; mental processing, information processing and levels of interest or preference.

- A high level of competence, or mastery, especially at the unconscious level can only occur in an area of natural aptitude or talent

- Some ways of thinking, learning and types of competence will be valued differently from one culture to another.

- There are universal leader characteristics and competences that make an outstanding leaders, but also some are culturally contingent.

REFERENCES

Asma, A. (1996). *Going Glocal* . Kuala Lumpur: Malaysian Institute of Management.

Buckingham, M. and Clifton, D. (1999). *NOW Discover You Strengths.* New York: Free Press.

Buckingham, M. and Coffman, C. (1999). *FIRST Break All Rules.* NY: Simon and Schuster.

Dawkins, R. (1989). *The Selfish Gene.* Oxford : Oxford University Press .

Drucker, P. (1954). *The Practice of Management.* New York: HarperCollins.

Gardner, H. (1999). *Intelligence Reframed.* NY: Basic Books.

Garfield, C. (1986). *Peak Performance* . New York : McGraw Hill .

Gazaniga, M. (1992). *Nature's Mind.* NY: Basic Books.

Herrman, N. (1996). *The Whole Brain Business Book.* New York: McGraw-Hill.

Hofstede, G. (1991). *Culture and Organisation.* New York: McGraw Hill.

Hoppe, M. (2007). *The Global Study Revisited: A Summary*. Retrieved from www.inspireimagineinnovate.com

House, R. (2007). *Culture, Leadership and Organisations.* London: Sage Publication .

Jacques, E. and Cason, H. (1994). *Human Capability.* USA: Cason Hall.

Kluckhorn, F. and Strodtbeck, F. (1961). *Variations in Value Orientations.* New York: Harper Collins.

Le Doux, J. (2002). *The Synaptic Self* . London : Penguin Books .

Maister, D. (1997). *True Professionalism* . London : Simon and Schuster .

McClelland, D. (1985). *The Achievement Motive.* New York: A Century Crofts.

McLagan, P. (1989). *ASTD Journal* .

Ornstein, R. (1993). *The Roots of The Self* . Harper Collins : NY.

Sternberg, R. (1988). *Beyond IQ: A Triachic Theory of Human Intelligence.* New York : Cambridge University Press.

CHAPTER FOUR

SOME CLASSIC AND EMERGENT LEADERSHIP THEORIES

LEARNING OBJECTIVES FOR THIS CHAPTER

By the end of this chapter, you will be able to:

- Contrast a range of early and contemporary leadership theories.

- Recognize that most theories seek a balance between a task versus a relationship orientation.

- Integrate the concepts of servant, ethical, moral and courageous leadership.

- Distinguish differences between some western and eastern leadership concepts.

- Interpret the various aspects of followership and 'groupthink' related to decision making in leadership.

- Differentiate between entrepreneurial and non entrepreneurial leadership and characteristics of the two.

- Generalise on some key differences between generational perspectives in leadership and the motivating of Generation Y employees.

- Identify a range of modern leadership concepts, including, mindfulness, leader-member exchange, coaching, mentoring, engagement and talent management, justice, ethics and principle centeredness.

- Recognize the key aspects of stewardship and leading a learning organization.

TABLE OF CONTENTS

SOME CLASSIC LEADERSHIP THEORIES

EARLY THEORIES

Douglas McGregor introduced the Theory X and Theory Y assumptions about people and leaders (1950s). Theory X assumes people are basically lazy and cannot be trusted to work hard if not tightly supervised (Snoopervision). This would equate with 'task' orientation. Contrastingly, Theory Y assumes people can be trusted to work hard and commit themselves to do work they care for (McGregor, 1960).

Following McGregor was a series of studies, again on western leadership, by the Universities of Michigan, Ohio, and Texas, that focused on the same dimensions of task versus relationship. Ohio University used the construct of 'initiating structure (task) and consideration (relationship). Then the Michigan University studies used the terms 'Job Centred' (task) and 'employee centred' (relationships). At the Texas University studies, (Blake and Mouton, 1991) developed the Leadership grid which also contrasted 'concern for people' (relationship) and for task concern.

CONTINGENCY AND SITUATIONAL THEORIES

These theories of the 50's & 60's were followed by the 'contingency' theories popularised in the 70's. Probably due to the failure of proving that a balance was the answer, behavioural scientists started looking at different situations where either task or relations would work. They focused on the maturity of employees ranging from low – with a high need for experience and learning – that determined a more task orientated approach to leadership. Whereas a high level of maturity called for a more 'hands off' or delegating style. Meanwhile in the UK, a similar model was developed by (Adair, 1968), where he considered the task, the team and individual and which style was best.

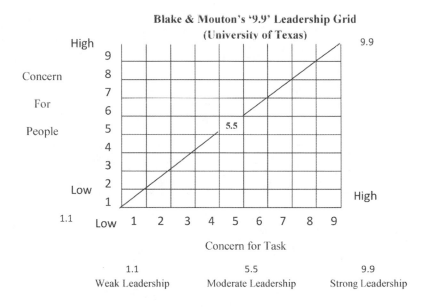

Source: Blake, R and McCanse, A.A. (1991) , Houston, Leadership Dilemma, Gulf Publishing

THE ONE MINUTE MODEL

A series of short and popular theories was written by Blanchard et.al. that started with the **'one minute manager'** and built on positive psychology. For example **'catch people doing something right'** or **'one minute appraisals'**. These books entered the realm of 'pop psychology' and become best sellers. They had a great impact due to their short, simple, yet effective principles and practises. They blew in a refreshing philosophy on how leadership could be, also even led to a book on 'one minute parenting'! This model contrasts significantly with many others.

SITUATIONS FAVOURABLE TO THE LEADERS

(Fiedler, 1967), together with Hersey and Blanchard, focused on situations in terms of whether they are favourable to the leader. For example, are the followers accepting of the leader or not, or how position power and the extent that authority is accepted? Then yet another American theory became popular. The 'path goal' theory where the leader classified the behaviour required (path) towards the achievement of the goal (task). Finally came the 'Vroom-Yetton' contingency model of 5 degrees of a leader participation in decision making (Vroom, 1969). On one end of a continuum was the maximum use of the leaders authority in making a decision, followed by the consulting of individuals and then groups, towards a more facilitative and participative style, giving the group a greater scope of freedom. However, each of these models is contingent on the situation. (Ibid).

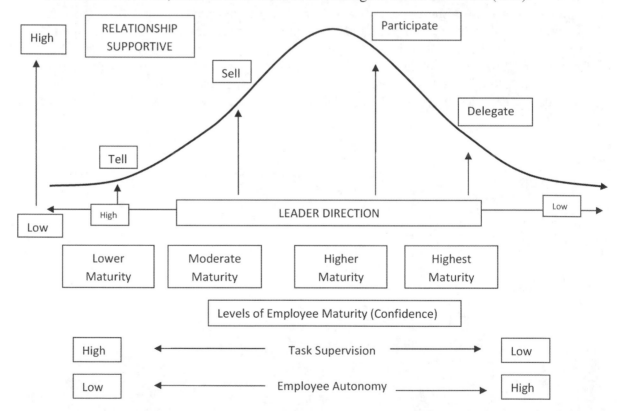

Source: Adapted from Hersey, K. et.al. Situational Leadership, 1981

CONTEMPORARY LEADERSHIP THEORIES

LEADERSHIP: STYLE VERSUS SUBSTANCE

Do we applaud our leader more for style or substance? Do we admire the charismatic leader, for their dynamic oratory and magnetism or the quiet, humble even introverted leader who gets results? Maybe it's what gets done and how, rather than the style of the who**! If shared values, vision and a sense of mission and purpose inspire the follower, then communication is the core behaviour.** With advanced technology, with virtual teams and E-business growing, then E– communication maybe as important as face to face dialogue.

EMERGENT THEORIES

New emergent theories have evolved, with concepts like collaborating more than competing, or empowering more than controlling, being ethical versus self-centred or diversity over uniformity or even humility over heroism, being more vital. In the books by Jim Collins 'Good to Great' or 'How the Mighty Fall', **contemporary theories have replaced the earlier classic theories**, that were popular in the 50's, 60's & 70's. At the time, each theory made sense and most fell into certain categories that looked at balance. Balance between 'task and relationship'! (Collins, 1991/2001).

LOVE AND PROFIT: CARING LEADERSHIP

Autry (1991) produced a book with many similarities to the 'Servant Leadership' concepts. As we conclude there, it's like 'upside down' leadership and other similar threads show up time and time again. In the popular book 'Zen and the Art of Motorcycle Maintenance, (Pirsig, 1979) or Jan Carlson's reorganisation of Scandinavian Airlines System (SAS), which turned the company around by turning the organization chart upside down. **Customers and those employees that have frontline contact with them should drive the company** and management and leadership are there to support them; the 'servant leaders'. The book showed "Moments of Truth" showed that **the bottom line was impacted positively when people interacting with customers were empowered** to 'fix' problems on the spot, assuming employees had sufficient competence.

Autry's thesis was the same as the Christian ideal – to show love to the employees, and they in turn would become as equally caring for the management. **It's the humanistic approach to 'caring leadership'.** Put the employees ahead of yourself – the love – and profits would pour in! In his book he cites not only his own corporate success and profits, but many other examples where if peoples' need for love, for recognition, for growth and realizing their full potential, for compassion and empathy (emotional intelligence) taps into their spirit and releases passion and commitment. This book addresses many good principles of leadership: from managing diversity and conflict, dealing with power, changing the 'job' to meaningful work, and the case for liberated leadership.

> *"Those who turn good into great are motivated by a deep creative urge and inner compulsion for sheer unadulterated excellence for its own sake".*
> *Jim Collins*

SERVANT LEADERSHIP

An interesting twist, on 'love and profit', which has been called **upside down leadership** is a novel approach developed by Robert Greenleaf in his book 'Servant Leadership' (Greenleaf, 1998). It is a more noble and higher ethical approach to putting service to those who are being lead, ahead of the leader. **Doing what is good or right for others ahead of one's own needs.** It is selfless and nurtures the followers in a caring way considering their mind, body and spirit in a holistic way. It is a supportive, facilitative approach that seeks the good in people and inspires trust and empowerment. It requires openness, vulnerability, compassion and even closure that take character and courage. The servant leader will **look for the best in people and affirm this**. The leader provides a climate of meaningfulness in work.

Obviously religious leaders would fall into this category and could be embodied in the Pope, Mother Theresa, and Mahatma Ghandi, Prophet Mohamed or Jesus Christ. But also typified as parent leadership where sacrifices are made for the education, growth and love of their children ahead self. (Often exists in small/family enterprises).

ETHICAL, MORAL AND COURAGEOUS LEADERSHIP

This logically builds on having a moral code of ethics that can take courage to assert against bribery or corruption and calls for the values of integrity, honesty and transparency. **The courage to speak up or speak out and even go against the grain**. There is a concept called 'group think' where for the sake of harmonious relations and solidarity with the group, members won't speak out. This can be similar in collectivist cultures, where to 'save the face' of others and for harmony, it is more important than 'rocking the boat'

LEADERS AS DECISION MAKERS

While traditionally, leaders have tended to make decisions or at least be accountable for their outcomes, leaders now are moving more towards participation and empowerment. With a great emphasis on democracy at the work place and knowledge workers being expected to think more on their own, **decisions are more group oriented**.

However, with the world becoming more global, complex and fast changing, we often don't have enough time to collect or analyze all the data we would like. Despite the sophistication of IT, it happens to present is with more data and options than ever before, but humans still have to make decisions. **Due to this, it is more a question of how to make decisions - rationally or intuitively?**

LEADERS NEED MORE CONCEPTUAL SKILLS (Percentages are approximate)

	CONCEPTUAL SKILLS	SOCIAL SKILLS	TECHNICAL SKILLS
Top Leadership:	70%	20%	10%
Front Line Leaders	50%	30%	20%
Operational Staff	10%	20%	70%

"Servant leadership is the essence of Quantum thinking and Quantum leadership".
Danah Zohar, Rewiring the Corporate Brain

RATIONAL VERSUS INTUITIVE DECISIONS

Jagdish Parikh produced a book based on some seminal research on how senior leaders make decisions. The study was done on 1300 managers from 9 countries. The dominant perception of managers is that intuition is the opposite of logical or rational reasoning. Words like 'gut feeling' sixth sense' or a subconscious process were used. (Parikh, et.al,1990).

Neuroscience puts intuition as a 'right brain' process (where the sub-conscious or non conscious mind operates). The whole brain model is both emotional and cerebral. The **'gut feel' resides in the right limbic or emotional brain,** which is where we connect the emotional feelings to our brain with links to the heart and stomach, thus the queeziness we may feel upon perception of certain types of information, produces the so called **'gut feeling'** (Childre and Martin, 1999).

A key finding from this research on intuition was a correlation between the age and experience of managers and intuition. The more senior managers made more intuitive decisions than the junior or less experienced. And as they got more used to using intuition, they came to trust it more. This is similar to saying that we can learn to trust the use of our non-conscious right brain more. However, that doesn't mean we should not try to gather and analyse data. **Intuition can be an option when we can't use rational analytic thinking.** It's the same option as using creative thinking, when logical rational analysis or critical thinking cannot find a solution to a problem.

INTUITIVE DECISIONS AND EXPERIENCE

Contrary to popular thought, the more we experience situations and, from process related information in the past, the stronger our intuition. **So intuition may not be a feeling or an idea that comes from nowhere!** Our non-conscious right brain is believed to store the vast reservoir of our experience and when we have to make a decision without data or information or that we cannot rely on? Our left brain function we have to use intuition from the right brain.

DECISION MAKING AND COURAGE

We often hear that it takes courage to make decisions, especially where outcomes may not be certain. Entrepreneurs take risks; innovation calls for experimenting with new products, services or even markets, which all entail degrees of uncertainty, fear or risk, and thus courage! **But if we don't make decisions, we cannot progress.**

NOTHING VENTURED, NOTHING GAINED!

Companies like 3M, encourage experimentation and risk taking, or taking a calculated risk. It's ok to make mistakes, but 3 principles apply. 1: Learn from mistakes 2: Share learning with others, so they don't make the same mistake, and 3: Don't make the same mistake again. Making a mistake "above the water line," is a tolerable mistake, but making it below the water line can "sink the ship".

"In the law of institutions, leaders evaluate everything with a leader bias".
John Maxwell

FOLLOWERSHIP

FOLLOWER ROLES

Most of us are followers in one way or another. The chairman of the board has to follow government directions or consensus of board members. The CEO follows the board and junior partners follow the seniors. Supervisors follow managers and other employees follow supervisors. Even children are supposed to follow parents, sometimes! And students may follow teachers or lecturers. **So every leader becomes a follower at some time.**

INFLUENCE PATTERNS

Leaders often influence followers, but sometimes the reverse occurs. If we are acknowledged as an expert, others may follow us! If we have information that others need, they may also follow. A leader, who is charismatic, may also influence others to follow. Even followers who have these powers may influence their leaders and even enhance their own leader performance. Actually **many of the qualities of an effective follower maybe the same as an effective leader – empathy, listening, clarifying roles and goals and confirming understanding.**

DIVERSITY AMONG FOLLOWERS

Leaders and followers who share a common set of core values and a vision can be more proactive and supportive. However, communication styles can differ. Follower personality and thinking styles may differ. For example, **a left brain follower may use more analytic and critical thinking styles,** and **a right brained leader may use a more strategic or creative style of thinking.** One may be a more independent, critical or creative thinker and prefer to operate with greater autonomy and freedom. The other may be more passive or cautious. This may be taken as being more 'lazy', but could be the opposite of being too impulsive or pessimistic! Often the need for a balance is useful.

EFFECTIVE FOLLOWERS

They need to be balanced and pragmatic. They should **be more 'whole brained'**! Both creative, strategic and critical. They should be 'mindful', sensitive, yet willing to take the initiative or even a risk, if needs dictate. Effective followers should know where they stand, understand how much they are empowered to act and have the courage to do so. Can they speak up or be assertive when needed? **They need the courage to challenge, participate, to serve, or even know when to exit a situation.** Such behaviour maybe difficult and rare, but can be admired.

MANAGING UPWARDS

Sometimes we hear the terms 'Managing Upwards' or 'Managing the Boss'. This is more a communication skill, based on expert or information power. While it can take courage, providing we have the facts, we can influence.

"The law of respect: people naturally follow leaders stronger than themselves".

John Maxwell

ENTREPRENEURIAL LEADERSHIP

ENTREPRENEURS AS SELF DRIVEN

Entrepreneurs are a good example of both 'self leaders', as they may have the idea, vision and passion to start up a business, or also may need to lead those whom they enlist to help. However, while they take the initiative to innovate and organise resources, especially funding, they also are willing to take risks. Here though, they may not always find the same traits in those they lead. Because **entrepreneurs by nature have drive, enthusiasm, persistence and put in long hours,** they can be very demanding leaders, and maybe hard to work for! So, do all great entrepreneurs make great leaders?

THE CHARACTERISTICS ARE COMPLEX AND UNIQUE

The action of entrepreneurial leaders are critical to the success of organizations, including institutions focused on education and training. Leaders can become entrepreneurial leaders in order to create an effective organization that move their goals and visions forward (Peck, 1993). Leaders, in both the public and private sectors can integrate the concepts of entrepreneurial leadership throughout their institutions, to strengthen the entrepreneurial inclinations of individuals, while also enhancing recruitment and retention efforts of people with an entrepreneurial flair.

IMPORTANCE OF INNOVATION

Even some administrators can become entrepreneurial leaders by recognizing that leadership and innovation are critical throughout every level of the organization. Leadership must no longer be defined solely by the position or traditional rank someone holds within the institution. Leadership must become everyone's job. (Kouzes and Posner, 2007). The **fundamental goal of entrepreneurial leaders is to create an atmosphere of innovation** while helping constituents themselves become more entrepreneurial. Innovation and entrepreneurial leadership are complex and challenging, however, both can be supported by creating and communicating a relevant vision, motivating and empowering individuals. Leveraging of human and social capital and developing a global mindset in their institutions **that embraces change, values diversity and cultivates continuous innovation, are also important.**

Entrepreneurial leaders are whole brained but with a strong bias towards the right brain.

Left Brain Orientation	*Right Brain Orientation*	
Critical thinking	Vision	Opportunism
Action oriented	Inspiration	Risk taking
Tenacious/Resolute	Optimism	Innovation
Cost conscious	Strategic	Passion
Planning Oriented	Driven	Resourceful

"Entrepreneurs are leaders of innovation and change. "

Daft, 2008

FROM WEST TO EAST

THE TAO OF LEADERSHIP

(Heider, 1985) authored a book called The Tao of Leadership, in a search for an eastern perspective on leadership. Lao Tzu, who also developed the example of wisdom for political rulers more than 2500 years ago with the 'Art of War' of military strategists. **Tao simply means 'How Things Happen'.** The method of leadership is really about how to govern or educate others in accordance with the natural laws and live in conscious harmony. It unifies the leaders wisdom and skills and views all behaviour consisting of polarities or opposites. It strives for balance. **The wise leader does not 'push' (Task Orientation) but allows processes to unfold naturally.** It encourages openness to learning, to innovation. Silence and reflection is as important as action, but one needs both. Coincidentally, this is **similar** to the **'Action Learning'** model developed by Revans (2011), where the manager acts and the reflects and learns, before continuing to act. But Tao itself has no polarity; it unifies opposites, seeking harmony and balance.

UNLEASHING ENERGY

As with Quantum physics, there is an energy which consists of positive or negative energy fields. Vibration consists of polar opposites, like co-operation (positive energy) or conflict (negative vibes). The enlightened leader sees the interaction between task and peoples energy field, with the potential for 'blocks' (negative) or for release (positive). **When leaders motivate positively they tap into and release energy** (The flow state). Leaders try to prevent blocks and unleash energy. Incentives and motives are the sources of internal energy that drive us. Thus the leaders, who imbibe Taoism, strive **for balance between, selflessness versus selfishness,** learning versus teaching, letting go versus control, substance versus style, simplicity versus complexity, creativity versus logic, humility versus arrogance, etc. (e.g. Tough-love).

INTERNAL VERSUS EXTERNAL RIPPLE EFFECTS

Influence starts within our self and ripples outwards. We are the muscle and growth spread outwards (The seed and the tree). The leader with Tao: knows existence is holistic, is a neutral observer, cannot be seduced by bribes, threats or fame, has integrity that is pragmatic and is not too idealistic. **Every law creates an outlaw**, so the fewer the rules, the freer people can to be more creative and productive. Good leaders practice silence, while group has high energy. They focus more on **doing less and on being more.** Or to sum up the Taoist approach, the leader is more a facilitator. This can be our mental model, our paradigm leader!

CHAOS THEORY APPLIED

In leading diverse personalities in teams, we often go through a cycle of convergent and divergent thinking. Especially in the process of transition from convergent to divergent, a form of 'chaos' can appear. This chaos is a natural organic process and if time permits, it can be useful to let it happen. One may need to provide some structure and boundaries, but think of it like a natural forest fire. Contain it, but let it burn itself out naturally. We need to walk the line between control and chaos, respecting that there is a high energy present in the chaos of divergent thinking.

"Radiance encourages people, but outshining everyone, inhibits them".
Lao Tzu

GROUP THINK

Individuals may not voice out their real feelings, so as to avoid conflict and save the 'face' of fellow team members. Notable research was conducted by Irving Janis (1982) into this phenomenon, where he cited the existence of 'group think' as a possible cause of the Challenger space craft tragedy that resulted in the loss of life of astronauts, scientists and even a teacher. Avoidance of this 'groupthink' syndrome was exhibited by John F. Kennedy when he deliberately absented himself from a high level meeting, surrounding the 'Cuba Missile Crisis'. **When a leader leaves a meeting, often people will speak up and out** as there is less fear about what the 'boss may say'. But this takes courage and trust that the group will be supportive. So group think may actually be more common in the East. (Janis, 1982).

SPIRITUAL LEADERSHIP

On the thread of spirituality, let's put it into a motivational context. **Spirit here means 'energy'** as with the child in high spirits or the 'spirited' race horse. It is not the more mystical view of spirits, as in 'ghost' or even 'alcohol', though these can have an effect on behaviour. Spiritual leadership is a bit like 'Tao' or 'Charisma', hard to define or even explain, but you know it when you feel it. In a book by Hawley (1993) entitled 'Reawakening the Spirit in Work', he talks about Dharmic Power. He provides a response to those leaders of deep integrity and decency, who seek to provide **a vision that infuses us with a feeling of spiritual energy**.

As with religious spirituality, the leader provides a sense of meaningfulness about work, and how through strong belief in positive values, – employees feel energized and committed to being productive and giving of their best. As with many models of inspirational leadership, it puts forward the idea that we can 'love' our work. Dharma at work is about: **Right Action, Courage and a Spiritual Connectedness**. Just as some derive a feeling of spiritual well being through worship and prayer, others may derive the feeling when in a forest or by a waterfall. It's from work, where we may spend more than 30 to 40 percent of our time that we can have an equal feeling of spiritual connectivity, harmony and fulfillment. Then we can conclude this aspect of Dharma is truly powerful.

THE SPIRITUAL LEADERSHIP MODEL

Leadership	*Spiritual basis*	*Leader is a:*
Vision	*Covenant*	*Sense make*
Integrity	*Dharma(truth)*	*Moral architect*
Values	*Virtue*	*Value steward*
State(of mind)	*Equanimity (inner peace)*	*Yogi*
Giving	*Service*	*Servant*
Energy and heart	*Spiritual awareness*	*Guide*
Culture :sense of community	*Unity/oneness*	*Whole maker*
Acknowledge	*Gratitude*	*Optimist*
Presence	*Inner/higher power*	*Warrior*

Adapted from: Hawley, J. 1993

"Most of us have jobs that are too small for our spirits"   Studs Terkel

QUANTUM LEADERSHIP

ENERGYFIELDS

Margaret Wheatley in her book, 'Leadership and the New Science', (Wheatley, 1992) she used the research on Quantum Physics to view **organizations as fields of energy** that could self regulate. Chaos theory emerged from this idea, where atoms, like people cannot be easily predicted and controlled. The motion of a **'flow state'** is where all things have a relationship with their environment, and form natural patterns to ensure adaptation and survival. Order emerges from this complex pattern of relationships.

The empty space between people is the field of energy that connect and bind them. For example, a set of values, an inspiring vision or important information. is where leaders must focus on the whole, the 'in-between' and the connectivity. Like the silence or even what is not said, to sense how people are relating and connecting and being energized.

GROWTH IS NOT STABLE OR PREDICTABLE

The reality is that we live in an uncertain, fast changing world, and quantum physics provides some laws that allow us to accept, adapt and cope with this reality. Today we say **'go with the flow' and 'strive for balance'**. When leaders have less stress, they can relate better with their team members. We must appreciate that the healthy growth of people and organizations are not stable or predictable, thus tolerance for uncertainty is important to possess.

NEED FOR MORE FLUIDITY IN STRUCTURES

Many organizations are experimenting with new organization charts that describe more fluid patterns of relationship. It is believed we are again learning "to manage in a world that is round", a world **not of hierarchies, but of encircling partnerships** (Hesselben and Cohen, 1999). Buckman Labs is moving from "a chain of command to a web of influence". And Gore Associates, manufactures of GoreTex, describes itself as a "lattice organization." One observer of Gore has noted that the issue is not who or what position will take care of the problem, but what **energy, skill, influence, and wisdom** are available to contribute to the solution.

In quantum physics, a homologous process is described as relational holism, where whole systems are created by the relationships among subatomic particles. Electrons are drawn into these intimate relations as they cross paths with one another, overlapping and merging; their own individual qualities become indistinguishable. We experience this when we say that a team has "jelled," suddenly able to work in harmony, the ragged edges gone, with an effortless flow of the work. We speak more these days **about fluid and permeable boundaries;** we know that organizations have to be more open to meet the unending pressures for change.

"Science outstrips other modes and reveals more of the crux of the matter than we can calmly handle".
                                                                              A.R .Ammons

DEVELOPING LEADERSHIP MINDFULNESS

CHANGING PEOPLE MINDS

Professor Howard Gardner (1999) a Harvard School of Education researcher, famous for developing the theory of Multiple Intelligences, more recently has been researching the role of leadership in changing people's minds. In his book, he puts forward the idea that leaders can use a number of 'levels of change'. Here are some of his findings (Gardner, 1999).

- Take time and approach change from many perspectives.
- Give messages in more than one way or context, eg. over a coffee, as against in the office, or via the internet or texting.
- Don't rely on reason alone. Leaders know they have to connect with peoples' emotions, which Gardner calls 'resonance'. E.g, telling stories can be useful, with imagery or real world effects.
- Don't underestimate the power of resistance to change. Gardner has identified several barriers to change and suggests leaders need to be familiar with them.
- Change can only be sustainable if people go along with it voluntarily and not have it forced on them.

FOSTERING MINDFULNESS

Mindfulness, which is conscious, should be a core for leaders to foster. This includes being open minded, using independent thinking and intellectual thinking and especially systems thinking. This is the ability to see the energy of the parts that make up the whole or 'big picture' thinking. Shell calls it, **'helicopter' thinking**. But also **described by Shell,** are being able to **analyze the parts that make up the whole synergistically**. This then allows the leader to reinforce or change whole systems through seeing the patterns and relationships of the parts. These are also similar to characteristics of 'Conceptual Thinking'.

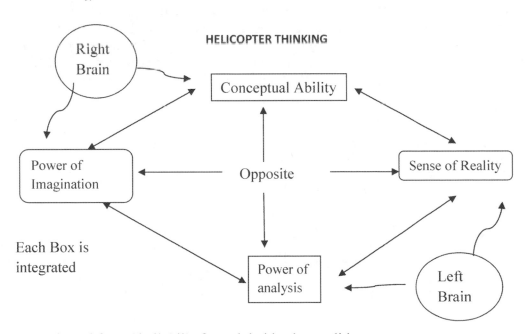

Adapted from Shell Oil's four global leader qualities

GENERATIONAL GAPS AND LEADERSHIP

GENERATION GAPS

In the past we tended to accept our role in life – according to gender and age – but now we have legislation to ensure fairness and non-discrimination. This is to protect from child labour at one end, fair wages for apprenticeships or internships at career entry and extension of the retirement age at the other end. As education has become more widespread and **technological change more rapid and complex** or 'replexity' to coin a word from Parikh, (1990) the **gap between generations can be more noticeable**. Younger people have become more literate in information technology, and our children are developing in a digital era. **One challenge that this presents, is the less exposure to human face-to-face interaction** with social-interpersonal skills becoming noticeably poorer, due to more time being spent inter-facing with computers and smart phones than socially with people!

GENERATIONAL ERAS

Those born after the turn of the century (year 2000 until now) have variously been labelled as **'Millennial'** or **'Generation Z.'** School, college or university graduates, born between 1981 up to 1999 are often called **Generation Y** and **pose a challenge in the leading and motivating of them - to the older 'Generations'**. Those born between 1946 and 1960 are called **'Baby Boomers'**. This was due to the millions of defense personnel returning home at the end of W.W.II, and a resultant explosion in the number of babies born. The **Traditionalists,** born before the end of World War II (1945) have mostly retired or passed away. Yes – there are even some 'oldies', between ages 75 and 100, who were never given a label! Now this **labelling of generations is not universally exact,** as for example, **'Millennials'** have been labelled as **late Generation Y**, but it doesn't follow the logic, if they were born at the beginning of a new millennium (2001).

Eras can overlap but a generation is usually defined by **eras of around 18 to 20 years,** where adults marry and produce the next generation. So what will we label those born after 2018/2020. In the US they refer to millennials as those aged 18 to 35 years of age. But in other parts of the world, the term "Generation Y" is used (born between 1988 to 2000). Someone born in 1981, would be 35 in 2016. In this book we use the term Generation Y. (See below).

ONE MODEL OF GENERATION ERAS
Traditionalist: *Born before 1945*
Baby Boomers: *Born between 1946 & 1960*
Generation X: *Born between 1961 & 1980*
Generation Y: *Born between 1981 & 2000*
Millennials/Gen Z: *Born after 2000*

"Leaders tend to favour those who are similar in age, gender, ethnicity and personality ".

Dr Fisher , Rutgers University , 2014

MOTIVATING GENERATION Y EMPLOYEES

GEN Y NEEDS, VALUES AND WANTS

Generation Y work values consist of being unique and competitive. They want to **standout from the rest and become the best** they can be in the organization. They want to **contribute towards something worthwhile** that draws from the best each unique Generation Y has to offer. **They want freedom in decision making** when given a task to complete. Generation Y **want to take the responsibility** and have the freedom to finish the task in their own way. This allows them to produce to a high number of possible solutions and consider a high number of alternatives. Moreover, **they feel responsible and motivated once challenging jobs are given**. Leaders who tend to adjust their human resource strategies to be more flexible and potentially accommodate to employee values, will more likely attract available talent, and ultimately become the workplace of choice.

LEADERS NEED TO CREATE A NEW CLIMATE

According to Jamrog (2011) recruitment strategies that employers need to use to attract, recruit, retain and motivate young people in the twenty-first century will need to rely less heavily on traditional pay and benefits (i.e. job security). Instead the focus is more on **creating a work environment that allows individuals to grow and develop**. Essentially, the ideal setting for Generation Y is where there is a combination of teamwork and mobility in the organization. Generation Y are particularly **attracted to organizations with non-hierarchical environments**, where the atmosphere is fun and exciting. As an example, Yahoo, an IT organization that encourages individualism and enjoyment, provides opportunities to employees to decorate their workstations in their own style. Since they enjoy work-life balance, therefore, leaders are expected to provide a mixture of environments such as a gymnasium, rest areas, cafeterias and creative workstations. This helps Gen Y employees become more motivated to work in the organization. In Malaysia, the Norwegian telecommunication company, (Telenor) **called "Digi" is an excellent case** study of how they changed from a hierarchy to a flat organization, bringing in a more egalitarian culture of empowered employees. (Shephard, 2008). This appealed to the Gen Y employees, and productivity soared. (www.digi.com.my).

Generation Y Employee Expectations

- *More flexible work hours and time to use social media*
- *Challenging work and opportunity to excel*
- *Work that is meaningful and significant*
- *More autonomy in designing own work and decision making*
- *More freedom to work in their own way*
- *More opportunity for learning and growth*
- *A work environment that is less hierarchical and more fun*

"We will have some things we don't like doing at work. Stick at it, and you might find that it makes you appreciate the good stuff even more".

Marcus Buckingham, 2007

LEADER MEMBER EXCHANGE THEORY (LMX)

DYADIC RELATIONSHIPS

Informal observation of leadership behaviour suggests that a leader's action may not be the same towards all subordinates. The importance of potential differences in this respect is brought into sharp focus by **Graen's leader-member exchange (LMX) model, also known as the Vertical Dyad Linkage theory**. The theory views leadership as consisting of a number of dyadic relationships linking the leader with a follower. The quality of the relationship is reflected by the degree of **mutual trust, loyalty, support, respect, and obligation** (Graen, 1976).

IN GROUP VERSUS OUT-GROUP

According to the theory, leaders form different kinds of relationships with various groups of subordinates. **One group, referred to as the 'in-group',** is favoured by the leader. Members of the in-group receive considerably more attention from the leader and have more access to organizational resources. **By contrast, other subordinates fall into the 'out-group'**. These individuals are disfavoured by the leader. As such, they receive fewer valued resources from their leaders (Veechio, 1997).

Leaders distinguish between the in-group and out-group members on the basis of the perceived similarity with respect to personal characteristics, such as age, gender, or personality. A follower may also be granted an in-group status if the leader believes that person to be especially competent at performing his or her job. (Gerstner and Day, 1997).

According to many studies conducted in this area, Manzoni, and Barsoux, (1998) found that leaders definitely do support the members of the in-group and may go to the extent of inflating their ratings on poor performance as well. This kind of a treatment is not given to the members of the out-group. **Due to the favouritism that the in-group members receive from their leaders, they are found to perform their jobs better and develop positive attitudes towards their jobs in comparison to the members of the out-group**. The job satisfaction of in-group members is high and they perform effectively on their jobs. They tend to receive more coaching from their superiors which helps them in their careers. For these reasons, a low attrition rate, increased salaries and promotion rates are associated with the in-group members in comparison to that of the out-group members (Claire, 1991).

'IN GROUP' PERCEPTION	'OUT GROUP' PERCEPTIONS
I am valued as an employee	Only on contract, so future is uncertain
I am engaged by my boss	Must work to contract terms
I have access to needed resources	I am often ignored by my boss
My boss recognises my contribution	I receive little in inspiration or encouragement
I feel competent and empowered	I don't feel included in any decision making
I am committed to my boss and organisation	People rarely ask me what I think or feel
I am helped in my career development	I am not committed to my work or job

"The ultimate goal in LMX, is that all employees have the same full fair treatment".
Conyngham, 2013

STRENGTHS OF LMX THEORY

- LMX theory is an exceptional theory of leadership as unlike the other theories, it concentrates and talks about specific relationships between the leader and each follower.
- LMX theory is a robust explanatory theory.
- LMX theory focuses our attention to the significance of communication in leadership. **Communication is a medium through which leaders and their followers develop, grow and maintain beneficial exchanges**. When this communication is accompanied by features such as mutual trust, respect and devotion, it leads to effective leadership.
- LMX theory is very much valid and practical in its approach.

IMPLICATIONS OF LMX VERSUS SX

It should be noted that Social Exchange (SX) has implications in all types of relationships from parents, teachers, siblings, colleagues, friends, team members etc. **Whereas LMX focuses more on the leaders**, and their team member's motivation, job satisfaction and resultant performance. Emphasis here is on leaders.

THREE DISTINCTIVE ROLES

The relationship between leaders and followers falls into three stages:

- **Role taking**: When a new member joins the organization, the leader assesses the talent and abilities of the member and offers them opportunities to demonstrate their capabilities.
- **Role making**: An informal and unstructured negotiation on work-related factors takes place between the leader and the member. A member who is similar to the leader is more likely to succeed. A betrayal by the member at this stage may result in being relegated to the out-group.
- **Institutionalization**: where policies, systems and practices, such as orientation, training and coaching become routine and normal and differences between 'in or out groups' are minimized.

EMPLOYEE ENGAGEMENT

LMX, when fully displayed is really a form of 'engaging' employees more. Engagement is a form of concern for the welfare and performance of employees displayed by empathetic listening and effective two way communication. It is one way of discovering employee talents, putting them in action and closely monitoring progress.

"The supreme quality for leadership is unquestionable integrity, without it no real success is possible..."
Stephen Covey

ORGANIZATIONAL JUSTICE

PERCEPTION OF FAIRNESS

Human resources strategies, policies and practices are powerful communicators regarding management's trustworthiness, fairness and commitment to employees. **If management is perceived favourably, employees reciprocate with increased commitment** to the organization. However, downsizing, restructuring, job insecurity with increased work pressure, have made many employees cynical. As a result HR managers increasingly must face issues of trust and fairness, particularly in the areas of recruitment and selection, performance appraisals, remuneration, promotions, demotions and terminations.

THREE TYPES OF JUSTICE

Three major perceptions of unfairness can be identified under Organizational Justice:

- **Distributive Justice,** refers to whether scarce resources (such as the merit budget, superior performance ratings, promotional opportunities and expatriate assignments) are perceived as being allocated fairly.
- **Procedural Justice,** refers to how the HR process is administered. For example, is the company's selection process seen as fair or biased?
- **Interactional Justice,** refers to how managers interact with employees. Are they warm and friendly, open and respectful, or are they cold, arrogant, aloof and abusive? This is also one key aspect of LMX.

UNDERLYING ASSUMPTIONS

1. Leaders usually treat individuals differently, according to their perceptions and values.
2. Leaders tend to favour those more like them. (Age, Gender, Ethnicity and Personality). Refer to research by Dr Fisher in this chapter.
3. Those favoured tend to join/belong to an 'In-group.'
4. Membership of this 'In-group' (followers) tends to receive more support and respect from the leader, resulting in more autonomy, responsibility and trust.
5. Members in return are more loyal, hardworking, committed, and respectful of their leader, which results in higher performance.
6. Members of the 'out-group', may feel de-motivated, have lower morale and show lower commitment to the task objectives, job, leader of the organization – resulting in lower productivity, quality and a higher employee turnover.
7. Recent research emphasizes how leaders can develop positive relationships with all followers, not only treating each employee as a different individual, each with their own unique characteristics of personality, gender, age, cultural background and ethnicity, but treating them all fairly (Daft, 2011).
8. Successful leaders have been found to be sensitive to all of these differences, and provide more coaching, mentoring and counselling, resulting in higher levels of employee engagement and productivity.

"All that is necessary for the triumph of evil, is that good men do nothing"

Edmund Burke

ORGANIZATIONAL COMMITMENT

Daft, (2011) defines Organizational Commitment as the employee's commitment to the organization. It has two facets; one of the organization's perspective and the other, employee commitments develop naturally. Commitment can be in the form of the nature of the relationship between an employee and the organization or relationship to a variety of entities including their superior and/or team members. **Commitment can be observed as an attitude or mindset where the commitment arises due to convergence of goals and values** and develops respectively. Organizational commitment is determined by a number of factors, including personal factors (e.g., age, experience in the organization, personality disposition, internal or external control attributions) and organizational factors (job design and the leadership style of one's supervisor). Thus, positive Leader-Member Exchange (LMX) strongly correlates with member commitments.

There are three components of organizational commitment. (Meyer and Allen, 1997).
1. **Affective commitment,** refers to employee identification, or strong emotional attachment and involvement in the organization.
2. **Continuance commitment,** refers to an awareness of the costs associated with leaving the organization. This is the economics of staying or leaving affected by commitment.
3. **Normative commitment,** reflects the obligation to continue with the organization.

SOURCES OF POWER AND INFLUENCE

There are various sources of power, which can be divided into 'organizational' or 'personal'. Personal sources can often be used to influence those not under formal authority.

Organizational: Position or Legitimate (eg: in your job title). Coercive (authority to punish), Reward (authority to give rewards/incentives), Informational (providing or withholding).

Personal: Expertise (a valued skill), Referent (accorded to you), Connection (know who) Persistence or Assertiveness.

COMPLIANCE	versus	COMMITMENT
Means that people follow the direction of the leader who has power, even if they disagree with the leader.		*Means that people follow the leaders view point and instructions enthusiastically.*
They will obey orders, and if they don't agree but they may do only just enough to satisfy the leader. If coercive power exceeds legitimate, people may resist or even sabotage leaders efforts.		*They want to serve, not merely because it is a duty, but because their "heart" is behind it. They are intrinsically motivated by the leader's vision.*

"Commitment is measured by the degree that the leaders view point is carried out enthusiastically by followers."

Daft, 2013

PRINCIPLED CENTERED LEADERSHIP

LEADERSHIP AND STEWARDSHIP

Covey (1991) the well-known author of the best seller "The 7 Habits of Highly Effective People", produced several titles, like "First Things First", and also "Principal Centred Leadership". Here the characteristics of these leaders are: **'Continuous Learning'**, which **is self-directed and self-reinforcing**; then 'service oriented' or the form of **stewardship** as mentioned by Greenleaf (1998) in 'Servant Leadership'. Next are leaders who 'Radiate Positive Energy', where they are optimistic and enthusiastic. This is the energy field, or aura that they can **radiate out magnetically**. Similar to the **energy fields** explained in Wheatley's book on Quantum physics (1999) in where they seek the unseen potential in others. They appreciate we are not all perfect, and have challenges, but when a leader believes in others, they in turn increase their belief in themselves. This is a form of **'Self Fulfilling Prophecy'** as typified by Prof. Henry Higgins in the classic movie 'My Fair Lady'.

LEADERSHIP AND A BALANCED LIFE STYLE

Another principle is leading a Balanced Life, striving for balance in many areas, as in 'The Tao of Leadership' They see **'Life as an Adventure, constantly adapting to change, newness and seeking flexible and creative answers.** Here the abundance mentality comes in. **They are synergistic,** as in the ability to improve almost any situation they get into, building on ideas, by putting things together (synergy). Finally, they **exercise self-renewal and strive for balance in their personality**: in physical, emotional, mental and spiritual aspects of their lives. For further exploration further read this leadership book by Covey, then read his later book, 'The 8th Habit: From Effectiveness to Greatness'(Covey. 2004).

In Covey's book the "8th Habit" (Ibid), he talks about **the 'voices' in us** and the need for leaders to find their 'voice' and importantly "inspiring" others to find their voices". This is where he enters the domain of leadership in an organization and presents three key points. **First** is the organization as a relationship with a purpose (its voice). The **second** point is that almost all people have a relationship with an organization, even if only at the simplest level as a member of a family. **Thirdly, the organization itself. For example, a self-employed** entrepreneur still works with an organizational purpose, in a 'Principle-Centred way and this is what Covey calls the 'Leadership Challenge'.

The book "Pygmaleon" by George Bernard Shaw inspired the popular movie"my fair lady".The story behind the success of Professor Higgins, who transformed a Cockney flower girl, to pass as a Duchess, is a classic example of the self-fulfilling prophecy or the positive "pygmaleon" effect.

Because the simple flower girl (Eliza Dolittle) believed in the linguistic professor's ability to change her, she in turn believed in herself. And had the faith and confidence to persist and work hard. Leaders can similarly inspire great determination in others when they show faith in the others capability.

"Leaders and Managers differ in their conceptions. Managers tend to view work as an enabling process involving some combination of people and ideas interacting to establish strategy and decisions. .... leaders create excitement to work"

– Abraham Zakznik

THE LEADER AS A COACH

ALL LEADERS SHOULD COACH

John Maxwell (2010) has extensively written on both leadership and coaching. He maintains that **all great leaders become coaches and mentors to their team members.** Maxwell is one of the most prolific writers on leadership, where he first produced the book '21 Irrefutable Laws of Leadership'. The very last law, No 21, is the 'Law of Legacy'. He states that a leader's lasting value is measured by succession. All great leaders should seek to be succeeded by someone, and they often have to spend a lot of time and effort in the coaching and mentoring processes. Since then he has gone onto review these laws and more recently has focused on the '**Leader as a Coach**'. Coaching he maintains is a feedback process, a helping process and focuses on getting followers to realize their full potential. It doesn't mean trying to change people from what they naturally are, **but draw out their inner talents, help with self discovery and strengthen their strengths**. As all great sports people have coaches to do this, so leaders also need coaches, yet they have to also become coaches to their own team members. **This is how they leave a legacy**.

COACHING VERSUS MENTORING

Mentoring on the other hand is much more focused on passing on your wisdom, and sharing your experiences and learning. Mentors look more into the future and may model the way. A CEO, who retires, may become a mentor to the new incoming CEO. **Usually a mentor is not your formal or line leader.** In fact they may help you understand how you can relate better to your leader, **so they need to be objective and isolated from the politics** and ideally should have had the experience to advise you. Coaching differs, because it may come from your direct leader – but of course can come from outsiders.

COACHES	versus	MENTORS
Facilitate learning		Expert and advisor
Ask Questions		Focus on long term
Elicit options		Help with career
Seek commitment		Motivate and guide
Maybe a line leader.		Not the line leader
Maybe an outsider		Must be an insider

CEO of Texas-based Virtual Solutions, and his managers accommodate the needs of the company's diverse employees, about half of whom come from outside the United States. He assigns mentors to new employees to help them adjust to U.S culture, such as understanding American slang. He sponsors international events featuring ethnic potlucks so employees can learn about the cultures of other employees.

"The law of legacy - the leaders lasting value is measured by succession. "

John Maxwell

THE LEARNING ORGANISATION

VISION SHOULD PULL US

Peter Senge well known for his work on the learning organization, also produced some valued insights on leadership and learning. He authored a book called 'The Fifth Discipline' (Senge, 1990) where he explores the 'Personal Mastery' of leaders, which includes three facets. **Vision, Reality and Creative Tension.** The personal growth and learning of a leader to focus on results (Vision) where they examine their own personal vision, dreams or aspirations. Next is facing reality and accepting the truth. Here they unearth mental models, mindsets or paradigms that maybe deceptive. They **challenge assumptions** or what Kouzes and Posner in their book "The Leadership Challenge" (2007) call "Challenging the Process". This takes courage. **They are committed to seeking the real truth.** The third facet is exploring the gap between their own vision of a desired future, and today's reality. This is where creative tension is managed. **Leaders creatively pull themselves towards their vision**, not settling for mediocrity. **The fifth discipline is systems thinking** and understanding the connectedness in circles of causality.

LEADING A LEARNING ORGANIZATION

Senge goes on to discuss a new view of leadership in a learning organization, where he says the **leader is a 'Designer', a 'Steward'** (see Servant Leadership) and **a 'Teacher'.** The Leader as a designer goes back over 2000 years, when Lao Tzu said "The good leader is he who people praise" and "The Great Leader is he who the people say, we did it ourselves". Design is something people don't see, as it is both ahead of, and behind, the task. It involves the planning and control functions and this is **where 'Systems thinking' plays a role, integrating and synergizing!** Many problems in organizations are ad hoc and often unrelated, so designers are always looking for the wholes.

The leader as a steward, as Senge states, **"is someone who develops a unique relationship to their personal vision, becoming a steward to the vision".** The leader as a steward is someone who is committed to describe their sense of purpose, which of course is aligned to the organization is purpose, and how becoming a learning organization is the context in which vision and purpose are shared. One way of doing this is by weaving them into stories. Thus the steward leader is a story teller.

Part of being a 'Leader as a Teacher' also includes the ability to tell stories, but they must be compelling and underlie the message that the leader needs to stress. For example, the source of the vision, thus giving a personalized meaning to the message.

One example of a leader who had this gift, according to Peter Senge, was William Gore, of the highly innovative and successful organization W.L. Gore and Associates. His company created 'Goretex', the fabric that has the magic to breath, keep us dry and either warm or cool. Your jogging shoes probably have some goretex in them!

"The good leader is he who people praise and the great leader is he who the people say, we did it ourselves"
— Lao Tzu

ALIGNMENT AND SYNERGY : McKINSEY'S 7 S MODEL
Back in the 80's Tom Peters and Bob Watermen wrote a book, called 'In Search of Excellence (Peters and Watermen, 1963). The authors, working with the giant consulting group, McKinsey and Co, developed a framework for assessing and monitoring changes in an organization. This model had at its centre the first 'S', which represented the '**Shared Vision and Values**' and super-ordinate goals of the organization. The remaining 6 S's were divided into **3 'Hard' S's – Strategy, Structure and Systems.** This can be viewed as providing a sound basis upon which to analyze an organization's structural design (Structure and Systems) and how strategy should influence this design. In other words, strategy, flowing from the shared vision, values and meta goals, should drive structure. It must not be subordinate to structure.

The 3 soft S's; Staff, Styles and Skills are of course the human side of the organization. Staff representing the employees or workforce. Styles represent their behavioural and personality characteristics, including leadership and communication styles. The skills element, represents talent and competencies.

The model is based on the theory that, for an organization to perform well, these seven elements need to be aligned and mutually reinforcing. So, the model can be used to help identify what needs to be realigned to improve performance, or to maintain alignment (and performance) during other types of change.

Whatever the type of change – restructuring, new processes, organizational mergers, new systems, change of leadership, and so on – the model can be used to understand how the organizational elements are interrelated, and so ensure that the wider impact of changes made in one area are taken into consideration (Wikipedia, 2014).

The seven inter-dependent elements - are based on the premise, that there are seven internal aspects of an organization that need to be aligned, if it is to be successful.

Harris Interactive, the originators of the Harris Poll, polled 23,000 US residents employed full time in a range of important government and industrial organization. They were also occupying key functional areas. The Findings were, only:

- *37% had a clear understanding of their organization's vision and mission*
- *20% were enthusiastic about their teams and organization goals.*
- *20% said they had a clear "line of sight" between their tasks and their team's and organization's goals.*
- *20% said they had a clear 'line of sight" between their tasks and their team's and organization's goals.*
- *50% were satisfied with their work done by the end of the week*
- *15% felt their organization truly enable them to execute key goals.*
- *15% felt they worked in a high-trust environment.*
- *17% felt open and respectful communication resulted in new or better ideas*
- *10% felt their organization holds people accountable for results*
- *20% fully trusted their organization.*
- *13% had a high trust, highly cooperative working relationship with other groups or departments.*

This is indeed a sad endictment on many U.S. organizations , especially those in government! This is where W.L Gore and Associates stands out as an innovative and empowering employer.

"We have to learn, unlearn and relearn." John Nisbett

THE LEADER AS A TALENT CHAMPION

CAPITALIZE ON TALENT

Marcus Buckingham, who co-authored with Donald Coffman, the classic book, 'FIRST; Break all the rules' (Buckingham and Coffman, 1999) worked for the gallup organization and used the mass of data to also co-authored with Donald Clifton, the book 'NOW, Discover your Strengths' (Buckingham and Clifton, 1999). More recent books: 'GO, Put Your Strengths to Work' (Buckingham, 2007) and the 'ONE Thing You Need to Know' (2005), also built on the same theme of discovering and building our strengths. The great quote **"Don't try to put in what was left out, draw out what was put** in, sums it up well. We all have strengths – or talents – and leaders need to discover and nurture these, rather than wasting time, energy, effort and money, trying to make someone what they aren't. I love the example of the Chicken and the Duck. They are both birds, have wings, feathers and two legs, but put them both into a pond, and only one has the talent to swim. Equally put them both on rough ground and throw out some corn, the chicken will race around and eat more than the duck, which will waddle and scoop up some corn and mud, with its bill! The essence of this series of books is what leaders need to be good at – **discovering, attracting, nurturing, unleashing and retaining the best talent.**

LEADERS CAN NURTURE TALENT

Talent Management, can include talent leadership. **Talent Management includes the processes of planning , recruiting, selecting, developing, compensating and retaining employees who have talent.** In short, it is ensuring there are no "square pegs in round holes", and requires the matching of talents to task and jobs. The leadership component is more with the leader's involvement is some of these processes, especially in the motivation of employees that comes from development activities. These can include **coaching, counselling, training and providing feedback** that ensures learning, growth and improved performance. In small organizations, the leader may take on all the roles of talent management. Whereas in a larger organization, recruitment and compensation may be handled more by the H.R department. But it is **still the leader's responsibility to ensure a good 'talent-job-fit'.** Thus, if employees are placed in jobs that do not match their talent, it can lead to disaster for both employer and employee. This may necessitate the use of personality profiling and aptitude testing and if the leader lacks the know-how in these, consultants or the internal HR people can usually assist.

TALENT	COMPETENCE
• Sense of rhythm and a musical ear	Can become a skilled singer or musician
• Naturally good and quick with numbers	Can become an accountant or financial analyst
• Linguistically gifted with an aptitude for Languages	Can become an interpreter or language teacher
• Very sociable with a high emotional intelligence	Can become an effective sales person
• Naturally adept in visual spatial calculations	Can become an architect, surgeon or landscaper

Talents are intelligences and where they are strong, it is easier for a competence to be developed .

"Don't try to put in what's not there, try to draw out what was put in".
Buckingham and Clifton

LEADERSHIP ENGAGEMENT

IMPORTANCE OF ENGAGEMENT

Engagement has been defined, as **"when employees are mentally and emotionally invested in their work and contributing to an employer's success"**. This is from the U.S. Institute for Corporate Productivity. Other descriptions include, **"the degree to which employees interact with their leader and the quality of this interaction, including the provision of support and guidance to improve job performance"**. This can include a wide range of engagement strategies, such as coaching, counselling, on the job training and mentoring. Studies in the US show that less than 30 percent of employees are engaged.

A gallup poll survey estimated the loss in productivity in 2008 to 2009 exceeded USD 300 billion. Also gallup research shows employees with the highest levels of engagement have an **83% chance of performing above company averages**. Those with the lowest level of employee engagement had only a 17% chance of performing well. Another study by the Watson Wyatt group showed that employees with high levels of engagement have a **26% higher revenue per employee.** Trade USA believes high engagement reduces employee turnover by 10%. Another study by Towers Perrin found that only about 21% of the global work force are engaged, and about 40%, disengaged. Unless leaders strategically engage with their team members, performance and productivity may suffer and staff turnover increase.

GAUGING ENGAGEMENT

It is not difficult to periodically gauge how engaged employees feel. Using the criteria in the table below surveys among employees can be given. For example, the large global consulting company, Accenture uses a very simple 3factor survey of its nearly 200,000 employees. Factor 1 "**SAY**". It asks them how proud they are of working for Accenture by **saying** this to others, or recommending the company to others. Factor no 2 "**STAY**". Is based on how long employees stay. And the 3rd factor "**STRONG**". For example, how hard they 'strive' to actively play a role in the company's success by doing the tasks that are, above and beyond what is the expected norm.

EMPLOYEE ENGAGEMENT
Employer/Leader's actions that make employees feel more engaged, was ranked by a Towers Perrin Survey., This is based on the percentages of agreement, by employees on their top 9 factors:

89%:	*Understand how my unit/dept contributes to company success.*
81%:	*Understand how my role relates to company goals and objectives.*
78%:	*Am personally motivated to help my company succeed.*
78%:	*Am willing to put in a great deal of effort beyond what is normally expected.*
77%:	*Really care about the future of my company.*
70%:	*Proud to work for my company.*
66%:	*Sense of personal accomplishment from my job.*
61%:	*My company is a good place to work.*
50%:	*My company inspires me to do my best.*

"In everyone's life, at some time, our inner fire goes out, then bursts into flame by an encounter with another human being".

Albert Schweitzer

STRATEGIC LEADERSHIP

While we have discussed several theories and models of Leadership, right brained strategic thinking is a vital precursor to strategic leadership. Strategic Management includes having plans, goals and objectives which are formulated into strategic decisions. The leader's role is to translate these into actions that fit the desired vision for the future. The word strategy comes from the Greek term 'strategos', which originally implied military leadership that positioned their forces so they could win the battle – and the war. Modern terminology uses the words 'competitive advantage'. It requires big picture (Helicopter perspective) and longer range planning and thinking (Future Thinking). Research by Finkelstein and Hambrick (1996) found that strategic thinking and planning for the future, can positively influence organisational success. Their study showed that **up to 44% variance in profitability of large organisations can be attributed to strategic leadership.**

The questions strategic leaders must ask: Where does the organisation want to be? (vision). Where is the organisation now? (Can use 'SWOT' analysis). What is occurring in the external competitive environment? (Can use 'PESTELIED' analysis) and, what resources and actions are needed to achieve the vision?

QUALITY MANAGEMENT CRITERIA

There are many national quality award. Note ability among them is the 'Malcolm Baldridge Award' (MBA-USA) and the 'European Quality Award' (EQA) developed by fourteen leading European companies, in collaboration with (EFQM). In both the MBA & EQA, leadership earns 10%.

Other criteria are shown in the chart below, with customer satisfaction ratings at 10% and people satisfaction at 9% respectfully, with business or key performance results rated at 15%, with processes at 10%.

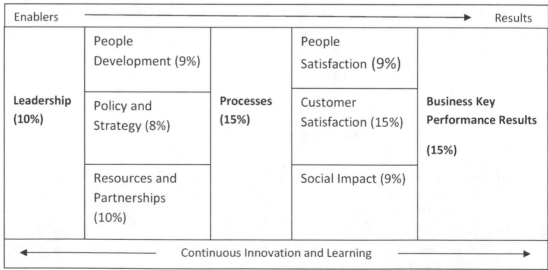

Source Adapted from EFQMind MBA

"He would be a leader, must be a bridge". A Welsh Proverb

SUMMARY OF KEY POINTS

- Most early theories of leadership, management and motivation were developed in the West, around the fifties to seventies, more than 30 - 40 years ago. Being strongly influenced by U.S. cultural norms and values at that time, many are not so relevant in other cultures, and now in a vastly different world.

- Some contemporary theories, especially for African, Eastern and Asian cultures, who have differing cultural values, are introduced and elaborated on. Spiritual leadership and treating employees more holistically are examples.

- The concept that 'leader-follower' relations have become increasingly more relevant, due to employees being better educated and informed, especially with the latest information technologies.

- Entrepreneurial leadership is contrasted to other types of leadership and emphasizes that innovation and risk-taking are essential for success – which not all leaders are comfortable with. It is concluded that not all leaders can be entrepreneurial, as it requires a higher level of 'right brain' thinking.

- 'Groupthink' is illustrated as a series of illusions that can cause groups and leaders not to challenge reality. Among them are the need for harmony, conflict avoidance and face serving. While groupthink evolved in USA, and was called the 'Abilene Paradox', it is perhaps even more relevant to the East.

- Energy fields are explored in Quantum Leadership, by looking at Quantum physics, and how leaders can tap into, or even design structures that have more fluidity, resulting in higher levels of the 'Flow State' that energizes team work. Leaders themselves must arouse 'spirit' among people at work as it is a form of energy.

- Mindfulness in leadership is suggested as an important paradigm for leadership. Using the power of the conscious left brain to build awareness around relational effectiveness. Balance in conceptual as well as analytical and creative thinking is depicted in Shell Oil's four global leader qualities.

- Leading across generational gaps is becoming increasingly critical, as leaders from one generation may not fully understand the motives and behaviours of team members from other generations. This is especially so when employees are from 'Gen Y' (age 20 plus) and the leader is from an older generation (Gen X or a 'Baby Boomer').

- Leader-Member Exchange (LMX) is described as a 'Vertical Dyadic Relationship' between the leader and individual team members. How members are treated can result in their perceiving if they are valued or not. Those favoured (the 'in-group') will be much more loyal and productive than others, who may form negative perceptions about the organization and their leaders (the 'out-group'). The ideal is that there should not be such gaps.

- When it comes to perceptions of fairness, there is the concept of Organisational Justice, with three types outlined. These are referred to as 'Distributive', where resources are allocated. The second is 'Procedural', which have more to do with H.R. Processes and if bias or prejudice exist. The third is 'Interactional', and whether leaders treat others with equal respect, warmth and friendliness, or not.

- Following this, there is the degree of commitment that employees show. Again, three types exist. Affective, Continuance and Normative. These depend on employee motivation, linked to perceptions of justice and whether leaders are 'Principled'. Do they see themselves as 'stewards', who can ensure employee interests are protected?

- A balanced life style, between work and personal life has been advocated by the late Stephen Covey, as well as the teachings of ancient Chinese philosophers, like Lao Tzu. This relates to energy and whether there is balance between mind, body and spirit. Stress must be well managed and people need to have belief in themselves and hope for their future.

- Based on this, the example of the 'Self Fulfilling Prophecy' or the 'Pygmalion' effect is outlined and the power of belief in one self and one's leader, trainer, coach or mentor. Coaching and Mentoring are shown as helpful interventions of employee engagement. The differences are explained.

- Leaders should develop a culture of learning and how 'Vision can pull' and how 'Systems' thinking can help. Again, it relates to the leader as a 'steward' of learning and the need to ensure organizational design facilitates this culture of continuous learning. Here the McKinsey's 7-S model can play a useful approach.

- 'Leaders as Talent Champions' is linked to their role of attracting, selecting, developing and retaining talent, and how competence development is an essential part of this. Leaders need to create a high level of employee engagement - both organizationally - and as individuals, as this has been proven to significantly increase loyalty, morale and productivity.

- Strategic leadership is often needed by leaders. It involves having mission, goals and resources that place the organization in a competitive advantage. This requires analysis of both the internal and external environment. Lastly, the role of leadership in quality management is shown by examining the criteria of the well known International Quality awards - such as the EQA.

SYSTEMS THINKING

More people are taking a systemic view of change. An increasing number of people are becoming familiar with the concepts of systems thinking. As a result, we will see fewer piecemeal approaches to address complex issues and more comprehensive approaches that consider multiple disciplines (e.g. engineering finance, purchasing, strategic planning). By taking into account multiple factors and disciplines, organizations and communities will be able to identify potentially conflicting strategies and also account for potential unintended consequences of strategic and tactical actions. They will also actively seek out high-leverage areas; those areas where a small amount of effort generates great returns.   *Tom Devane: The Change Handbook.*

"Man has a limited biological capacity for change. When this capacity is overwhelmed, it results in future shock."
    Alvin Tofler, in Future Shock, 1971

REFERENCES

Adair, J. (1968). *Training for Leadership*. London: McDonalds and Company.

Autry, J. (1991). *Love and Profit*. NY : William Morrow.

Blake, R. and Mouton, J. (1991). *The Managerial Grid*. Houston: Gulf Publishing.

Blake, R. and McCanse, A. (1991). *Leadership Dilemma*. Houston: Gulf Publishing.

Blanchard, K. (1981). *One Minute Manager* . New York: Library of Congress.

Buckingham, M. and Clifton, D.E. (1999). *NOW Discover You Strengths.* New York: Free Press.

Buckingham, M. and Coffman, C. (1999). *FIRST Break All Rules*. NY: Simon and Schuster.

Buckingham, M. (2007*). GO Put Your Strengths To Work.* USA: Library of Congress.

Childre, D. and Martin, H. (1999). *The HeartMath Solution*. London: Piatus Publisher.

Collins, J. (1991). *How the Mighty Fallen*. NY: Collins Business Essential .

Collins, J. (2001). *Good to Great*. NY: Harper Collins.

Covey, S. (1994). *First Things First.* New York : Simon & Schuster.

Covey, S. (1991). *Leadership is a Choice* . NY: Simon & Schuster.

Covey, S. (1990). *Principle Centred Leadership* . NY: Summit Books.

Covey, S. (1991). *The 7 Habits of Highly Effective People* . NY: Simon and Schuster.

Covey, S. (2004). *The 8th Habit* . NY : Simon & Schuster .

Daft, R. (2011). *Leadership.* Singapore: Cengage Learning.

Fiedler, F. (1967). *A Theory of Leadership Effectiveness*. NY: McGraw-Hill.

Fisher, H. (2014). *Rutgers University Research Paper*. NY: Rutgers University Press.

Gardner, H. (1999). *Intelligence Reframed*. NY: Basic Books.

Gardner, H. (1999). *Mindful Leadership*. USA : Library of Congress.

Gerstner, C. and Day, D. (1997). *Meta-analytic review of leader-member exchange theory: correlates and construct ideas. Journal of Applied Pscychology,* 56-60.

Graen, G. (1976). *Role Making processes with complex organisations. (1st, Ed.) Handbook of Industrial and Organisational Psychology,* 1201-1245.

Greenleaf, R. (1998). *The Power of Servant Leadership.* San Francisco: Berrett-Koehlar.

Hawley, J. (1993). *Reawakening the Spirit in Work*. San Francisco: Berrett-Koehler.

Heider, J. (1985). *The Tao of Leadership*. Atlanta: Bantam Books .

Herrmann, N. (1993). *The Creative Brain*. USA: The Herrmann Group.

Herrmann, N. (1996). *The Whole Brain Business Book*. NY: McGraw-Hill.

Hersey, P and Blanchard, K.H. (1979). *Situational Leadership*. New Jersey: Prentice Hall.

Hesselben, F. and Cohen, P. (1999). *Leader to Leader*: Enduring Insights of Leadership. UK: Jossey-Bass.

Jamrog, J.J. (2002). *The Coming of the Employee.* Human Resource Planning. Vol 25. No.3

Janis, I. L. (1982). *Groupthinki: Pyschological studies of policy decisions and fiascos*. Boston: Houghton Miffin.

Kouzes, J. and Posner, B. (2007). *The Leadership Challenge*. USA: Library of Congress.

Manzoni, J. and Barsoux, J. (March-April , 1998). *The Set-Up-To-Fail Syndrome*. Harvard Business Review, 101-113.

Maxwell, J. (1998). *The 21 Irrefutable Laws of Leadership*. Georgia: Maxwell Motivation.

McGregor, D. (1960). *The Human Size of Enterprise* . NY: McGraw Hill .

Meyer, J and Allen, N. (1997). *Commitment in the Workplace*. Calif: Sage Publications.

Nisbett, R. (2004). *The Geography of Thought*. USA: First Press.

Parikh J.et al. (1990). *Beyond Leadership.* London: Blake Well Publishers.

Parikh,J et.al. (1996). *Institution, The New Frontier*. London: Blackwell.

Peck, S. (1993). *The Road Less Travelled*. Great Britain: Random House.

Peters, J. and Watermen, R. (1963). *In Search of Excellence*. USA: Library of Congress.

Pink, D. (2005). *A Whole New Mind*. London : Penguiin Books .

Pirsig, R. M. (1979). *Zen and the Art of Motorcycle Maintenance*. London: Vintage.

Revens, R (2011). *ABC of Action Learning*. Gower Publishing Co. USA

Senge, P. (1990). *The Fifth Discipline* . NY : DoubleDay .

Shephard, P. (2003). *Leading Diverse and Multi-Cultural Teams*. Kuala Lumpur: Brain Works Media .

Shephard, P. (2008). *Personality Matters*. Kuala Lumpur: BrainWorks Media.

Shephard, P. (2001). *Whole Brain Thinking and Learning*. Kuala Lumpur: Brain Works Media.

Veechio, R. (1997). *Are you in or out with your boss? In R. Veechio, Leadership: Understanding the dynamics of power and influence in organisations.* (1st ed). Notre Dame: University Press

Vroom, V. (1969). *Work and Motivation*. NY: John Wiley.

Vroom, Y. (1969). *The Vroom-Yetton Contigency Model of Leadership*. New York: John Wiley.

Wheatley, M. (1992). *Leadership and the New Science*. SFO: Berrett-Koehlar.

Zohar, D. (1997). *Rewiring the Corporate Brain*. USA: Berrett Koehlar.

CHAPTER FIVE

LEADERSHIP, CULTURE AND DIVERSITY

LEARNING OBJECTIVES FOR THIS CHAPTER

By the end of this chapter, you will be able to:

- Define and describe culture and recognize the main underlying laws for cultural behaviour.

- Differentiate between African, eastern and western values and their underlying assumptions.

- Identify the dynamics of time, task and relationships in terms of cultural patterns.

- Recognize how the values of harmony and respect influence the concept of 'face'.

- Identify the essential competencies for communicating across cultures.

- Distinguish how the concept of religion and spirituality differs in secular or non-secular cultures.

- Contrast between the range of diversity among employees, including gender, generations, ethnicity and personality types and traits.

- Define how the management and leadership of diversity requires matching jobs, policies and how the use of best practices ensure high levels of morale, motivation and performance.

- Integrate best practices to ensure minorities are ethically and legally protected from discrimination.

TABLE OF CONTENTS

ELEMENTS OF CULTURE

INTRODUCTION
- *Why are people different?*
- *Why do some people like to work alone and others prefer to be in groups?*
- *Why do some people like to build relationships before they get down to work, while others believe that the 'task' is the boss?*

The answer lies in both nature (our genetic predisposition) and nurture (our upbringing, schooling, socialization or culture) and how they both interact. Our differences are found in both our **genetic endowment or inheritability and our environment and culture.**

CULTURE AS MENTAL PROGRAMMING
Our behaviours are due to the complex interaction of our 'personality', temperament, personal and cultural values or norms. Our mental and emotional preferences have a strong genetic component, with, our personality remaining fairly stable throughout our life. Whereas **our cultural practices are influenced by the environment in which we live.** This means that the way we do things is to a large extent dependent on the degree of cultural 'programming' from our parents, peers or role models.

CULTURE AND GROUP BEHAVIOUR
Culture is based on what we have learned and acquired as a member of a group, community or nation. To understand a culture, we identify those cultural practices which are more 'learned' or collectively programmed into us, often from birth. These **practices are based on a set of values and underlying assumptions** that will differentiate one group of people from another. These values are the 'shoulds, musts or oughts' in life, and guide us on what we are expected to do, in order to be accepted.

SOME KEY CONCEPTS
To help us learn more about some key aspects of culture, we will look at 8 key concepts. Each of these concepts are in 'pairs' which are at opposite ends of a continuum. Each concept can be described with many characteristics. Broadly they can be clustered under **Culture A** (More 'Eastern' or African') and **Culture B** (More 'Western').

VALUES
Based on the underlying assumptions, different cultures will transmit sets of values to their members in order to maintain and preserve their identity and uniqueness.

"We are captives of our own culture and the values we internalize in the process of growing up have a significant influence on our lives. This knowledge becomes even more important when we interact with people from other cultures. "   *Hall, E, Beyond Culture. Doubleday, New York, 1976.*

8 Cultural Concepts:

The 8 key concepts and their 'opposites : Each pair can be seen on a continuum

CULTURE A (Collectivist)   CULTURE B (Individualist)

A	B	A	B	A	B
1. Harmony.......................Control,		2. Relationship......................Task,		3. Shame................................Guilt,	
4. High Context.................Low context		5. Polychronic.................... Monochronic,		6.Collectivism....................Individualism,	
7. Hierarchy.........................Equality		8. Spiritual/Religious .... Secular			

GENERATIONAL VALUES DIFFER

DIVERSITY OF VALUES ACROSS GENERATIONS

Employees are regarded as valuable assets for organizations to develop and grow. It is the duty of an employer to ensure that the right workforce is selected to sustain the growth and development of their organizations. The dilemma many organizations face today is to have loyal and highly skilled workforce in the business. An increasing number of Generation Y (Gen Y) is a good sign as they have up to date information technology capabilities to make business and organizations successful. Proactive Generation Y employees exhibit innovativeness, future orientation and self-motivation required to add real value to organizations. So, older generation leaders, (eg: Generation X) will need to understand the generation Y values and how they differ.

Since Generation Y employees are dominant in the job market, many employers have to understand their needs and characteristics so that they can provide their best services to the organization. In an increasingly competitive, dynamic and unpredictable work environment, employers have to pay particular attention to develop Generation Y employees who are willing and able to work proactively. Generation Y's characteristics put them in high demand in today's job market, but leaders are having a challenge understanding how to motivate them.

LANGUAGE AND DIVERSITY

Theories, almost all, are expressed in language. Language is learned in the brain, but shaped by both our personality, gender, upbringing, education and importantly our culture. The language of leadership therefore is shaped by all of this diversity. Rules of grammar, sizes of vocabulary and word preferences differ for English, Fench, German, Arabic or Chinese etc. Language also evolves with new words being invented and added to our dictionaries every year, just as 'old fashioned' or rarely used words fade from our everyday usage.

Language is a way of connecting sound to internal ways of seeing and thinking. Left brain language is more logical and likely to follow rules. (Spelling, Grammar and Concrete choice of words). Whereas, right brain language is more abstract, artistic and poetic. Semantics is the study of meaning of words, with modern youth abbreviating much of it, for texting or twittering, for speed and instant response or gratification. With business priorities around time and money, internet memos become less personal, less flowery and less wordy. With minimal face to face interaction, it lacks the emotions that are needed for leaders to engage and motivate. For leaders who need to engage with diverse groups from generation Y or Millenial Employees, with people of a different gender or culture. How should they communicate to embrace all these differences? Are there universal rules? Perhaps not, except, to empathize, choose words carefully and moderate delivery – appreciating the diversity of your audience.

So if Gen Y want messages to be as short as possible. Woman may want them to emote a little more. A busy male leader, under stress, may even shout out a command, more aggressively. An extrovent may use more visual and contextual language, and an introvert may prefer more reflective language.

"The World is just a click away" Deloitte Consulting

CULTURAL VALUES AND ASSUMPTIONS

COLLECTIVISM AND INDIVIDUALISM

In some societies, people are affiliated to a group or collectivity (Group Loyalty). Members in **a collectivist culture** tend to be concerned about the impact of their behaviour on other people. They are **more willing to sacrifice personal interest** to attain collectivistic interests and harmony.

An **individualistic** culture would tend to make people more concerned with their own behaviour, needs, interests and goals ("I did it for myself"). The spirit of competition, individual achievement, independence, assertiveness and pursuit of material success are highly valued. **Personal freedom, autonomy and self**-interests are regarded as the best impetus to advancement. **Hofstede (2001) calls this 'Low Power Distance'.**

HIERARCHY AND EQUALITY

Some cultures are more able to tolerate differences in status and wealth and believe that those at the top of the social hierarchy are entitled to more privileges. Inequality in power is accepted and considered normal: "A place for everyone and everyone in their place." In this case they are more likely to receive instructions from their superiors and would be cautious about expressing disagreement with them. But in other cultures, members regard each other as equals and that inequalities in society should be minimized. In this instance, people are seldom afraid to disagree and expect to be consulted before decisions are made. Hofstede refers to this as 'High Power Distance'.

HARMONY AND CONTROL

Some cultures dictate that **people should live in harmony with the environment** and the world around them, while others believe **in taking control and being in charge**. The former are more inclined to adopt an accommodating posture to their environment. As a result, this belief tends to promote a healthy co-existence with other people and a willingness to accept things the way they are.

RELATIONSHIPS AND TASK

In some cultures, it is important to recognize that the basis of establishing contracts with others is to **initially cultivate good and friendly relationships with people.** They believe that by understanding and having a "feel" for the other party that they are able to live and work smoothly with them. But in other cultures, they **would prefer to firstly attend to the task** by entering into a contractual agreement with the other party.

Harmony versus Control
Western, Industrial and Scientific - and Urban societies increasingly believe that the forces of nature must be harnessed through technical and scientific devices to meet the needs of man. Goodness for those in the latter, means separating themselves from Nature and establishing mastery by looking for ways to control and manipulate it to human advantage. Many less developed or rural areas believe in harmony with nature, and not in trying to control and manipulate it to human advantage.

"Culture is like water to the duck or swan. Remove them from the water and much of their context is missing. They may survive, but will never be the same".
Conyngham, 1999

LOW AND HIGH CONTEXT-CULTURES

LOW CONTEXT

In some cultures, communication means that what is said is what is meant, i.e. 'Mean what you say, say what you mean'. The message containing, facts and information means everything; hence the more detailed and specific, the better. ***Meaning is more explicit or direct.***

In this case the sender and the receiver of the message **shares only little stored information** about the people and things involved in the newly transmitted information. Therefore, the receiver of the new piece of information needs many details in order to understand the meaning of the message. Even then, he will probably still not be able to understand the full meaning of the given information.

HIGH CONTEXT

However, in other cultures which are homogeneous, the meaning of the message is also conveyed through shades of tonal qualities, modes of non-verbal channels, and the use of imprecise and ambiguous language to say more or to say less. What is not spoken may be just as important as the spoken word in building and maintaining relationships. ***Meaning is more implicit, indirect or hidden.***

In some cases, both the sender and the receiver of the message, **share some implicit information** about the people and things involved in the newly transmitted information. Therefore, the interpretation of the new piece of information does not need much detail in order for them to understand the meaning of the message. A few words or gestures are enough for the receiver to understand the full meaning.

SHAME DRIVEN

In certain cultures, members are driven by a sense of shame as they are expected to demonstrate an acute sense of social sensitivity towards others in the group. These feelings tend to discourage them from misbehaving because of the adverse social consequences on their group (External locus of control).

GUILT DRIVEN

In other cultures which are driven by feelings of guilt, individuals are taught to be internally driven and to take control of their own destiny and to do things on their own volition (Internal locus of control). For example 'I may feel guilt, but not shame'.

High vs. Low Context Cases
Some processes or tasks have in themselves a tendency toward high or low context, e.g.:
High Context Conditions
* two old friends meet and talk about their mutual business plans.
* a reporter on a US sports TV program comments on a baseball game to Americans.
* a son writes a report about his stay in Australia in a letter to his parents.
Low Context Conditions
* two potential business partners meet and talk about their business plans.
* an American tourist tries to explain baseball to Malaysians.
* an astronaut writes a report about his stay on planet Mars for a magazine.

"Culture is a silent language........... which influences the individual behind his back, without his knowledge".- Eric Fromm

POLYCHRONIC AND MONOCHRONIC TIME ORIENTATION

POLYCHRONIC VERSUS MONOCHRONIC

A polychronic orientation is where one sees time as not so significant and where constraints and failures to meet deadlines are often tolerated. **Polychronic time people don't interpret time as a concrete commodity** which can be negotiated. Punctuality and deadlines are not absolute or made of concrete chunks (Hall, 1993).

Those who are **monochronic see time as a scarce, indeed finite, resource;** communication between business people is done with directness and speed. In this setting, work is planned and executed within the time specified. And this is seen as most important.

A person's orientation towards time also clearly connotes the economic values placed on the other resources used to create wealth and prosperity. As a result **monochronic time people will compartmentalize their lives and accept the schedule as sacred** and unalterable with an ordered life.

MONOCHRONIC TASKS

Examples of monochronic tasks: Building a house, assembling cars in a factory or organizing the flight schedule of an airline.

All of these can and must be scheduled carefully by the person(s) in charge. Each phase of the process has a fixed time frame during which it has to be completed as other phases precede and follow it. If one of the phases moves out of its time frame, the whole pattern or process will be seriously damaged. The reason: these processes are mostly **Task Oriented** and/or **Technical.**

POLYCHRONIC TASKS

Examples of polychronic tasks: Successfully making a new business contact, a doctor seeing a patient for diagnosis, discovering a new technology (duration is flexible).

All of these cannot be exactly scheduled by the person(s) in charge. Instead, they have their own rhythm and include a dose of luck or coincidence. They demand patience, flexibility, multitasking and the capability to react quickly and appropriately.
The Reason: These **Processes Are Mostly People Oriented and/or Organic.**

DIVISION OF TIME -APPOINTMENTS

In a global study done on business and government meetings or appointments, the following general trend of averages were:

* *Dutch/German/Japanese*	* *Very definitive*
* *British/Australian/ USA*	* *+5 Minutes*
* *Hong Kong/Singapore/New Zealand*	*+10 Minutes*
* *Italian/Spanish*	* *+ 15 Minutes*
* *Malaysia/Thailand/Indonesia*	* *Usually Late*
* *Arabs/Africans*	* *Much Wider Span*

'Time goes, you say? Oh no! Alas, Time stays, we go'
A Dobson, The Paradox of Time

TASK OR PEOPLE FOCUS

Some cultures put task achievement ahead of relationships (eg: American) others favour the building of relationships and trust, before emphasizing the task. (eg. Africa, Middle East, and most of Asia).

While both task and people are a **focus - one is an 'end' and the other the 'means'**. The end result (task achievement) may still be the same. It is merely which values are emphasized first. Where time and money - and short-term results are more important - relationship building comes later. It is still important, but merely comes later.

Relationship oriented cultures tend to be more collectivistic. Harmony and face are core values here. **Task oriented cultures on the other hand** tend to be more **individualistic and competitive**. Relationship oriented Cultures (African, Middle Eastern or Asian) emphasize 'face'. This includes 'giving face', 'saving face', 'losing face' or 'showing face'. In Western cultures, we call it 'self-esteem'.

In some cultures these prescriptive influences also come from more formal, external teachings - such as school, teachers or religious indoctrination. Hence it is critical for members in a society to know their cultural values as they mirror their culture. Those individuals responsible for their socialization have defined various situations.

A 'Task' oriented group.
* Focuses on self-achievement ahead of relationships with others.
* Seeks to control the environment.
* Communicates in a 'low-context' style (explicit) using specificity & directness.
* May be more 'monochronic' and plan activities in a linear way & according to set time schedules.
* Puts the 'task' ahead of the 'boss.'

A 'Relationship' oriented group
* Focuses on harmonious or long-term relationships ahead of self-achievement.
* Prefers 'harmony with nature' and 'going with the flow'.
* Communicates in a 'high context' style (implicit), being indirect or obtuse, seeking to save face and maintain harmony between people.
* More 'polychronic': doing many things at one time, according to feelings or at the spur of the moment, rather than in a linear, sequential way.
* May put the 'boss" or people of status or older age, ahead of task efficiency.

SOURCE OF VALUE ORIENTATION
The earliest and strongest source of values come from our primary social group, the family. The most influential figures are parents, aunts, uncles or cousins with whom we have the greatest contact in our formative years. Parents and significant elders are often venerated as repositories of communal and family wisdom.
It is through interactions with them and the normative and prescriptive instructions received from them that we learn the values of task or relationships.

"As life is action and passion, it is required of man that he should share the passion and action of time......"
                                        Oliver Wendell Holmes -

THE MANY FACES OF FACE

THE MEANING OF FACE

The concept of 'face' is a term used more in Eastern and Asian cultures and can be closely linked to the concept of 'shame'. In a Western context it may be thought of more as Pride or 'Self Esteem'. If our self-esteem is lowered, such as when we are criticized, or belittled, we may say we feel guilt or embarrassment - and not know how to look others in the 'face'. We may want to 'hide our face'. In an Asian context, we talk about 'losing face'. But here it has more to do with 'group shame' rather than individual guilt.

Thus 'face' can mean 'self'. We talk **of 'saving face'; 'giving face'; 'showing face'; as well as 'losing face'.** As a value, harmony therefore plays an important role, as harmonious relationships ensure face is preserved.

MANIFESTATIONS OF FACE

This is one reason why many Asians may not be so 'direct', frank, blunt or even specific. Conflict is avoided if possible, and people are reluctant to criticize openly, or directly confront the conflict. **Being vague or non-specific means that if we have a problem, it is easier to save face while dealing with it**. If relationships are harmonious, we are more likely to have cooperative teamwork and feel motivated. Job satisfaction will be higher, thus contributing to higher productivity.

FACE, JOB SATISFACTION AND PRODUCTIVITY

Western studies of job satisfaction and productivity have found that motivation and satisfaction come from being productive. Achieving the task may well be more satisfying than having good relationships. As we've already stressed, Asians may put relationships first. If we like and trust the people we work with and enjoy harmonious relationships, cooperative teamwork will come naturally and the task will still be achieved. The case is similar for Africans and Middle Eastern people.

The main drives for such productivity in Africa or Asia therefore comes from the values of harmony, face and trusted or respected relationships. This is opposite to the more task oriented Western drives or norms.

This task orientation also helps explain why Asians are more likely to show loyalty to people, such as the 'boss' or team rather than putting loyalty to the organization first. It is also one of the factors that strengthen the importance of 'cronyism' among Asians.

Expressing Feelings Openly

In a 10 countries survey, people were asked how openly they would express their feelings. Here is low exhibiting is unacceptable.

Country	%	Country	%
Italy	59	Netherlands	59
France	61	Norway	61
USA	71	UK	71
Singapore	42	Indonesia	75
Hong Kong	55	Japan	83

"One cannot be human by oneself. There is no selfhood where there is community...... We are who we are in relating to others".

Carse, J. 1986

CULTURE AND RELIGION

HOLISTIC OR SECULAR

Some cultures believe that there has to be a separation of state from religion and therefore promote a secular approach to development. Religion here is not such an important factor to be considered in one's daily work.

Other cultures incorporate a more holistic approach which combines both religious and material dimensions in one's outlook towards life. The whole person, mind, body and spirit, has to be taken into consideration. It is important to blend spiritual and material dimensions, in order to have a sense of interconnectedness with the world around.

CULTURE OR RELIGION

Culture however, is group or society based, rather than individual or genetic. If the culture is a large group who follows a particular set of religious teachings, beliefs and practices, then we can see how it is possible to confuse and attribute behaviours to both or either. For example, **some practices that are culturally Arabic - predate Islam -** yet often may be believed to be Islamic. Female genital mutilation is one example.

In collectivistic cultures, religious practices that are more relationship-based, like communal prayers, may be valued as more important than staying at work and finishing the 'task'. Regardless of deadlines, productivity or profits; prayers, going to the mosque or temple or respecting a religious holiday, are valued as more important.

In individualistic cultures, state and religion may be superseded by commercial or materialistic pursuits. In such secular states or societies, religion is kept separate and is often merely up to the individual to decide how to follow.

DEGREES OF RELIGIOSITY

How do 'Relationship - Task' values relate to the 'Spiritual-Secular' values? Spiritual and religious belief systems can have an immensely strong influence on behaviour. Of course, this depends upon each individual's own degree or strength of religiosity. From new research on genetics and the brain, we know there are special areas and mechanisms in the brain where we experience spiritual or religious feelings. Also, that there is a differing intensity of beliefs - from atheistic, agnostic, accepting to dogmatic. Some research indicates that this intensity may be more genetically predisposed than cultural.

In families with the same cultural and parental influences, one child may evolve as highly or strictly religious, while another sibling (but not an identical twin) may be less religious. In fact , that other sibling may even 'rebel' against the religious programming and teaching, going as far as becoming a disbeliever, even with the same parenting, schooling and peer pressures. Once free to express or believe on their own, the two siblings can differ significantly. In studies done on genetically identical twins, there are surprisingly strong correlations of belief or disbelief, regardless of upbringing. Thus the degree of religiosity may have a genetic predisposition.

'Culture.....is an infinate game. Culture has no boundanes... for this reason it can be said that where society is defined by its boundaries, a culture is defined by its horizons'

Carse, J

CULTURE AND COMMUNICATION

Values, therefore, are the most important elements to a deeper understanding of a particular culture. They are derived from the underlying assumptions and beliefs of its members which are not easily seen and can only be inferred from the behaviour of its members. They are from the heart of a culture and guide the behaviour of its members at the unconscious level.

Very often we learn cultural values so early in life that we are usually unaware of their influence. We communicate them verbally and non-verbally and often unconsciously. **An integrated value system therefore provides a sense of purpose and meaning for living**. Values reflect the norms that rule a society and are based on the underlying assumptions of how we relate with the world around us, that is, communication.

HOW WE SEE THE WORLD

From this broad mental orientation, group members develop a set of beliefs and convictions about how the world actually is. Attitudes, which are predispositions to and perception of ideas, feelings and specific opinions, are concrete expressions of particular issues. For most Asians, regardless of ethnic group, their cultural values are clear and uncompromising statements about the importance as a specific group member.

These values guide individual behaviour, provide meaning and serve as social bonds among those who belong to the same ethnic group. They become shared practices that members demonstrate through symbols and rituals. **These values are important because they govern our daily behaviour,** both in our work and non-work areas. They strongly influence how we communicate.

CULTURAL EXPRESSION

To understand a culture, sayings, compliments and proverbs can also be a reliable source of information and oral tradition. Cultural values of good manners, group orientation and shame are often expressed through sayings communicated in local folklore, poetry, art and, lately, social media.

VALUES AND PERCEPTIONS

Communication is an attempt to transfer ideas, pictures and meanings between peoples' minds. At the core is the process of perceiving. Communicating across cultures is sometimes difficult, not only due to differences in values, but also in perceptions.

In one study among managers from 8 countries, they were asked to rate their degree of agreement with the following statement. "It is important for a Manager to have at hand, precise answers to most questions that subordinates may raise about work".

Nationality	% Agree	Nationality	% Agree
1. Swedes	10	5. German	46
2. Americans	18	6. French	53
3. British	27	7. Italians	66
4. Swiss	38	8. Japanese	77

"Let us not be blind to our differences - but let us also direct attention to our common interests - and the means by which these differences can be resolved" - John F. Kennedy -

CROSS – CULTURAL COMMUNICATION

SKILFUL COMMUNICATION

The skillful communicator is highly tuned or sensitive to the clues that display both their own, and the other parties' emotions. The cross-cultural communicator may sense these, but may not always interpret them accurately.

Non-verbal signs, can differ from one culture to another. For example, in one culture, a smile may depict a friendly disposition. In another culture, it may be a defensive mechanism or a way of hiding embarrassment. We can appreciate therefore, how challenging it can be to learn the non-verbal nuances and subtleties of another culture.

STEREOTYPING AND GENERALIZATION

We need to avoid 'the all too easy trap of describing people as typical of'...or labelling them in general terms like hard working or lazy This is stereotyping, based on using a set of assumptions that all people of a certain race or profession or even gender, are alike.

TESTING ASSUMPTIONS

This stereotyping comes from not testing our own assumptions, or from strong in-built prejudices or biases we have formed. We often make judgements about someone from a culture, based on a guess, misinformation or inexperience. We may label people of a particular ethnicity or nationality, as not punctual or not specific. Here we may be judging them from our own world view, based on our different values about time or specificity. (Asma, 2001).

These are dangerous traps when we are interacting cross culturally. We need to avoid judging, stereotyping or evaluating others based on our own untested assumptions.

NEEDS FOR FLEXIBILITY

This quality includes a high degree of addictiveness to the different ways of others. In fact, one of the key qualities for overcoming culture shock, is to possess a high level of curiosity and genuine interest in learning about the 'so called strange ways'. When we are interested to learn, we display an openness that others can relate to.

Instead of ignorance breeding arrogance, it stimulates awareness, builds knowledge and helps us learn useful new skills. These become the critical tools for both building our inter-cultural bridge, and living comfortably on both sides of it. (Ibid, 2001)

TOLERANCE FOR AMBIGUITY

Another quality of the inter-culturist, is having a high tolerance towards ambiguity. When things are ambiguous, it means that things are not clear cut or predictable. Perceptions, interpretations or meanings may seem very different. We need to appreciate that communicating cross-culturally will be full of such uncertainty.

A high level of ignorance or lack of awareness about other cultures can produce surprise or even shock. I'm sure we've all heard of 'culture shock'. This really is a form of stress, when we experience things that are new or strange. We don't have the same frame of reference to interpret. We are therefore sometimes arrogant, because of our ignorance.

"Cultural empathy is the ability to see the world, as members of another culture can see it."
- Moran and Stripp -

DIVERSITY MANAGEMENT

INTRODUCTION

The word diversity in organizational terms, refers to the mix, variety and differences among the workforce. Due to demographics, workforces are changing. From rural to urban to global migration, the mix of ethnic diversity has grown in many countries. This is especially so in large cities.

At the operator level, we have new migrant labour groups filling jobs in the manufacturing and construction industries, as there are insufficient numbers among the local populations for that. At the senior management, professional and technical levels, we see multi-national and international companies moving people regionally and globally and this level of people also employ foreign domestic workers.

MAIN AREAS OF DIVERSITY

These can vary even more in cultures or cities that value or permit freedom or individualism. How we behave in London, Los Angeles, Singapore, Sydney or Tokyo can be strongly influenced by the cultural norms in those cities. Whereas, in the small town or village, social pressures to conform may be stronger.

When studying diversity and the main sources of it, gender, personality traits, age and ethno-cultural differences would head the list. Language, religion and marital status are also aspects of diversity. Sexual orientation and preferences, socio-economic and occupational preferences, food and eating preferences are also further aspects of diversity.

Dress codes, styles and preferences or other physical traits, such as hairstyles, would be additional elements of diversity. While culture and religion may dictate what people eat, drink or wear, there are still strongly individualistic personalities who may deviate from the norm, or the culturally dictated and acceptable behaviours.

ORGANIZATIONAL CULTURE

Similarly now, the corporate or organizational culture can determine the degree of diversity which is permitted or encouraged. While ethnicity, gender, age or personality may be diverse in some organizations, the dress code or hair style, and types of behaviours may be more uniform. In the military, some schools, hospitals or large government bureaucracies, dress, hairstyles or behaviours may be more regimented. Whereas in other organizations, like advertising agencies, or manufacturing companies, diverse dress styles may be quite acceptable.

Characteristics Associated with a Diversity Program's Long-Term Success

* *Top management provides resources, personally intervenes, and publicly advocates diversity.*
* *The program is structured.*
* *Capitalizing on a diverse workforce is defined as a business objective and necessary to generate revenue and profits.*
* *The program is evaluated.*
* *Manager involvement is mandatory.*
* *The program is seen as a cultural change, not a one-shot program.*
* *Managers and demographic groups are not blamed for problems.*
* *Behaviours and skills needed to successfully interact with others are taught.*
* *Managers are rewarded on progress toward meeting diversity goals.*

Rynes, S. & Rosen, B. 1994

WHY DIVERSITY MANAGEMENT

DIVERSE TEAMS

Leading and building a diverse work team is a major challenge. It is much more challenging than when team members are all similar. However, once one is able to produce synergy in a diverse team, their performance can vastly outshine a homogenous team. Especially when it comes to problem solving or decision making. Here, diversity of thinking styles, talents, perceptions or experience, bring to the team a wider and richer perspective. The quality of decisions is usually higher and the range of creative solutions to problems are greater.

The development of team cohesiveness calls for a very special leadership style. The leader of such a diverse team needs to have the qualities of openness, objectivity, flexibility and a high tolerance for ambiguity.

ADVANTAGES OF DIVERSITY

Organizations that have sound policies and practices for managing diversity, will find that they can both attract and retain talent from a wider pool. **Highly talented people, who may be from a minority group, may feel more attracted to, secure and motivated when working in such an organization or team.** There is a cost advantage in investing in such a policy, especially in reduced absenteeism or staff turnover, as recruiting and training to replace skilled staff can be a costly process.

From a marketing perspective, insight and sensitivity to diversity issues, particularly for the diverse consumer, has obvious advantages. Organizations that have flexible policies and systems for attracting, recruiting, developing, rewarding and motivating a diverse workforce, are said to be managing diversity well.

MOTIVATION

Not everyone is equally motivated by the same factors - such as money, job security, or a challenging job. Needs differ and are sometimes as diverse as the group.

Single versus married people, single mothers and fathers, disabled people, migrants, senior citizens, all have differing motivational needs. The key word is 'flexibility'. Flexibility in work and leave schedules, job design, job sharing, even compensation and benefits. For example, the financial security needs of a married couple with a single income, children, home mortgage and a car loan will differ greatly from young, single people living with their parents.

Advantages and Disadvantages of Diversity

Advantages	Disadvantages
- *Multiple perspectives.*	- *Ambiguity.*
- *Greater openness to new ideas.*	- *Complexity.*
- *Increased flexibility*	- *Confusion.*
- *Increased creativity.*	- *Multiple interpretations*
- *Increased problem-solving skills.*	- *Difficulty in reaching consensus*

"A great many people think they are merely re-arranging their prejudices." - William James-

KEY DIVERSITY ELEMENTS

AGE DIVERSITY

Another major source of diversity lies in age. With each generation, values and behavioural norms change. More than ever before, **due to globalization and IT, the younger generation have become exposed to a wider variety of behavioural choices**. As teenagers tune into E News, MTV - on TV - a new set of 'global' and 'western' values are being embraced. Thus new, overseas-educated college graduates may have very different mind sets from their parents, or older employees at work.

DIVERSITY OF TRAITS

What's important here, in attempting to manage diversity, is both the interplay between nature and nurture, and which traits are more strongly genetic. This gives some understanding of which traits will remain stable and unchanged, and therefore a predictable component of diversity. Once these have been isolated, we can better conclude which behavioural patterns are more learned and culturally or socially programmed. Albeit difficult to change mindsets, it is almost impossible to change personality.

ETHNO-CULTURAL ELEMENTS

Cultural diversity, while still falling under the category of behavioural patterns, differ from personality traits; which are individual and more biological. Culture is the study of social groups of people and **how the patterns are similar within a given group or society**. In culture, we measure the behavioural patterns that are normative across groups of people. They are 'learned' patterns of behaviour, usually not conscious, adopted as a result of the need to conform or be accepted by our social groupings.

There are small social groups, like the family, the team, or committee. And there are larger groupings such as ethnic, racial, religious, organizational or even national.

ETHNIC VERSUS NATIONAL CULTURE

We may loosely refer to American, British, Chinese, Japanese, German or Australian cultures, but such stereotyping is dangerous. While Japanese can be an ethnicity, it can also be national. In many national cultures, we may have distinctively different ethnic groups. Even among ethnically diverse cultures - like Australia or the USA, there can be Australian Chinese or American Chinese - who's culture is very different from the Chinese in China. It is not as much colour or race, as it is the society into which we were born and raised that determines the degree of diversity acceptance.

Age Discrimination
Age is another major aspect of diversity. The so called generation gap can produce a dramatic difference in values, preferences and behaviours. In the US, although the Civil Rights Act of 1964 prohibited discrimination in employment, it was only later that an upper age limit was eliminated. The recently amended Age Discrimination Act of 1978, now means that men or women can remain in active employment, as long as they are physically and mentally able to work.

"I'm not interested in age. People who tell their age are silly. You're as old as you feel."
- Elizabeth Arden

DIVERSITY IN PERSONALITY TRAITS

PERSONALITY AND DIVERSITY

Some strong personality traits are shown in the paragraph below, as pairs of opposite traits. Some are more strongly genetic in predisposition than others, and these are usually evident when we come under pressure. Often called our 'back-up', or 'fall-back' style, they tend to reveal our 'true self' when we are under stress. As the well known American phrase illustrates "When push comes to shove", our true colours are revealed.

Over recent years, one clustering of traits has come to be called the 'Big Five'(Costa, 1990). These have been found to change very little after the age of 30. They certainly are a major factor in helping us understand diversity in personality, especially as they have been found to appear in all cultures. I favour the physiological models of traits, like the CPP. (www.credotrust.org).

Personality differences are a major factor in diversity. What makes each of us a unique person is a combination of both nature and nurture. The age old debate is, how much of our personal traits are due to nature (our biological and genetic self) and how much they are shaped by nurture (socio-cultural conditioning). All leaders are individuals with diverse traits, but leadership also requires some strong traits.

One definition describes personality traits as**: "observable patterns of behaviour, that remain stable over time**, **which distinguish one person from another, and are thus quite predictable"**. In order to differentiate these traits from cultural patterns of behaviour, we need to observe them consistently displayed across all cultures, especially outside of our 'mother' culture.

TWIN STUDIES

A way of viewing the 'nature-nurture' paradigm, is to examine the findings of the now **well-known studies of identical twins**. Those who have been brought up apart, in different cultures and by different parents, for over 20 years. Many who have gone on to live apart for over 50 years, **still have been found to have remarkably similar traits**.

Most behavioural scientists now agree that genes play a significant role in shaping personality. They claim that just about every trait and behaviour, including behavioural disorders, have a genetic component. While not every behaviour trait is equal in genetic influence, they now are believed to range from 30% to 80% in genetic predisposition.

DIVERSITY IN PERSONALITY TRAITS
* While there are hundreds of different personality traits, most can be plotted on a continuum of opposites.
* Where employees - such as members of a team - display these opposites, we can say that such a team is highly diverse in personality. One early study that has stood the test of time, has become known as the 16 PF list (PF= Personality Factors). Here are 12 of them. 1.Reserved vs. Outgoing, 2. Submissive vs. Dominant, 3.Serious vs. Happy-go-lucky, 4.Expedient vs. Conscientious, 5.Timid vs. Venturesome, 6.Tough-minded vs. Sensitive, 7.Trusting vs. Suspicious, 8.Practical vs. Imaginative, 9.Forthright vs. Shrewd, 10.Conservative vs. Experimenting, 11.Uncontrolled vs. Controlled, 12. Relaxed vs. Tense

SOCIO-CULTURAL VERSUS INDIVIDUAL

SOCIAL VS. OCCUPATIONAL

Society could be ethnically pure - or ethnically very diverse. To manage diversity, we want to understand it in terms of different values and norms that each group possess. Gender, age, marital status or occupation may be common to both individual personality or within a group culture and some differences may be unique to that group. These can include language, religion, leadership style, food, clothing and sexual or relational norms.

GROUP CULTURE

Where any of these values and norms is unique to all the members of a particular group, we say they are the cultural. **If most members of that group follow a consistent pattern of behaviour, we can also conclude that it is cultural**.

Therefore we can have cultural diversity in a group when different cultural values and norms exist. And in the same group we can also have individual diversity represented by differences in gender, age or personality. From an organizational view point, we can also have groups that are similar within themselves, but different from other groups in the same organization.

OCCUPATIONAL DIVERSITY

For example, the culture of the sales department, can be very different from the culture of the production or finance department. Inter-departmental diversity does exist. Ned Herrmann calls these 'tribal cultures', and their collective values and thinking styles can be very unique to that group. (Herrmann, 1996)

Sales people stereotypically are very different from accounting people. In fact, even outside the organization or country, their differences can still set them apart. Attend any international conference of sales people, and contrast this with an international conference of accountants. These occupational or professional cultures are very different, even if the employees come from the same organization, ethnic group or country.

PERSONALITY - JOB FIT

Therefore we can conclude that diversity in personality can be as varied and complex as diversity in jobs. Truly managing diversity can be as challenging as diversity itself. Achieving a good personality - job fit can be an even bigger challenge for leadership.

PERSONALITY - JOB FIT

Analytic Types	Social-Interpersonal Types	Organized Types	Conceptual – Ideational Types
* Legal	* Sales	* Secretary	* Strategist
* Financial	* Teaching	* Supervisor	* Visionary leader
* Medical	* Social Work	*Operations	* Entrepreneurs

"I tried to treat them like me, and some of them weren't". - Bill Russell, Sports Coach -

DIVERSITY TRAINING

CLARIFYING POLICIES

Now that we have an idea of the scope of diversity in our organization, department - or even our own team - what precise policies exist to address this diversity? Can you find out, or articulate clearly what policies address the issues of equal employment opportunities? Does discrimination exist against minorities? Are all employees treated fairly, especially where it relates to appraisal, pay rates and promotion, training or career development?

DISCRIMINATION AND BIAS

Are people given selection or personality tests that are culturally fair or free? Some tests in English, or developed against western norms, may be biased towards people who have a higher level of English Language competency. Or those exposed more to western culture, may do better.

For example, in many Asian organizations, selection of foreign educated graduates may be favoured, over the locally educated. Are we testing, selecting and promoting employees fairly and without bias or prejudice? **If you can't answer positively to all the above questions, then your organization may not be articulating Diversity Management policies clearly or fully.**

DIVERSITY TRAINING

Where the organization is found to have a very diverse workforce or when it decides to become more diverse, conducting training programs or workshops may be very valuable. As with any training, it is useful to identify the key learning or competency development needs that exist. Who needs more knowledge or skill in managing diversity?

At the policy and strategy level, managers may need more knowledge, whereas in front line supervision, skills in handling a diverse team may be more important. **Those who are involved directly in recruitment, selection, testing, appraisal or in H.R.D**, would need specific knowledge and social skills training.

For example, training in areas of empathy, where we need to be able to put ourselves 'into the shoes' of others. Empathy, while coming more naturally to those with a high EI (Emotional Intelligence) can still be learned to some extent. Through simulation and role play techniques, we can learn to try and see things from another's view. Although it is not possible for a man to fully empathize with a women and vice versa .

OUR 'MAP OF THE WORLD'

Perhaps you saw the movie, where Dustin Hoffman dressed up, and played the role of a woman. As he admitted after, he didn't realize the degree of discrimination - or privileges - that exist for a member of the opposite sex. This is true empathy when you can see the world from the other's "map". What we sometimes call, entering the other person's 'Map Of the World', or 'MOW'.

"Organizations need to ensure that employees understand how their values and stereotypes influence their behaviours toward others of different gender, ethnic, racial or religious background"
- Raymond Noe, 2002 -

DIVERSITY MANAGEMENT - FOUR STEPS

CREATING AWARENESS

Those involved in formulating diversity management policies and practices need to be aware of diversity issues before they can be committed. An educational process in the nature of diversity and then in the diversity management process itself, needs to occur. We have discussed a wide range of elements and aspects of diversity, but how will they be shared widely among managers or policy makers? It'll help if we can show the benefits in 'bottom-line' terms. We need to understand the advantages in human resource management or talent attraction and retention in terms of diversity.

LEARNING

Approaches to Diversity Management (DM) requires a formal learning process. Holding DM workshops or forums are one way. Doing a survey of the workforce demographics and then showing these numerically and graphically can help. Informing management about the ethnic and gender ratios is also a start. This should be at all levels.

How many migrant workers, single parents, disabled or other minority groups comprise the employee base? We need to factor in the natural attrition and staff turnover rates. Often the ethnic and gender ratios of elder people retiring, are not the same as the replacement ratios. The advantages of balance and mix at all levels, needs to be learned.

SCOPE AND DEGREE OF EMPLOYEE DIVERSITY

If you have no breakdown of employee diversity in your organization or department, try doing a small survey and make a table of percentages on this. The table should include all aspects of diversity - such as , gender, age, ethnicity and personality traits . However, you might not be able to discover these so easily.

CONTENT OF TRAINING

One area of diversity in training is learning styles. Preferences for the way we like to learn - not only differs based on our personality traits - but also have cultural influences. If a group or organization is widely diverse in age, gender or ethnicity, each of these should be addressed. Whatever the desired outcomes of diversity training may be, the initiative to train should be highly applauded. Any organization with a diverse workforce will reap multifold benefits from such training.

HIGH ETHNICALLY DIVERSE COUNTRIES

Countries who have a history of extensive migrant settlement would rate higher in ethnic diversity.. For example: Australia, New Zealand, Canada, United Kingdom, USA, Netherlands. It is useful to note that these top six are primarily English speaking nations, four of which are members of the British Commonwealth.

Rapidly Diversifying Regions
Many European Community nations, the "new" South Africa

Low Ethnically Diverse Countries
Japan, China, Korea, Taiwan and most Arab* countries.

* By ethnically, we are using nationality as much as race
Note:: *Most wealthy Arab nations continue to use Foreign labour, from India, Pakistan, Bangladesh, and the Philippines, which adds to their diversity.*

BIASES: INDIVIDUAL or ORGANIZATIONAL

DISCRIMINATION: CONSCIOUS OR NON CONSCIOUS

We must realize that some discrimination, especially ethnic or racial, may exist more at a non-conscious level. People may not be intentionally biased, but may have been programmed from young, to only mix with their own race, class or even gender. When these norms have never been challenged or tested, they **may naturally feel discomfort when mixing with others of a different race, colour, class or gender.**

Some Diversity Management workshops deliberately throw people together in very mixed groups, in order for people to learn to adjust or accept.

HOW WE ARE SOCIALIZED

From a personal view, I was raised in a 'WASP' (White Anglo Saxon Protestant) ethic. Yet my parents and the schools I attended, welcomed children from any race, creed or colour. I even remember the Boy Scout Oath, that encompasses this acceptance of diversity. I remember even better, going to dances or parties where I socialized closely with people of many nationalities, colours and religions. Did this make me more culturally sensitive and accepting? Perhaps! I'd like to think so.

LEGAL VERSUS ETHICAL OR MORAL

The other area of awareness, other than skill training, relates to the legislative factors. We have already mentioned that these differ from country to country, **but leaders and policy makers need to be very familiar with any laws that relate to discrimination.** Whether these laws relate to employment, safety, welfare or sexual harassment, codes of ethical conduct should also be clearly spelt out.

TRAINING HELPS

All employees or team members will benefit from such training, by gaining an appreciation of employee differences. They will learn to understand and respect the uniqueness of each employee. They will become aware of how generalizations and stereo-typing can so easily be made - and be inaccurate or unfair.

They will understand how and why people think differently (thinking styles), or why personality clashes can occur so easily. If a group or organization is widely diverse in age, gender or ethnicity, each of these areas of diversity should be addressed.

ORGANIZATIONAL DIVERSITY

This can be divided into different types, such as the workforce composition, or the diversity in structures, systems and business policies or practices.

   a. *Workforce diversity- Working with those who are different from us in terms of thinking styles, personality, ethnicity, social class, occupation , gender, age, disability and sexual orientation differences.*
   b. *Structural Diversity- Differences in structures, systems and styles often show up when people from different organizations come together. And during mergers, acquisitions and joint ventures, these differences become more marked.*
   c. *Business diversity- May include markets, products, services and professional specialists in the various disciplines which are all now impacted by globalization, and management processes and systems. Thus they need to be appropriate for each culture, within the global context.*

DIVERSITY AND EEO

LEGAL ASPECTS
In some societies, there are forms of legislation on Equal Employment Opportunities (EEO), and anti - discriminatory practices. In some cultures that are more male-oriented, women may be discriminated against. Sexual harassment is one example. Similarly, economic, ethnic, racial and religious minorities may be discriminated against. Sometimes there are 'affirmative action' policies to redress these inequities.

Some examples could include, the Aborigines in Australia, the Bumiputras in Malaysia, the Maoris in New Zealand, the Native American or Indians in USA and Canada. In each of these countries there is legislation or political guidelines to ensure indigenous minorities are assisted or protected or even majority ethnic groups are not economically disadvantaged. In these cases, it has more to do with poverty and economics.

POLICIES AND PRACTICES
Managing diversity in organizations would include formulation of policies to address diversity. The core values of the organization, especially those upheld by top management, or in recruitment and appraisal, would play an important role in diversity management.

Human Resource planning would determine the type of employees that will be required to fill jobs, or receive training, perhaps as far as five years ahead. The attraction and retention of talent necessitates that non-discrimination may be an important policy. Similarly, if the organization wishes to be seen as, and become recognized as an employer of choice, it will need to ensure equal employment opportunities exist (EEO).

MORAL AND ETHICAL VALUES
Policies and practices that do not discriminate against minorities should be morally and ethically valued by the management. This is regardless of legal or market forces.

DIVERSITY AND GENDER
There may well be greater diversity between men and women than between many ethnic groups. As more women enter the workforce at all levels, gender differences become more noticeably important to address. Men and women differ anatomically, physiologically and socially. Brain structures and hormones differ significantly, and new research shows that thinking styles differ accordingly. Yet traditionally, socialization patterns have not allowed for these.

List for possible inclusion in an Equal Opportunity policy

-Women	*-Caring Responsibilities*
-Ethnic minorities	*-Class*
-People with physical disabilities	*-People with HIV/AIDS*
-People with learning disabilities	*-Political affiliation*
-People with mental health problems	*-Employment status*
-Ex-offenders	*-Regionalism*
-Older people	*-Appearance*
-Sexual orientation	*-Accent*

"Organizational racism and sexism are embedded by management thinking and behaviour". -

Swan & Martin, 1994

CHARTING DIVERSITY IN YOUR TEAM OR ORGANISATION

Assess Diversity in your Team by using this chart

Gender : Female .... %   Male .... %

Marital Status: Married ....%   Single ....%   Single Parent ....%

Thinking Styles: More Left Brained ....% More Right Brained ....%

Personality Styles: More Introverted .... %   Balanced .... %
More Extroverted ....%

Occupational Groups – How many exist: a) .... %   b) .... %   c) .... %
d) .... %   e) .... %   f) .... %

Handicapped – How many employed: Full Time:............... Part Time:.............

Ethnic Groups. a) .... %   b) .... %   c) .... %   d) .... %
e) .... %   f) .... %

Nationalities/Citizenships: 1) .... %   2) .... %   3) .... 4) .... %
5) .... %   6) .... %   7) .... 8) .... %
More than 8 ....

Language/Dialects (commonly used): a) ....   b) ....   c) ....   d)...............
More than 4 ....

Structural Diversity: Tall Hierarchy (More than 11 levels) .... levels
Medium Hierarchy (5 – 10 levels) .... levels
Flat Hierarchy (< 4 levels) .... levels

Overall: High Diverse: Yes/No   Moderately Diverse: Yes/No   Less Diverse: Yes/No

Does your organisation provide diversity training? Yes – Regularly/ Yes – Occassionally/
None

SUMMARY OF KEY POINTS

- Culture has been defined as the "Collective mental programming of the mind, which distinguishes one group from another". The group can be a nation (national culture) or an organization, tribal or ethnic, or a team (team culture). It has also been described as "the way things are done around here"

- In attempting to understand culture, it is useful to first know some of the 'laws' of culture. These are based on the strongly held values of each culture and their underlying assumptions. This gives us the 'why' or reason for a value being strongly held.

- Cultures can also be described as either 'High' or 'Low' context. High context cultures are more 'natural' - having evolved from an agrarian history. They are general and more in harmony with the natural environment (context). Where as low context cultures are more 'man made', in terms of industrialization, or urbanization.

- Time can be perceived and valued differently. High context cultures are more 'being' and relationship oriented. Time in low context cultures relates more to 'doing' and task completion. Here preciseness, specifics, linear thinking, planning, deadlines and punctuality are valued (monochronic).

- Just as cultures differ in task versus people focus, they also can be described as more 'collectivistic' or more 'individualistic'.

- Collectivistic cultures are more relationship or 'we' oriented, and behaviours are often driven by an external locus of control.

- Individualistic cultures are more task focused or 'I' oriented. But the achievement of the task is more internally driven (internal locus of control). Emphasis is more on the individual rather than the team.

- Face is another core concept of culture. Due to this emphasis on face, and the value of harmony and relationships, people tend to be more polite, soft or indirect. Negative feedback is often given through a respected third party, often an elder person.

- Some cultures integrate in a more holistic way – into work and life. This would be especially so for spiritual beliefs like Feng Shui, or the religious belief system of Islam.

- Diversity includes individual, social, cultural and ethnic differences among employees and can include gender, age, personality, and occupational differences. They can stem from genetic as well as learned beliefs and behaviours.

- Diversity - while existing in our personal make-up, can equally apply to group, ethnic or organizational cultures. Diverse work teams tend to be more creative and higher performing, but more challenging to lead and manage.

- Diversity in personality traits is one of the widest areas of influence. It includes the variety of motivational drives, temperament and talents, including a range of intelligences.

- Managing diversity requires matching the job to the individual. There are as wide an array of jobs or occupations as there may be "personality types" that need matching.

- Managing diversity includes organizational initiatives such as clarifying employment and development policies. These policies must address the equity in employment opportunity, and ensure minimum biases, prejudice and discrimination exist.

- Diversity can be managed in a number of steps. These include an awareness of the nature of diversity and its need to be managed. Then the policies and strategies, which may include training, must be clearly articulated.

- Discrimination may exist at a 'non-conscious' level, so people can be unaware that they have been programmed to have biases or prejudices. We need to be aware of our socialization and how learning may have shaped our values and attitudes towards others.

- There may need to be legalized codes of protection, especially towards minority groups or those most likely to be discriminated against. These groups could include age, gender or ethnic minorities, or physically and mentally underprivileged people and those suffering poverty or economic inequities.

- Typical of some minority groups that may need special attention, could include those who are handicapped by an inability to speak the local language. Also those of a religious minority, who may have special dietary, dress or behavioural norms that don't 'fit' the main culture of the larger group.

"Every society produces its own truth which has a normalizing and regulatory function."

-Tanton, 1994

REFERENCES

Asma, A. (1996). *Going Glocal* . Kuala Lumpur: MIM.

Deal, T. & Kennedy, A. (2000). Corporate Cultures: The Rites and Rituals of Corporate Life.
   USA: Persues Books Publishing

Hall, E. (1976). *Beyond Culture.* New York : Double Day Pub.

Herrmann, N. (1996). *The Whole Brain Business Book.* New York: McGraw-Hill.

Hofstede, G. (1991). *Culture and Organisation.* New York: McGraw Hill.

McCrae, R. and Costa, P. (1990). *Personality in Adulthood* . NY: Guildford .
Noe, R. (2002). *Employee Training and Development.* (Second, Ed.) New York: McGraw
Hill.

CHAPTER SIX

ORGANIZATIONAL CULTURE: DEVELOPING THE ORGANIZATION CULTURE FOR A GLOBAL WORLD

LEARNING OBJECTIVES FOR THIS CHAPTER

By the end of this chapter, you will be able to:

- Describe how to map and diagnose organizational culture.

- Clarify the role of managers and leaders in developing a 'strong' organizational culture.

- Discover how our collective styles of thinking can influence the behaviours of a culture.

- Differentiate between global and local organizational cultures.

- Distinguish how we can synergize the best from both east and west - in shaping a 'glocal' culture.

- Recognize the effect of shared values and vision on the leadership of a strong culture.

- Identify the core competencies essential for the multi-cultural leader.

TABLE OF CONTENTS

DIAGNOSING ORGANIZATIONAL CULTURE

INTRODUCTION

One popular description that is simplistic, yet effective, was described by Marvin Bower, former CEO of the large consulting company. He referred to the more informal cultural elements of an organization as: ***"The way we do things around here"*** (Bower, 1966)

Another definition, based on the work of Ned Herrmann, (1996) deals with the **'collective ways that people may think, especially the leaders'**, owners and managers of the organization. He describes organizational culture as, **"the common pattern of behaviours influenced by our thinking and feeling preferences"**.

SYMBOLS

The onion, as a metaphor itself, and peeling back the onion's layers to reveal its core, are already symbolic of the understanding of culture. The outer layer or skin represents those visual symbols of culture. These include the larger physical artifacts such as a flag, building, airport, or even a Jumbo jet. The size, shape, colour or location are all physical and visual symbols of strength, power, status, wealth or success. At a more micro level, the logo, a slogan, a tag-line, a song, a jingle, a poster, calendar, diary or other 'give-aways' can be symbolic of the culture. It is a form of 'Culture Branding'.

HEROES OR ROLE MODELS

Heroes may include the founders of an organization, or possibly the CEO, key top managers or performers. (Deal and Kennedy, 1982).

For an R&D company, it might be a senior scientist, a Nobel prize winner or the employee that has the most innovations, patents or published articles. For a sales organization it may be the top sales performer. For a University, it maybe a top professor who has a best seller book. All organizations have such heroes, many of whom may be role-models. **All leaders should be role models.**

In larger organizations they may be personified by the Steve Jobs, Bill Gates or Henry Fords of the corporate world. In smaller organizations the visionary or entrepreneurial leader. For a team, it may be the supervisor who is a team leader.

RITUALS

Rituals are the more regular functions, such as greetings, how we address people or even how we dress. They may include having coffee at all meetings, or all presentations being done with power point slides. **It often depends on the leader.**

Evolving a culture is a socialization process, that operates at the non conscious level. It is hard to change things in the non conscious, as we are often not aware. It's like the water to the tadpole. Until the tadpole grows new legs and lungs, and becomes a frog, it cannot live outside the water. But later it learns how to do so. It rapidly adapts to its new environment, but is versatile enough to return to the water, even if only to lay eggs.

"The aggregate of the thinking preferences and resulting behaviours of people in a group, particularly of those who manage or lead it."
Ned Herrmann 1996.

STRONG CULTURES

RITES AND CEREMONIES

Rites include those regular or periodic actions such as safety campaigns, courtesy campaigns or the quarterly appraisal of performance. **There is seemingly a grey area in distinguishing between Rituals and Rites**. (Deal and Kennedy, 1983).

Rites may be more symbolic of certain values that need to be promoted or upheld. They tend to be more irregular or adhoc, but having experienced their process, behavioural norms are reinforced. They each serve to symbolize and strengthen the culture.

Ceremonies however are usually less frequent, yet still symbolize core values. The company picnic, or CEO's 'open-house', prize giving, annual awards or dinners may typify these ceremonies. **They each serve to symbolize and strengthen the culture.**

CULTURAL NETWORKS

These are the webs of communications. Members of a culture network with each other. They share common norms and values, perhaps speaking the same language or jargon. They reinforce or follow similar patterns of communicating and behaviour, **and this strengthens their culture**. Employees are the key resource of the network, but information technology serves to link them.

Informal gatherings, meetings, forums or training programs are good examples. Presentations by top management, visits to head office by branches or affiliates, or vice-versa, are additional ways. Extensive friendships emerge.

Significant components of these networks include the legends, folklore and stories of the culture - especially its history and traditions **- thus strengthening the culture.**

SHARED VALUES

Values form the core of the culture as with the onion, it is the deepest layer and therefore harder to see. We can infer what these values might be - by observing the shared practices and the cultural networks at play - especially the heroes or role models.

Sometimes these values are formally stated in organizational documents, like the annual report or promotional literature. Sometimes they are written up in large letters, framed or mounted, and hung on walls in boardrooms, reception areas or factories. **These can then said to be 'shared'**, but still not necessarily so widely, that all employees can articulate them.

Strong Cultures
Widely Shared Values
*People Are Paramount   * Pro active
*Shared Clear Vision   * Knowledge sharing
*Inspiring and Meaningful   * Shared learning
*Flexible and adaptable Mission or Purpose * Innovativeness
 *Customer responsiveness

* Effective Leadership   (at all levels)
* Strategic Thinking
* Cooperative Teamwork

"Strong corporate cultures create heroes for employees to emulate." Moran & Stripp, 1991

CULTURE AND MANAGEMENT

INTRODUCTION

If a culture is the collectivity of values and behaviours, then 'mapping' the culture would require ways of measuring these. By **clarifying and prioritizing values** - the strong beliefs shared by employees - we **can obtain a 'value map'**. Further, we can group and classify them as productive or progressive etc. depending on our criteria for these. There is however a possible paradox here - as criteria for productivity or effectiveness in itself - is a value judgement.

BENCHMARKING

We may need to benchmark highly successful or competitive organizations first. And in doing this benchmarking, it is important to ensure a comparison within a similar context, industry, and the environment of the larger culture. For example, we don't want to compare the small retail outlet in a rural village, with one in a busy urban environment. The context and the customer base would be very different. The values and norms that make each retail outlet effective - may differ. **It's back to leadership!**

HI-TECH AND HI-TOUCH

Can we have a culture that embodies both - in a synergistic - and yet measurable way? In mapping a culture, these are two often opposing variables. The rural village store would embody the 'Hi-Touch' culture, where people are friendly, have time to chat, know our name and probably the needs of ourselves or even our children.

Conversely, the culture of the busy urban store probably has a larger and diverse clientele. It may also need to promote the friendly and pleasant service, but with an efficient system for this service. Knowing the names and faces of the clientele may be less easy, and perhaps a lesser criteria of effectiveness, than speed.

This store may need to be more hi-tech, in terms of bar coding products, quick cash / credit card service and storage or dispatch of produce. Systems and policies for tracking inventory, purchasing, security, return of merchandize etc. may need to be more hi-tech, than the smaller 'Mom and Pop' corner shop in the village. This is what management includes. So organizational culture differs due to size, location and technology.

CONSISTENT PATTERNS

Strong cultures display a consistency in both easy or difficult times. Friendly service, quality decisions or reliable products must be predictably consistent, year after year.

PROFESSIONAL CULTURES

Some jobs - like that of an air-traffic controller - calls for a very high level of pressure and stress tolerance. This would be very different from the job of a farmer or gardener. While there may be climatic or natural demands, there is not a high level of stress or ambiguity. This may seem therefore to be more a 'personality' difference between the type of temperament and talent required for air traffic controllers or farmers. Yet each profession represents a different group culture. The culture of the professional society for air traffic controllers, would be very different from that of the state farmers association.

> *"If we are to live in harmony - and work together - we need to better appreciate each other's diverse make up. Tolerance is superficial, whereas appreciation comes from understanding. We can then respect and celebrate differences."*
> *Conyngham, 1999*

MAPPING THE CULTURE

MAPPING BEHAVIOURS

Mapping Behaviours on an individual basis, while easy if we have the time to track and measure the behaviour, maybe impractical, time consuming and costly. We would need to study and compare trends or **repeated patterns of behaviour**. The consistent - and therefore more predictable behaviour that are common to a group - would be what we mean by norms. That is, **what most people of the group do most of that time, under differing conditions.**

MACRO LEVEL

Ethnic, national or geographical factors would form the larger or macro influences. Knowing what the strong values and norms of an ethnic group, or a national culture, can be very important in understanding the group's culture. These can include the degree of patriotism, loyalty to king, queen and country, or a religious belief system. This can include moral and ethical codes of behaviour.

Then there are the industrial influences. For example, **the values and behaviour prevalent in a hi-tech manufacturing company, would again differ from that of a government department, responsible for agricultural, forestry or rural development**. Equally, those of a multinational oil company or bank may be different from local or national companies in the same industry.

MICRO LEVEL

By micro, we mean here, the smaller groups, where employee behaviours maybe influenced more by **their leadership, or by technology, organizational structure and systems**. Here, the operational technology can be a strong influence. Again, is it Hi-tech, safe or hazardous, or has it to do with the Hi-tech demands or friendly and courteous service.

CULTURE MAPPING

Culture mapping has more to do **with studying the general patterns of behaviour** of a group, rather than an individual. It is similar to the difference between a clinical psychologist and a social psychologist or anthropologist. Most psychologists deal more with individual behaviour, whereas sociologists and anthropologists are more interested in cultural norms of groups, tribes, organizations or whole societies.

Most, if not all organizations, want a culture that is both innovative, progressive, profitable and globally competitive. They also want all stakeholders to be equally satisfied. From the owners or investors, the employees and ultimately the customer. The new paradigm now includes a balance of life-work experience. A high quality of private life and a high quality of work life (QWL). Culture mapping helps us see the gap between what we are and what we want.

> *"There can be a pervasive and strong culture of an occupation or profession. Accountants, Engineers, Doctors, Lawyers maybe more alike in their profession - than in their gender or race."*

> *Herrmann, 1996*

THINKING STYLES AND CULTURE

THINKING PREFERENCES
One of the most effective determinants of how a group will behave, which is quite new in its nature, is the study of a groups collectivity of thinking preferences. The measurement of the how and why of thinking differences, can now be done with validity and ease. Using personality profiles gives us some valid indicators of how a given group may behave.

The collective thinking styles of employees, especially the leaders, can be very different. By measuring those, we can achieve a very accurate and reliable 'map' of the culture. **A left brained culture differs from a right brained one.**

LEFT VERSUS RIGHT BRAIN CULTURES
In the CREDO Personality Profiling system, we can plot the strong cultural influences by measuring such thinking preferences as: Factual versus Emotional, or Logical versus Creative or Bureaucratic versus Entrepreneurial. Or Safekeeping versus Risk taking and Innovative. For example, an organization may have a vision and values statement that requires it to be creative, innovative, entrepreneurial and customer friendly. This organizational culture would be labelled as more 'right brained'. An advertising agency would exemplify this. Conversely, a 'left brained' culture would be more bureaucratic, rigid, structured and perhaps conservative, safe and technically oriented. A large bank would typify this left-brained culture. (Shephard, 2001)

THE THINKING STYLE MODEL
If the leader is a 'right-brained' innovative, strategic and visionary thinker, and the culture of the group or organization is 'left-brained', it is a big task to change the culture. **By nature, the left-brained style of thinking and behaving is cautious and conservative and typically resists change.**

However, within each organization, there can also exist a range of different 'sub-cultures'. We can call them 'tribal' cultures. For example, the Production or Manufacturing, or Accounting departments would be more 'left-brained'. Whereas new product development or marketing departments would be different 'tribal sub-cultures' and more right-brained.

Therefore, a large, diverse or multi disciplined organization would also have a different overall culture, from the single disciplined or narrow specialist organization.

What is required for the change effort to work is a series of parallel strategies that include:
(i) Selling the benefits of change (Mindset).
(ii) Equipping people with new competencies (Skillset).
(iii) Providing incentives for and rewarding change.
(iv) Changing the structure, especially the power structure.
(v) Providing lots of information and autonomy
(vi) Walking the talk (role modelling)
(vii) Promoting and hiring only people who are open to change and willing to experiment, to innovate or take risks.

> *"Even some cultures seem more 'left' or 'right' brained in the collectivity of thinking styles."*
>
> *Conyngham, 1999.*

ORGANIZATIONAL CULTURE
AND LEADERSHIP

LEADING VERSUS MANAGING
Leadership here is deemed to be different from management. While many managers have to lead as well as manage, not all leaders have to manage. Leadership areas can also include, Scientific, Technological, Political, Economic, Academic, Commercial or Sports, etc. etc.

In the context of organizational culture, we are looking more at leadership of people, groups, teams or corporations. Cultures are built, strengthened or weakened by leadership. This includes the human factor and socio-cultural elements that influence leaders.

A CONTINUOUS CYCLE
Strong cultures produce strong leaders, yet those strong leaders influence these same cultures. We can contrastingly conclude that the opposite may equally be the case. A 'weak' culture may produce weak leaders who in turn maintain the status quo. While the organization may have shared values and vision, how positive and productive are they? The effective leader will display a high level of enthusiasm, pride and be a positive role model. The culture will be one of high performance and high morale.

CULTURAL ASPECTS OF LEADING
How do we assess these cultural components of leadership? More importantly, how do we ensure we have the most appropriate and effective leadership style for the building of a team or organization and its culture?

There is a danger of using symbols from one culture that may not translate into the context of another culture. Sensitivity to this would be a critical starting point. **Neglect of the cultural aspects of organizational leadership can be the main cause of the failure to translate vision into reality.**

STYLE VERSUS SUBSTANCE
The substance, the nature of the mission, purpose, strategy and goals may be solid. Unless the style or form of leadership are congruent with the culture, we may see more failure than success. Weak cultures don't succeed and eventually crumble or die. Weak leaders don't last long either. **So both style and substance must be congruent** and also reinforce or strengthen each other. Substance includes structure and systems to help achieve the strategic vision or mission.

LEADING CULTURAL CHANGE
Leading cultural change can take a lot of time for a culture to change. This is one reason why so called 'Change Management' initiatives often fail. Making a transition often requires a lot of education, patience and persistence. It requires a lot of 'unlearning' and relearning, before things change. It's like changing the direction of a floating iceberg or super tanker.

> *"The cultural aspects of leadership is possibly the most pervasive,*
> *yet least visible of leadership effectiveness"*
>
> *Hofstede, 1991*

A GLOCAL HYBRID

HYBRID VIGOUR

Hybrid is a term that is usually associated with genetic mutations. When two different species crossbreed, they tend to each pass on the strongest genes to their offspring. Because of a new set of mixed, yet stronger genes, the progeny is invariably superior. This has become known as **'Hybrid Vigour'**. Examples are endless, from animals, humans, fish or plant life. **So thinking global and acting local - or 'glocal' - is hybrid!**

Why is it that pictures of Eurasians often featured more in TV and magazine adverts in Asia? Are they more beautiful or handsome? Or is it more culturally acceptable to have a pan-Asian face? How does this 'Hybrid' look in African or Eastern Cultures?

In nature and commerce we find many examples of genetic re-engineering. Be it the Dutch friesien milk cows, crossed with the Indian Brahmin bull, or a hybrid hibiscus or orchid. This metaphor of 'hybrid vigour', can be used for organizational cultures. **We cross fertilize when we benchmark, merge or form a joint venture.**

GOING GLOCAL

As we go 'global', there a is risk of losing some of the best of the strong traditions that are 'local'. There is the old expression that; "if you can't beat 'em, join 'em".

If we accept that globalization is like the slowly rising sea level that won't fall - then how are we adapting and accomodating. We can use the hybrid vigour model and go 'Glocal'. This word is itself a hybrid - so very apt. It means a marriage of global and local. It mirrors quantum thinking. **It is not global versus local, it is global and local.**

THE GLOCAL HYBRID

While the West may seek a more spiritual balance, and the east has become more individualistic, what are the cultural values that we can promote? What can we immediately inculcate into our new organizational paradigm?

Do we 'think global' yet respect local values and norms? How does your organizational culture live up to these? Globally competitive; sensitive to local cultures (home or abroad). Respecting tradition, yet open to change; Diversity of work force and teams; Hi-Tech and Hi-Touch; Respecting loyalty and long service, yet rewarding knowledge and performance. (Asma, 1998).

Have you heard of or seen a 'Labradoodle? This is a cross between a Labrador dog and a Poodle. They are bred and trained as 'blind seeing' dogs. They combine the superior intelligence, temperament and smaller size to form a new breed that is easier to train, manage and maintain.

A key feature is that they retain the gene that prevents the moulting or shedding of hair. This was found to be a great asset to blind owners of a dog. As they are also smaller and more agile than the labrador, they eat less and fit better in small cars.

"Think global, Act local"
Andre Laurant

BEST OF EAST AND WEST

EAST - WEST SYNERGY

Rudyard Kipling once wrote a poem, which had a line that said, "The east is east and west is west, and ne'er the twain shall meet". Perhaps he was inspired when the British rulers left India or the Afghan's massacred the British. However, the world has changed.

California has its Silicon Valley in Bangalore, the British Commandos went back to fight in the Afghanistan mountains and the Japanese are in the Multi-Media Super Corridor (MSC) in Malaysia, over nearly seventy years after World War II occupation by the Japanese. Most of the surviving giant telecommunication companies have joint ventures all over the world.

COMMON GOALS

The common factor in all of these, is the crossing of cultures, the building of bridges that are both flexible and strong. **So how might our Glocal Hybrid Model look?** This can produce a strong, new organization culture?' "It could be the marriage between the wisdom of the East and West-is Best"

BEST OF EAST

African and Eastern leaders and organizational cultures tend to put more stress on long-term and harmonious relationships, with a more wholistic and high context view. They embrace a more 'spiritual' component in daily matters, where traditions such as 'feng-shui', or tribal dances maybe used.

Leadership style balances with a more nurturing, paternalistic or benevolent mindset. The culture of the organization can still retain the best of the extended family spirit. How many of these traditional elements do we wish to retain?

BEST OF WEST

Much of western culture epitomizes a new technological and knowledge-based revolution. We talk of a k-economy and of k-workers. What then do we need to adopt or adapt? Creativity and innovation could be one. Transparency and less bribery or corruption would be another.

However, it maybe less prevalent as a cultural phenomena in a collectivistic culture. Perhaps greater 'monochronic' or 'low-context' behaviours lend themselves to increased speed, efficiency and quality. If these are indeed what customers want - we have to learn how to weave them into our cultural web regardless of geography.

Willingness to take risks, to become more entrepreneurial and to evolve a learning culture where experimenting and mistakes are acceptable, is a major challenge. Here, some US and UK organizations have evolved a culture where this is not only accepted, but even encouraged.

Classic examples are the 3M company, which still leads in product innovation. Others, in toy inventions or software development, such as Microsoft or companies like GE. H.P., Intel, Samsung or Apple. All these companies have a culture that combines innovation, quality, productivity and shared learning.

> *"East is East and West is West and ne'er the twain will meet".*
> *Rudyard Kipling*

SHARED VALUES AND VISION

LEADERSHIP AND VISION

By exhibiting a leadership style that is visionary, which gets employees excited by this vision, so it is also strongly shared. This requires a style where the leader is highly articulate and enthusiastic about the vision. **Thus the vision must be perceived and believed to be both achievable and meaningful.**

LEADERSHIP AND VALUES

Values, similarly should be clearly articulated by the leader. If they are also meaningful, or perhaps even 'noble', leaders can help ensure they are shared widely and strongly. It is through these beliefs and actions that leaders can be inspirational. This is one key element of effective motivation. This is a more right brained' approach to leading.

STRATEGIC THINKING

Strong cultures are strategic in their thinking and intent. Leaders and managers who naturally think strategically are more right brained. **They are able to integrate and synthesize vision, mission and strategy**. They have a more holistic or 'total picture' view of the world and their organization. (a 'Helicopter' view).

STRATEGIC PLANNING

Such strategic thinking leads to strategic planning and resource utilization. This in turn helps the organization position itself, its resources, products or services in a more competitive way. When competitor products may be similar in nature and cost, service and employee competence and motivation may be the only competitive advantage. Strong cultures ensure such strategic leadership. Strategy has to do with positioning oneself for future competitive advantage, thus it can include **future or scenario thinking.**

GLOBAL COMPETITIVENESS

As we become more globalized, building on a strategic leadership requires a dynamic or strong culture. The degree of customer delight comes from a responsiveness to the customers needs and wants and the quality and speed in which they are met. Cost, value, speed, time are all critical factors in providing a competitive edge.

If we agree that the goals of innovation, progress and profits are common then we need to combine these with an ability to attract, develop and retain a talented and highly motivated work force. And, of paramount importance is the attraction and retention of a loyal and highly satisfied customer base. And, that's the leadership challenge!

KNOWLEDGE SHARING AND KAIZEN

Building and sustaining a strong culture needs us to manage knowledge in a more systematic way. In this fast changing competitive world, learning faster than our competitors is another edge. We can gain. But learning faster is not so value added, unless we can share this learning -widely yet relevantly. A learning culture is one where learning is continuous, so that improvement is continuous or 'Kaizen' - as it is popularly known. Kaizen has its routes in the 50's, where in Japan, it came to represent ongoing improvement involving everyone, Kaizen should be everybody's business. From a cultural perspective, the Japanese approach it as a 'process-oriented' way of thinking.

"It is one thing to respect the organization and adaptiveness of cultural systems, but quite another to insist they are equally admirable or adaptive."

Murdock, 1965.

THE MULTICULTURAL EMPLOYEE

CORE COMPETENCIES

We have already covered some aspects of the leader of a strong culture. However, if the employees - be they leaders, managers, professionals or technicians - need to function cross culturally, then an additional repertoire of competencies is needed. **When communicating across cultures**, be it leading, motivating, negotiating or training, such **multicultural competence becomes critical.**

KNOWING OUR OWN CULTURE

In one study done by INSEAD, a number of specific competencies were identified and ranked in order of importance. **Top of the rank was the knowledge competency of 'Knowing one's own culture'.** While learning about the others culture is useful, it may be extremely time consuming. Some anthropologists believe one can never truly or deeply understand all the subtleties or nuances of a foreign culture. Unless of course, one is born into, and grows up in, that culture. And, if the primary language of that culture, is fully comprehended.

RESPECTING OTHER CULTURES

By becoming more aware of our own culture, we are more able to recognize quickly those differences we see in other cultures. We can be sensitive to, and respectful of, those values, norms or behaviours that are different. While similarities can become the building blocks of a cross cultural bridge, we must appreciate that the land across the bridge is different. **It is these differences that can lead to misperceptions of 'reality'.**

Until we question the underlying assumptions of our values and practices, we may not truly understand them. How well do we really understand our own culture? Often we are like the fish in its own water, and we take it for granted until we are removed from it. **Culture is like the water to the fish.**

LISTEN AND OBSERVE

A key interpersonal skill set, **is the ability to listen with empathy**, and to observe with acuity. Empathy means being able to see situations, and read emotions or feelings, as others do. It literally means being able to put oneself into another person's shoes. Acuity is the degree of perceptive accuracy and interpretation of the other persons view, beliefs, feelings or behaviours. It does not mean you share or agree with them, but that you understand them.

NON VERBAL CLUES

A very large component of communication is non-verbal. This includes vocal, such as the emotional 'flavour' of the voice its, tone, volume, pitch and pace. It also includes body language, which is how the physical and physiological aspects of the body display emotions or meaning. Emotions can produce changes in body temperature, skin colour or texture. Goose pimples or a cold sweat can be examples of such emotions manifestating how we feel at the moment of communicating. Such skills in reading body language can help us interpret how the other person is feeling. Some people reveal and some conceal emotions.

"Always assume differences, until similarities are proven."
Asma Abdullah
'Going Glocal', 1998

SUMMARY OF KEY POINTS

- In diagnosing organizational culture, **one can use the analogy of an onion**. In the centre are the core values of a culture which are unseen. Each layer represents different aspects of cultural depth from the cultural networks, rites, rituals, heroes and role models. The outer layer - visible to the world - are the symbols that represent the culture, in a more public view.

- **Cultures can be described as 'Strong' or 'Weak'.** Strong cultures are represented by clear values and vision that are strongly shared. They produce strong leaders, who in turn keep the culture sustainable and attractive. They are driven by a sense of mission or purpose.

- One way of diagnosing and understanding how and why a culture is the way it is, is **through culture 'mapping'**. By assessing the values and thinking preferences of its leaders and managers, we can predict certain behavioural patterns. The organization - or its various departments - can also be described as either **more left, right or whole brained**.

- Organizational cultures can be either more global or local in their outlook. A culture that wishes to become globally competitive can do so, by both benchmarking global best practices, and by developing a more global mindset - and **"Think global, yet act local". It can become a 'glocal' hybrid.**

- Part of becoming globally competitive, yet locally respected, can come from **synergizing the best from the eastern and western values and practices.** They need to be appropriate and pragmatic, and can be produced by knowledge sharing. **Through effective knowledge management and shared learning, leaders can produce an effective set of shared values and inspiring vision.**

- As organizations are increasingly and inescapably affected by globalization, we need to develop employees - especially leaders - with **competencies in cross cultural management and communication. Such competencies include knowing their own culture, having a global mindset, being flexible and having a high tolerance for ambiguity.**

Globalization has produced a surge or tidal wave of change - especially in new technology which has become our servant. Structures and systems are designed to: accommodate cross-functional, multi-disciplinary and globally instant sharing of knowledge, experience and learning. These are truly a new feature of a strong organization culture in the 21st century. Such systems are more open to feedback, and the 'double-loop' or duetero learning characterizes a learning organization culture. These improvements often come from the strategy of benchmarking

" Culture represents the behaviour patterns or style of an organization that new employees are automatically encouraged to follow....."
John P. Kotter

REFERENCES

Asma, A. (1998). *Going Glocal.* Kuala Lumpur: Malaysian Institute of Management.

Bower, M. (1966). Management Review; May 66, Vol. 55 Issue 5, p4

   The way we do things around here: A new look at the Company Philosophy: USA

Deal, T.E. and Kennedy, A.A. (1982). *Corporate Culture: The Rites and Rituals of Corporate Life.* Mass: Addison Wesley.

Herrmann, N. (1996). *The whole Brain Business Book.* New York: Mc Graw Hill.

Hofstede, G. (1991). *Culture and Organizations.* New York: Mc Graw Hill.

Kotter, J. (1990). *What Leaders Really Do.* Boston: HBR Press.

Laurant, A. (1994). *Voyages en Seire-et-marne.* Amazon Books.

Moran, R.T. & Stripp, W.G. (1991). *Dynamics of successful Business Negotiations.* New York: Gulf Publishing.

Shephard, P.C. (2001). *Leading Diverse and Multi-cultural Teams.* Kuala Lumpur: Brainworks Media.

CHAPTER SEVEN

LEADING TO MOTIVATE

LEARNING OBJECTIVES FOR THIS CHAPTER

By the end of this unit, you will be able to:

- Differentiate that leadership and motivation are inseparable and that effective leaders produce high motivation.

- Clarify the complex relationship between needs, drives, perceptions and their influences on behaviour.

- Identify how motivation and behaviour are brain related and where they interact in the brain, through chemical signals, between our sense organs, the emotional (limbic) and cognitive (cerebral) brains.

- Assess the main criteria for our job satisfaction and how this can differ for diverse individuals and groups.

- Recognise that motivational patterns may not be the same across all cultures.

- Distinguish the role of the leader in fuelling positive motivation for people diverse in personality and culture.

TABLE OF CONTENTS

MOTIVATION AND LEADERSHIP

LEADERSHIP AND MOTIVATION

Leadership and motivation are inseparable. If we feel highly motivated, either we have a 'boss' who leads effectively or we are leading ourselves effectively. **If those who work for us are highly motivated, we are probably an effective leader.**

How we interact with others can have a positive or negative impact on their motivation. All parents are a leader of their children. Teachers are leaders of their class. At work, the team manager is a leader and in sports, the captain is a leader of the team and the coach is the leader of individual players. The salesperson leads the customer.

The common denominator for all of these leaders - is how well they motivate those with whom they interact, supervise or serve. **Motivation is truly the key to successful leadership.**

WHAT IS MOTIVATION?

The term motivation comes from the Latin word **'Movere'**, which means: 'To Move or Moving'. Motivation has to do with our internal drives or energy forces.

NEEDS AND MOTIVES

What produces our behaviour - including natural or innate drives or instincts - are our needs. Such reasons for behaviour, that is, purpose, are often called 'motives'. We can conclude that behaviour is caused, it doesn't just happen, there has to be a need, reason or purpose and when felt, it becomes a drive.

CONSCIOUS OR NON CONSCIOUS

Some behaviour may be instinctive, and operate at a non conscious level, but others can be consciously directed or controlled. They can be cognitive and thought out (cerebral), or they can be driven by emotions unconsciously (limbic).

Motives are the reasons, purpose or intentions of the behaviour - once the needs/drives have been recognised or felt. Primary needs and drives are largely instinctive and non conscious. While some motives may also operate at the non conscious level, most are conscious, pre-planned and deliberate. Leaders must therefore learn to recognise which needs/drives or motives are instinctive or non conscious and which are conscious.

HOMEOSTASIS

Need-satisfaction is a physiological process of homeostasis or restoring the chemical balance in the brain and body. Incentives are any perceived rewards or benefits that satisfy the needs and reduce the drives. Thus, satisfying a need will restore the bodies' physiological or psychological balance. The technical term is 'homeostasis' or producing a normal and stable state balance. Stress or tension from need deprivation are reduced or removed. Put another way - we are now motivated, energized and satisfied.

"The only thing 'stable' is that nature is not stable"   *Zen Buddha*

PRIMARY AND SECONDARY NEEDS AND DRIVES

PRIMARY NEEDS

Needs can be divided into primary or secondary. **Primary needs are natural and unlearned** and are necessary for survival. These include the need for oxygen, nutrition, liquid, protection from excess temperatures and pain. They include biological needs such as maternal needs in women. There are also social needs, such as to belong to or be accepted by other human groups. By nature, man is a social and gregarious animal.

An additional social need is for influence, control or to dominate others. This is often called our power need. **Along with the affiliative or belonging needs, these power needs may be strong or weak.** They differ from person to person, but are essentially unlearned and mainly innate. These are among the genetic influences that are often labelled as 'Personality Traits'.

SECONDARY NEEDS

Secondary needs on the other hand are learned and are socio-cultural rather than biological. They have to do with ego, status and esteem. They include those that are often expressed as values. Here we learn about moral codes of behaviour and the need to conform or be treated with respect and dignity. They are called secondary, because we can survive without them being satisfied, but we may not feel so motivated, happy or successful.

DRIVES

Drives are also natural, innate and genetically predisposed. **While universal** to the human species, **they differ in strength or intensity** from person to person. Their strength depends upon the brain chemistry, and the degree of mix of various hormones produced in the brain. Drives are located in the limbic system of the brain (the centre for direction and control of emotions). It is the location where our primitive selves are experienced. It is our non-conscious self.

WHAT ARE THESE DRIVES

Such drives include the drive **to defend** ourselves, **to learn, to bond** to attract a mate and also **to acquire certain physical and material possessions** essential for survival and protection. They serve to energise and influence our behaviour. They can direct our reasoning processes (cognitive) and how we perceive and make sense of our world. (Pink, 2011).

PERCEPTIONS TRIGGER DRIVES
Perceptions of danger, friend or foe, would be strong triggers. They can influence our memory and recall capacities as well as the whole range of multiple intelligences and preferred styles of thinking and learning. How we differ in our internal processing of information would be examples of the influence of drives. They can be likened to a genetic code of laws or rules.

"Work is made visible. And if you cannot work with love but only with distaste, it is better that you should leave your work and sit at the gate of the temple and take alms from those who work with joy".
Kahil Gibran

MOTIVATION IN THE BRAIN

FIRING THE NEURONS

If motivation is an inner force that directs and sustains behaviour, what stimulates or triggers it? And where is this energy source, and how is it sustained? If **it is like a 'fire within us',** what fuels or dampens this fire? In this section we will explore the neuronal, influences on motivation. This will give us some insight into the basic mechanics of motivation in the brain. So the next time we are either **'elated'** or **'depressed'**, or cause someone else to feel the same way, we will understand that some neurons were 'fired up' one way, and others, another way.

SENSORY STIMULI

We interact with our environment. This environment can be friendly, neutral or hostile or at least - perceived to be so. It may be perceived as one of these, but in reality it maybe the opposite. Yet **if that is how we perceive** it and believe it to be so, even if imagined, **the brain reacts accordingly**.

Our five senses of **sight, sound, touch, taste or smell,** or even our intuitive 'sixth' sense, receive various signals or stimuli from the environment. These sense organs or functions relay signals to the brain, where they first enter our limbic system. This is the centre that processes emotions and short-term memory, among its various functions. Within a **millisecond** these perceived signals are directed to the pre-frontal cortex.

PROCESSING DATA

Here, the information is processed with our stored memories, which search for past related experiences or emotional associations. This is often thought of as a type of 'working memory'. Cultural learning and other stored representations help us analyse a range of possible actions or perceived consequences of our behaviour.

RESULTS OF BEHAVIOUR

This resultant behaviour can have either positive or negative consequences. They either 'fit' the environmental situation or demands (positive) or fail to do so (negative). **In terms of motivation, we can say that the felt needs that set up drives, are either satisfied or not satisfied**. If unsatisfied, the needs can set up even stronger drives to behave. Such behaviour can therefore make us feel elated or frustrated. Our persistence to behave may depend upon the intensity of the drive we feel. So the need-perception-drive-behaviour process is a cycle.

THINKING SPEED
These 'thinking' processes occur in a few milliseconds, and help us determine some intended actions. They are first processed in the emotional brain (limbic), then the thinking brain. Next, these reactions or associations re-enter the limbic system and trigger an appropriate drive or drives. In turn, messages are relayed to the various parts of the brain to act or behave. These decision processes can occur in less than 80 milliseconds (that's about the time it takes to blink an eye!).

"Where the brain is wired up - we can be fired up"   *-Conyngham, 2001 -*

MOTIVATION IS CHEMICAL

BRAIN HORMONES
When we feel euphoria, calmness, clarity or confidence, we can say we feel motivated. Such states of mind are produced by brain chemicals - called hormones.
Two hormones in particular are important. The sex hormones of testosterone and estrogen and the hormone dopamine are discussed later.

AN EXAMPLE: VISUAL MEMORY
Let's illustrate how the complex chemical processes work in the brain, by giving a practical example. Imagine you are needing to buy some canned tuna fish in a supermarket. You visually scan the shelves for canned tuna.

If you have purchased this product before, you already have a memory and association, located in the brain. Assume you want a brand that is free of potentially hazardous toxins like mercury, this is another need.

The **working memory and decision making takes place in the pre-frontal cortex**, you where can recall a brand name, label or colour. The label, colour and a picture of a tuna fish is perceived as a signal. **The message is relayed through the limbic system into the cerebral cortex**. The visual cortex sends the pictorial information to the pre frontal cortex where it makes a decision on the intention to buy.

MAKING A DECISION
Your working memory processes the previously stored association influenced by your motivation to buy (the purpose or reason for buying). Lets also assume that you want a reasonable price value, but health is a more important value. **Your key drives of the 'hunter-gatherer', combined with your drive to get a good price, is activated in the limbic system**. A message is now relayed to direct your motor cortex to pick up a can that matches your internal representation, in terms of colour, size or perhaps brand name. (Memory-Drive-Behaviour).

Another message instructs your visual system, to read the label. Your logic-maths intelligence in your pre-frontal cortex assesses the price. This cycle of **neurons firing and zapping information from one part of the brain to another, ends up with your decision to buy - or not to buy!** The same processes may be repeated, if you want to select and compare data of other brands. Once a final decision is made, we can say your need is satisfied, and the motivational energy in purchasing your tuna is complete. Positive hormones make you feel satisfied. (Need/Drive-Act-Satisfied).

THE CHEMISTRY OF HORMONES
Some hormones increase our positive attitudes and optimism. Conversely, if we find our behaviour had not satisfied our needs, others hormones cause tension, stress or even depression. We can then conclude we feel 'de-motivated' the positive hormones are called 'endorphins' and negative ones are endocrines, like cortisol. So, feelings of motivation have a chemical basis. Emotions produce chemicals and chemicals produce emotions. The secret of motivation then is to ensure we produce the right mix - as much of the time as possible.

"Emotions produce chemicals, and chemicals produce emotion".
Conyngham, 2001

DIVERSITY AND MOTIVATION

WE CANNOT MOTIVATE OTHERS

From this view of motivation, we can see that the decision to act relates to our own internal needs, perceptions and drives. We can only motivate ourselves. Others can provide incentives, suggestions, directives or advice. However the choice of what and how - or even when and why we behave is internal. **"Motivation is the fire within"** Others, or incentives are externals. While they may serve as **"fuel for the fire"**, we still control whether we allow it to **"fire us up"**.

HOW DIVERSE ARE OUR NEEDS

Are all people motivated similarly? The answer clearly is 'No'. As we have already explored, people are diverse in age, gender, personality and ethnicity. In addition, their socio-economic status differs. What motivates a young, male, single, new employee who lives at home with his parents will be very different from a mid-career married female, with a home mortgage and children.

EQUITY THEORY

One contemporary theory of motivation, which builds on 'Expectancy' theory, is 'Equity' theory. **It argues that a key aspect of job satisfaction and motivation to perform, concerns the perceived equity of rewards**. A male and female employee, doing the same type of work, with a similar level of work responsibility and competence should be equally rewarded. This is equity. **Leaders can do this!**

Sometimes however this is not the case and one party maybe unfairly discriminated against. Perhaps one is older, or has a larger family responsibility, or out performs the other. Perhaps one has worked many years longer for the same organization. Should people be rewarded differently for loyalty, service, age, marital status or superior results? This is a challenge for employers. Treating everyone equally may not be equitable. (Adams, 1965).

INPUT VERSUS OUTPUT VARIABLES

Input variables include age, sex, education, qualifications, position, and effort. Output may include pay, status, title, promotion, intrinsic job satisfaction, promotion and benefits. Here, **the real challenge is the perception of the value and fairness** of these. Now, these are 'internal' equity factors. We must also factor in 'external' equity. This includes the value of a position in the labour market influenced by a shortage of qualified applicants for a specific job.

EQUITY VERSUS EQUALITY
Equality is not the same as Equity. The word equality infers that all people must be treated equally and all would have equal opportunities for promotion, selection and even the same work or conditions. It would mean all ethnic groups or males and females would not be discriminated against. Equity however means fairness or justice. It means that the selection and criteria was fair and the most qualified people are promoted or paid according to their responsibility or performance. If employees do not perceive that treatment is fair, they may be de-motivated and feel a grievance. Often the actual quantum of pay may be less important than the 'fairness' of it.

"We need to give different 'strokes' for different folks."   Anon

MOTIVATION AND JOB SATISFACTION

JOB SATISFACTION

In study after study on job satisfaction, we find people differ in their level of work satisfaction. **What satisfies one person may not satisfy another**. It again depends on the diversity of the employee needs. Although there are common satisfiers, their priority of order may differ from person to person.

Let's assume equity, vis-a-vis, job, or person exists, but individuals have some similar and some different needs. Similar ones will include the basic instinctive biological or physiological needs and drives shown earlier. The different needs will depend upon a person's age, talent level, personality, socio-economic status or qualifications etc.

The ten needs in the box below have been found to be highly significant need-drive satisfiers, essential for a well-motivated employee. What is important is how they differ culturally, ethnically, socially and individually - in terms of personality, age, marital and economic status. But also they can differ between team members and their leader.

While some are very important to the lower paid group, they may be the same for the highly paid group. Yes, there are some cause-effect relationships, and several are interdependent. For example, a good boss and peer relationships should contribute to job satisfaction. **What are significant are the differences in the perception of what the boss has about the employee and reality. (See table below).**

JOB SATISFACTION AND PERFORMANCE

Does high job satisfaction lead to high performance? Are happy people more productive? Research shows there is no guarantee of this. **Happy employees can be lazy but not necessarily motivated to be productive.** One classic study showed only a .17 correlation between job satisfaction and performance. What is really interesting is that a sort of 'reverse' situation occurs. **High performance which produces results, leads to high job satisfaction** and increases motivation. **"Productive people are happy, rather than happy people being productive".**

Another factor is that a leader perception of what their employees need or prefer can be very different. General studies have shown these perception gaps are remarkably similar. (See table).

In one study of employee motivation conducted at George Mason University, USA, 1000 employees were surveyed. They were asked to rank order 10 possible incentives or rewards. The leaders (supervisors) of these employees were also asked to guess what their 'subordinates' preferred. These can be seen here. (E=Employees, S= Supervisors)

"He, who has a way to live for, can bear with almost Anyhow" . - Nietzsche -

	Ranking	
	E	S
* Interesting work	1.	5
* Appreciation of work done	2.	8
* Being kept informed	3.	10
* Job security	4.	2
* Good wages	5.	1
* Promotion & growth	6.	3
* Working conditions	7.	4
* Employee loyalty	8.	6
* Tactful discipline	9.	7
* Help with Problems	10	9

JOB SATISFACTION VERSUS LIFE SATISFACTION

OPTIMISM AND SATISFACTION

Most of us see the world more positively than perhaps it really is. We tend to forecast a more optimistic view of the world, or what Kahneman (2011) says is a cognitive bias. The bias towards optimism is normal; however some people are genetically endowed with this bias ("Born optimists"). This attitude which is really a personality trait is largely inherited. Optimists are normally cheerful, happy and therefore more popular. They are more resilient and able to adapt to failures and hardships. Their immune systems are stronger and they take care of their health better and tend to live longer.

OPTIMISM AND LEADERSHIP

Optimism has often been associated with great leaders, not average people. They take more risks, are more innovative and seek out challenges. This optimism is a trait that comes under the group of personality dispositions called 'Temperament'. This genetic or inheritability for well-being is as inheritable as height or intelligence, as shown by twins who were separated from birth. Now, while leaders may tend to be more optimistic, it does not mean that all their team members may have the same temperament. If life satisfaction embodies the wants and wishes that we have for ourselves, and is a complex synergy of what we are, what we want and how we feel now and about the future.

Kahneman also links such cognitive bias to entrepreneurial optimism as similar to leadership optimism. His book, Thinking Fast and Slow, uses a paradigm of thinking which he describes as 'System 2' (Fast Thinking) which equates to our right brain, which is more liberal, intuitive, metaphorical and non-conscious. His 'System 1' (Slow Thinking) is conscious, deliberate, focused, attention and effortful. These are 'left' brain functions. So while leadership may call for more System 1 (Fast, effortless and intuitive decision making, other employees life satisfaction can differ. So again, it comes to how well leaders know their team members

What do employees really want? (From a gallop poll survey on over a million employees from a range of companies, industries and countries).

1. *Having the opportunity to do what I do best*
2. *Knowing what is expected of me in my job*
3. *Having the materials and equipment I need to do my job properly*
4. *Receiving weekly recognition or praise for good work*
5. *Having a supervisor or someone at work who cares about me personally*
6. *Having someone at work encouraging my development*
7. *Having my own opinion at work accepted*
8. *Having a company mission that makes me feel my work is important*
9. *Having co-workers committed to doing quality work*
10. *Having a best friend at work*

Source: Buckingham & Coffman, 1999

MOTIVATION ACROSS CULTURES

CULTURAL DIFFERENCES

What might be some significant cultural influences in motivation, especially motivation to perform? Also how leaders could influence this across cultures? **One of the main differences would be between individualistic and collectivist cultures.** In some cultures, hierarchy and relationships are the norm - including Africa, Asia, Middle East, Latin America and some Southern European countries. These would be patterns that differ from 'Anglo-Saxon' or 'Western' cultures.

Most of the management motivation theories put forward since World War II, have been developed in, and for, the West. What motivates an employee in a highly individualistic culture, such as Australia or the USA, could differ from highly collectivistic cultures like China, Japan or Indonesia. The classic motivation **theories of Maslow, Vroom or Alderfer do not apply so well in Asian or Eastern or African cultures.** (Note: These earlier western theories are not included in this book).

RELIGIOUS INFLUENCES

Many of these theories were related to the 'WASP' cultures (White Anglo-Saxon Protestant) and their work ethic. **In Asian cultures**, Buddhist, Catholic, Confucian, Hindu, Muslim or Taoist philosophies have pervaded for centuries. In such cultures, the work ethic and **how leaders motivate can significantly differ from the West**.

Religious, spiritual or family values of 'caring', nurturing and paternalism can have a direct - or indirect - impact on people's motivational patterns. Respect for elders or people in a high position, concern for harmony and face saving, or the extended family values of collectivist cultures, impact strongly on relationships.

RELATIONSHIP OR AFFILIATION NEEDS

In studying the western 'content' theories of motivation, the 'hierarchy' of needs may need to be re-arranged. For example, **in the collectivist cultures of Asia, social, affiliative or belonging needs probably should be placed ahead of self-esteem and self-actualization needs**. Even safety-security needs may be of a lower priority to the needs to belong in some cultures. So the understanding of motivation means we must study the meaning of work among people across cultures.

MEETING SPIRITUAL NEEDS
Relationship with 'god', with nature or with others can be strongly influenced by the dominant religion in a given culture. How we were brought up, and naturally programmed can remain a strong force at the 'non conscious' level. Religious beliefs and values are among the strongest, and people will not readily shift from those. Real motivation will use these - or build on them - not try to change them.

For example, devoutly religious people will be more highly motivated by the employer who cares for their spiritual needs. Allowing people time off for religious obligations, or providing facilities such as a prayer room, will often contribute to higher motivation, than depriving them of these.

"The hierarchy of the importance of our needs differ across cultures" -
Nietzsche -

FUELLING POSITIVE MOTIVATION

POSITIVE VERSUS NEGATIVE MOTIVATION

In reality - unless we are asleep - **we are all motivated all the time**. Every human has needs and drives that must be satisfied, continuously, until they die. The challenge for leaders or the self-led is whether our motivation is positive, healthy and constructive. If we do not like our job, or our boss, we may be destructive, 'attack' our boss or sabotage the organization. Thus **motivation at work is about channelling or releasing energy towards positive or productive behaviour and results**. This energy is the fire within - and motivation is finding the right fuel to sustain this fire.

LEADERS ROLE

Leaders who are effective can provide such a climate and fuel to feed the fire. Climate can be a nurturing environment in which the fire can burn healthily. **The leader must know each employee's personality type and traits**, their unique needs and drives and what "turns them on". Next they will need to ensure that each employee is well suited to their job. This means knowing which natural talents fit each job or task type. If we have adequate knowledge of both, this matching process should be easily achieved. Matching such talents can only be done after objectively assessing and measuring talent or talent potential. **Ability to analyse personality and competency is a quality that leaders must possess.**

JOB DESIGN

We cannot redesign people - at least the mature adult that comprises most employees. By the time we are in our early adulthood, our brain is fully matured and our personality is pretty well fixed. What we can do though is to **redesign the job** that we are assigning to an employee, as it's **too late to 'redesign' the employee!**

CULTURAL APPROPRIATENESS

As our feeling or self-worth and value is important, we need to ensure our self-esteem and personal dignity is enhanced and protected. However, how we do this may differ culturally. Depending upon what culture we are from - more collectivist or more individualist - motivational policies and strategies may need to differ. The concept of 'self' differs from culture to culture. How we view the concept of self, must be done with respect to the cultural, ethnic or religious values of each employee. There is a 'related-self' and 'separated-self.' E.g.: I am the son or daughter of ... (related-self).

The benefits of job design or redesign are numerous. They include allowing peoples' talents and energy to be fully utilized. This also builds employee morale and loyalty. We know that people are more highly motivated when they can be productive and show positive results. Job satisfaction is increased with such results. Boredom - which is stressful - will also be reduced. This reinforces the importance of knowing which satisfiers motivate each employee. We need round pegs in round holes - not square pegs - or misfits. Selecting the best job fit for one's unique personality and motivational needs or drives is the key.

"Motivation is the fire within. Finding the right fuel to sustain this fire is the challenge"
-Conyngham, 2001-

MOTIVATION: INTRINSIC VERSUS EXTRINSIC

REWARDS AS SATISFIERS – INTERNAL VERSUS EXTERNAL

If we agree that motivation is the force that arouses feelings and behaviour of enthusiasm – we can see why theories on this are so abundant. From a leadership perspective, there are multiple theories, from classic traditional ones that attempt to explain what leaders should or shouldn't do (external) to affect these feelings of enthusiasm (internal) among employees. Among earlier models would be the concept of Intrinsic (internal) motivational rewards, versus Extrinsic (external).

The internal or intrinsic rewards are the satisfiers that are felt from performing self-directed actions, like doing work that feels rewarding, due to one's own efforts, talent or skill. Extrinsic are those rewards given by others, such as a leader. These might include system wide incentives or benefits, like promotion, more money or pride in belonging to a winning team or organisation.

HOW APPLICABLE IS THE 'INTRINSIC– EXTRINSIC' MODEL?

Critics suggest that many extrinsic rewards are insufficient as full motivators. They may actually diminish intrinsic rewards. Employees may in fact focus more on extrinsic factors and less on the intrinsic satisfaction from the work itself. When this occurs, they lose interest in what motivates people internally; the challenge, the drive to achieve, to learn, grow and excel. Further, critics maintain that extrinsic factors can only be temporary, and assumes people can be driven by lower needs rather than the higher needs of self-fulfilment. There is also the likelihood that extrinsic rewards may inhibit collaboration and teamwork and foster selfish competition. The key is to empower employees with adequate learning, knowledge, skills, autonomy and meaningful work.

THE ACQUIRED NEEDS MODEL AND LEADERSHIP

Harvard Psychologist and Motivation Guru, Professor David McClelland (McClelland, 1953) pioneered a model that suggests people are social animals that each have **social needs for affiliation (belonging), achievement and to influence others (power).** These needs, while common to us all, differ in intensity between people, which are probably more genetic in nature, than learned (Nurture). Leaders, especially those at high levels in larger organizations, usually have stronger influence and power needs than those of achievement or affiliation. McClelland is one of those rare behavioural scientists who tracked these need patterns for more than 40 years.

SELF-DETERMINATION THEORY (SDT)

Deci & Ryan (2000) studied the 'intrinsic' personality and psychological needs that are universal and innate. They are; Autonomy, Competence and Affiliation (see McClelland above). When met, people will function optimally, but Leaders must nurture them.

CULTURE AND ACHIEVEMENT

McClelland's motivation theory is more 'personality' based, and therefore less prone to cultural influence. However, emphasis on individual achievement ahead of group achievement, would differ between the US and Asia. The highly achievement motivated employee in Asia will still exist, but the achievement should be within the 'acceptance' of a highly affiliative or supportive framework. Achievers in Asia should not stand out so much as an individual in the USA. In Asia they should be members of the team, not a 'lone wolf', which might be acceptable in the USA.

"What lies behind us - and before us - are tiny, compared to what lies within us".
Oliver Wendell Holmes.

GENDER AND MOTIVATION

GENDER DIFFERENCES IN McCLELLAND'S MODEL

For many women, hidden psychological traps make them deal with achievement and competition differently from men. It can cause them to under rate themselves, feel less competent and lose out when they don't need to. Leaders of both gender need to appreciate this. Research has shown that women's need for achievement differs in two crucial ways. **First, the psychological 'button'** that pushes men to achieve is 'competition'. For women, the button is 'social acceptance'. **The second, their need to achieve is focused on their 'affiliation' needs**. This means that concern for acceptance or to please others. This is one reason why women tend to achieve things better through 'collaboration' and 'co-operation', rather than competition. This enhances their **'Relational' and 'Transformational'** leadership. Men will tend more towards a 'Transactional' leadership style. The same applies in gender differences in the power motive.

GENDER, MOTIVATION AND HORMONES

Continuing with McClelland's work on the **3 social needs** (achievement, affiliation and influence), he found that the sex hormones of testosterone and estrogen can also influence behaviour towards the power motive. Testosterone can make male leaders more aggressive, task oriented and confrontational. Their approach may favour a more authoritarian style. Contrastingly, the higher levels of **the female hormone of estrogen, produce a leadership style that is more caring, empathetic or transformational**. Women leaders can display a higher level of 'people' sensitivity in their emotional intelligence. This results in gender differences in leader behaviour, due to genetics and hormones. From more recent research (Fisher, 2013) those leaders with higher testosterone levels, not only are more dominant and competitive, but also more analytic. Conversely, high estrogen people are more nurturing and introspective.

Key leadership behaviours that motivate can therefore be summed up as also relating to personality and style preferences. And the research showed each type were more drawn towards those who have similar personalities. How leaders should relate to employees, by listening with empathy, coaching, counselling, giving supportive feedback and delegating more autonomy. Each will stimulate positive motivation, performance and productivity. Job enrichment, provides more responsibility, recognition, growth, learning and development and actual achievement and is at the core of leadership motivation.

GENDER AND OUR BRAIN

Males have stronger linkages or connectivity between the frontal lobes (our executive brain) and the visual cortex. This increases the speed between perception and visual spatial ability. Whereas in the female brain, connections are wired more strongly between cognitive, (thinking) and emotional (feeling) parts of the brain especially in the language cortices. This strengthens linkages between rational and emotional control. (Fisher, 2013). So again, there are cross dynamics, here at play! **Knowing how men motivate women and vice versa** is able to help leaders of each gender, better select different motivation approaches that work.

"Leaders are people who do the right thing. Managers are people who do things right"
Warren Bennis

SUMMARY OF KEY POINTS

- Motivation is the 'fire' within us. It is that which gives us the energy, drive and enthusiasm to behave. In short, it is the 'Why' of behaviour.

- The word motivation comes from the Latin term 'movere', which means 'to move'. It is the actual needs and drives we each possess that move us. Once satisfied we can say we are motivated.

- Motives are the reasons or purposes we have that cause us to behave. They can be either conscious or cognitive, or they can be non-conscious or instinctive. It is useful to know how they operate at these two levels. The instinctive needs for food, shelter, safety and security are referred to as basic, primary or lower order needs.

- Needs are primary or secondary. Primary ones are more natural, instinctive and unlearned such as our physical and physiological needs. Secondary ones are more socio-cultural, and are learned, such as what we value or believe to be morally right.

- Drives are however more emotional, lying in our limbic system. They direct the brain to behave in a particular way, subject to our needs and the perceived consequences of our behaviour. (The need for love or recognition). Above the basic are higher level (secondary) social needs. McClelland calls these needs for achievement, influence and affiliation.

- Incentives are the rewards or positive consequences that when perceived as being valued or desired, may strengthen our drive to behave and satisfy needs.

- Some higher needs may be classified as Intrinsic (internal) and Extrinsic (external), as with many incentives or rewards. We need a healthy balance between these but many criticize this model, saying real motivation is only intrinsic.

- Job satisfaction is a feeling of being motivated from the work we do. This is why money per se is not a motivator, but what the money can buy. Money can be an incentive, out only if it provides what satisfies or drives us.

- Food may be a primary need which money can buy (extrinsic). But a job well paid, while providing the money to buy food may not necessarily be satisfying, or meet our secondary needs. Extrinsic rewards may inhibit the drive towards the intrinsic.

- Needs differ from person to person due to personality gender and age so we cannot assume the same things are equally strong in motivating everyone. Hormonal influences, which influence motivation, differ in individuals and gender.

- Need patterns, or a hierarchy of needs may differ from culture to culture. Attention should be paid to the different personalities who differ in the need for the hormones that stimulate (Dopamine) or those that calm (Serotonin).

- Due then to the diverse range of differences between people and what motivate them; the leader really has to treat each employee as a unique individual. Gender, personality or even ethnicity that dictates that what stimulates one person, may not do the same for others.

- While listening to people motivates, adequate learning and growth, challenge and need to achieve or belong differ in each person. Leaders must realize this and motivate people through coaching, counselling, providing intrinsic rewards matching their leadership style to maximize motivations of each type.

INSPIRE OTHERS

THE "GOLDEN CIRCLE" AND
WHOLE BRAIN THINKING AND FEELING

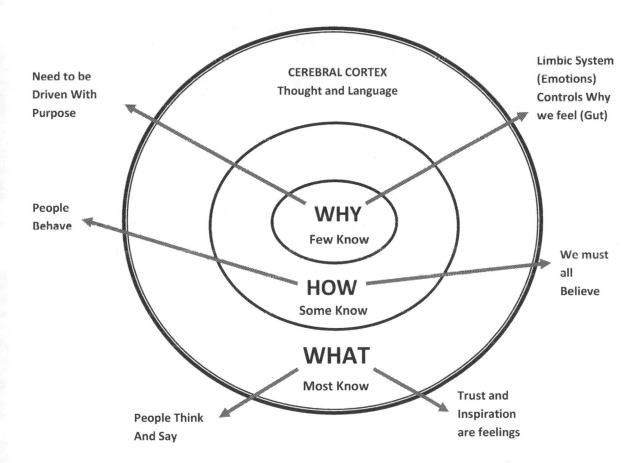

Adapted From: The Golden Circle
By Simon Sidek

REFERENCES

Adams, J. (1965). *Inequity in Social Echange in Adv. Exp. Social Psych* .

Buckingham, M. & Coffman, C. (1999). *First Break All The Rules: What the World's Greatest Managers Do.* New York: Simon & Schucter.

Fisher, H. (2014). *Rutgers University Research Paper.* New York : Rutgers University Press.

Kahneman, D. (2011). *Thinking Fast and Slow.* London: Penguin Books.

McClelland, D. C. (1953). *The Achievement Motive.* New York: Century Crofts.

Pink, D. (2011). *Drive: The Suprising truth about what motivates us* . London : Penguin Books.

CHAPTER EIGHT

LEADING HIGH PERFORMANCE TEAMS

LEARNING OBJECTIVES FOR THIS CHAPTER

By the end of this chapter, you will be able to:

- Describe the nature of teamwork and team effectiveness.

- Recognise and apply the main techniques of 'Participative Design' in team development.

- Differentiate between conventional, creative and high performance teams.

- Identify how to select and apply any, or a combination of, four teambuilding models.

- Detect the key characteristics of a leader as a team facilitator.

- Judge the effectiveness of team member interactions and apply whole brained team work.

TABLE OF CONTENTS

TEAMS AND HIGH PERFORMANCE TEAMWORK

A HIGH PERFORMANCE TEAM

"A group of two or more people, who are highly committed, motivated and supportive, working together in harmony and synergy, to achieve shared high performance goals and standards." What distinguishes high performance teams from normal ones is the degree of precision and standards achieved.

Synergy is one feature, where the end output is greater than the sum of the parts or individuals. Members are highly skilled and supportive of each other. There is a high degree of inter-dependence. Trust and loyalty is high. Goals, roles, responsibilities and relationships are clearly defined and understood.

A system can be defined as a group of organized parts working together in an orderly, yet interdependent whole. This whole is more than simply the sum of its parts. Systems thinking is a disciplined approach of scientific enquiry. It seeks to understand why any system works. It does this by analyzing all the parts and their relationships to one another.

PARTICIPATIVE DESIGN (PD)

Emerging from the work done by Emery (1969) and his associates, a more highly structured and participative design evolved. Earlier designs lacked the sense of ownership required for open systems to be self-managed and sustainable. They should enable teams or organizations to know how systems function.

When team members have an appreciation of each other's roles, responsibilities and relationships, they perform with a higher level of respect and commitment. People feel empowered to redesign structure - a form of 'Kaizen' – directed at organizational or team renewal.

STRUCTURAL REDESIGN

This would include self-control mechanisms to ensure alignment and coordination of values, vision and mission. Job/task rotation or sharing and multi-skilling would be a feature, but their benefits need to be understood by all. As an incentive, 'Pay-for-skills' programs might help.

Realizing that it is normal to resist change, commitment to change can only come where there is an exciting or energizing vision of the future. Structure must be designed to provide for the above, and participation increases commitment.

OPEN SYSTEMS THINKING

High Performance Teams or Teamwork (HPT) comes mainly from the early work done by the Tavistock Institute in the UK, in the 1940's. Pioneers like Eric Trist and Fred Emery did research work on Coal Mining teams who worked under often difficult, dirty and hazardous conditions. They noted that when certain effectiveness criteria was present, the morale and the productivity of the teams was extremely high. One criteria was the harmony between man and machine (Social and Technical Systems or 'STS' Theory). It stemmed from a type of thinking called 'Open Systems Thinking' and Ergonomics emerged from this.

> *"Whenever there are problems….a master of systems thinking automatically sees them as arising from underlying structures, rather than from individual mistakes or ill will"*
> *-Peter Senge - The Fifth Discipline*

SOCIO TECHNICAL SYSTEMS (STS) DESIGN

STS (Emery, F. & Trist, E, 1981) views the organization as an open system that interacts with its environment (Systems Thinking). It consists of the 'social' system (people) and 'technical' system (Technology), which both must be jointly optimized for best results. It infers there must be a form of harmony or balance between these two systems.

Metaphorically it is like the 'horse and rider' moving in perfection and synergy. Several change lessons have evolved from the STS experiments. Most notable would be the 'Quality of Work' Life (QWL), where labour and management participate in self-directed teamwork, with resultant quantum leaps in productivity. The main conceptualization initially emerged from the U.K. Tavistock Institute's work and research into the coal miners motivation in 1947.

Trist observed how teamwork among the miners, which they themselves directed, worked so much better than in traditional assembly lines. This spun off a whole new approach to human systems design, including SAWG (Semi-Autonomous Work Groups), Survey Research, Action Research, Action Learning and a new view of Human Relations'. In the spirit of STS, came the idea of ergonomics, which was the redesign of equipment, machinery and even entire assembly lines. (Volvo, The British Mini, to name two classic examples from auto manufacturing) to match the movement, posture and manual functions of workers. All of these initiatives were based on employee motivation, job satisfaction and human performance enhancement, and resultant improvement in work quality and productivity.

PARTICIPATIVE DESIGN (PD)

A sense of ownership of a project and also of the design of processes for the work flow, have be found to greatly increase teamwork commitment. Participative Design was an off shoot of STS as an attempt to foster democratization of the workplace. The idea of Quality Circles, as empowered and semi-autonomous work groups, are good examples of self-directed high performance teams (Emery and Devane, 1999), One of the outcomes is efficiency, and many teams that deal with simple, routine tasks or linear work processes can often be handled by any team member. A job rotation and multi-skilling schedule enables team workers to easily replace each other when needed. It also greatly increases work variety, which has been found to enhance job satisfaction. These are highly structured but very participative systems. They are called 'Techno-structural' interventions. However, where tasks and technology are highly professional or specialized, such interventions may not be so applicable.

ATTITUDES AND BEHAVIOURS

High Performance teams adhere to high standards, Many of their behaviours are influenced by a set of values and winning attitudes. These would include dedication, commitment, patience, persistence and intolerance for apathy or mediocrity. Behaviour would be exemplified by energy, enthusiasm and cooperation. Team members often have their own language or jargon - for efficiency - as well as to appear special or elite. They communicate well and listen fully to each other, respecting all ideas and contributions.

> *"We are born for cooperation, as are the feet, the hands, the eyelids and the upper and lower jaws"- Marcus Aurelius Antonius.*

TEAM EFFECTIVENESS CRITERIA

SIX EFFECTIVENESS FACTORS

Research done by the Centre for Creative Leadership, in the USA, identified six characteristics of successful teams. These were:

- Having a clear mission and high performance standards. Each member knew what their team was trying to achieve and how well they had to perform.
- Leaders knew what resources, facilities, technology and opportunities were available to help the team. Leaders were enablers or facilitators.
- Leaders assessed the level and scope of competencies needed by the team's members and ensures they secured or achieved these.
- Leaders spent considerable efforts to ensure planning and organizing was done by the team – not merely by the leader alone.
- High levels of communication took place, to ensure group maintenance and interpersonal relations were effective.
- Potential for dysfunctional conflict was minimised and interpersonal conflict was managed to ensure a healthy level of tension. This produced practical ideas and win-win outcomes. Negative conflict was not allowed to de-energize or de-moralize the team. Leaders developed skills in conflict management and negotiating.

FURTHER CRITERIA

Additional research by Ginnet, (1993), building on work by Hackman (1980) found four critical variables need to exist. Those were:

- **Task Structure**. All team members know what their tasks are. They are aligned with the mission. They believe them to be meaningful, with sufficient autonomy and feedback on results.
- **Group Boundaries & Size.** The group collectively possess sufficient knowledge and skills to achieve the tasks. The group avoids duplicated roles, so it is optimally efficient.
- **Norms**. Team members share an appropriate set of behavioural norms. Their ways of working together contribute to high performance. Here the technique known a Interaction Process Analysis (IPA) can be used (Bales, 2014).
- **Scope of Authority.** The team members have sufficient authority to feel valued, respected and empowered. Too little authority inhibits initiative and creativity, and the team may not be flexible or also responsive enough and they may not feel empowered. We need a balance between too much and too little authority.

TEAM PERFORMANCE

High Performance Teams (HPT) tend to foster a climate of informality, comfort and flexibility. They have structures with simultaneous 'loose-tight' properties. High levels of humour and laughter co-exist with the seriousness of task achievement. Demanding performance standards are challenging and energizing. Teams are flexible and responsive to change, and to the customer demands of quality, speed and cost. HPT's invest a lot of time and effort in exploring their purpose, value, contribution and effectiveness. Members communicate extensively between themselves, to ensure reflection on, and development of, the ways they work together. Again, the 3R's of Roles, Responsibilities and Relationships, become critical.

"The leaders job is to create conditions for the team to be effective" - (Ginnet, R.S., 1993)

HIGH PERFORMANCE TEAMWORK

HIGH PERFORMANCE TEAMS (HPT's)

Who are these HPT's? What are their attributes? These are the critical questions we will explore here. Examples of HPT's would be where high precision, competence and interdependence are required. From the fiction and movies they have become easily recognized – with Hollywood stars as their heroes and role models. They might include:

- Mission Impossible
- The 3 Musketeers
- Robin Hood
- The "A" Team

In real life they exist in a wide range of areas and might include from the Sciences and Arts:

- An Astronaut Crew
- The Red Arrows
- A Surgery Team
- A Circus Trapeze Group
- A Rowing Eight
- A 'Pit Stop' Crew
- A SWAT Team
- A Jazz Band
- A Choir
- A Dance Group
- An Orchestra
- A Yacht Crew

ATTRIBUTES OF HPT'S

These can be seen by their high standards of excellence in both performances and results. We can divide their characteristics into behaviours, use of technology and the environment, which are fully exploited. Emotions felt or displayed are very strong. They celebrate with exuberance and joy.

SYNERGY

We have already indentified that effective teams are highly synergistic – where the end output is far greater than the sum of the parts. This comes about by members being highly supportive and helpful to each other. While roles maybe distinctly different, they are clearly understood and each role player is respected for their unique competence and contribution. Members will help others complete tasks or projects, if in the interest of the team.

As with many team sports, like hockey, soccer or rugby, players know each other's strengths and weaknesses. They will pass the ball to others if it strategically helps position the team to win. They will do this ahead of trying to score points for themselves or to be seen as a hero, or for self glory. Often, members are multi-skilled, and therefore not only can they help others, they can replace them when absent.

SHARED EMOTIONS

If things go well, they show excitement and pride. There is passion, enthusiasm, joviality and fun. A sense of humour pervades and is balanced with purpose.

"One for all and all for One" - *From the book, The Three Musketeers, by Alexander Dumas*

BUILDING HIGH PERFORMANCE TEAMS

WHY TEAM BUILDING

Who 'invented' teambuilding? Many concepts of team building have become popular over the last 30 years. The more common models are evolving in western and individualistic cultures, especially the USA. In the more collectivistic Asian cultures, particularly Japan, we can see that teamwork is natural. Values of harmony, respect for the leader, and cooperation are an intrinsic part of the Japanese work ethic and culture.

Perhaps 'Teambuilding', as we've come to understand it today, emerged mainly for individualistic cultures. Where self esteem and self actualization are the norms, or where competitiveness and standing out among others is valued, the need for team building may be greater.

EVOLUTION OF TEAMBUILDING

Historically we can look back to the concept of a team, which might include a hunting party, a band of minstrels or a football team of 100 years ago. Team work, even then, still relied on common goals, shared competence, cooperation and trust. Loyalty to the team, esprit de corps and passion for excellence, were the drivers for winning teams.

GLOBAL COMPETITIVENESS

While these norms exist, even to today, the world has changed. Due to increased globalization, competitiveness and the higher demands for quality, speed, services and cost, teamwork has taken on a new priority. Higher performance standards are often the only competitive edges. Computers, cameras, jets or cars are all built to satisfy higher customer expectations. Yet it is teams of people who do the building. So increasingly these teams need to also be built to perform higher. And it is usually their leader who is entrusted with these processes.

Here are four team building models. Each has its applicability to different phases of development, and the types of problems or situations, the team face.

Model One: Clarifying Values, Vision, Mission, Strategy & Goals.
Model Two: Clarifying Roles & Responsibilities. (Perception, Comparisons and Clarification).
Model Three: Interpersonal Relationship Building (Building Communication Skills and Trust).
Model Four: Analysis and Development of Needed Competencies.

TEAM BUILDING PROCESSES
If we use the system thinking concept, teambuilding can be divided into these phases – Input, Teamwork and Output. The Input phase examines all the input criteria, and what it lacks from the external and internal environments. This is a diagnostic phase which assesses the available resources and whether the climate is conducive. For effective teambuilding, we can use techniques like SWOT (Strengths, Weaknesses, Opportunities & Threats), PESTE (Political, Economic, Social, Technical & Environmental) or FFA (Force Field Analysis). The next phase evaluates the actual teamwork processes. Here a technique like IPA (Interaction Process Analysis) can be used.

"Vision is only a dream if it does not have commitment and support from the people involved" -Lou Quast & David Lee-

FACILITATING TEAM CREATIVITY

THE NATURE OF CREATIVE PEOPLE

Creative people tend to be more right-brained, specifically right cerebral dominant. They like to experiment, use imagination and intuition and are often more artistic and musical. By their nature they are more open to information, ideas and new experiences. They may take risks and even 'bend the rules' being seen as non – conformist. Naturally more optimistic, they are opportunity seeking, prefer to have more freedom and independence. They impulsively follow new ideas that attract them.

Creative people are more idealistic than realistic, often coming across as impractical or even 'crazy'. They are less concerned about money and are more intrinsically motivated. They're driven to prove themselves, often emotionally and stubbornly. They tend not to be good 'followers' and can be difficult to lead. They may not make good team players, unless the team members and leader are themselves creative.

LEADING CREATIVE TEAMS

Because organizations today have to be more innovative, leading and motivating creative individuals and teams has become a critical success factor. The following leadership practises and styles will help facilitate creativity in a team, producing the ideal climate for innovation.

- Set clear goals, yet flexible in structure and time frame. Reduce time pressure, but monitor progress in a loose and supportive way.
- Provide adequate resources and a wide scope of authority on how to use them. Give budget limits, but provide autonomy or freedom on how to spend – within a broad limit.
- Consider non-monetary incentives or rewards as well as monetary ones. Recognition, freedom and self actualization are often as, or even more important, than financial security.
- Recognize that creativity is more an evolutionary than revolutionary processes. Creativity can produce small and continuous improvements to products and processes, as well as big breakthrough ideas.

Too much structure – rules and regulations – can stifle creativity. Opportunity to experiment and freedom to make mistakes, must be allowed for.

NURTURING CREATIVE TEAMS

The nurturing of creativity requires specific skills. These include: Being a good listener – patient and with genuine interest in the thoughts, ideas or needs of team members. Listening can be highly motivational. Being open, receptive and supportive. Creative problem solving can often be more satisfying than the solution itself. Reserving judgement, withholding negative reaction and not or using 'killer' phrases, are also very important. These skills of being open and deferring judgement are the same that are critical to successful 'brainstorming'. Encouraging self censorship is better. Asking members how they feel about their efforts and progress, rather than telling them, unless of course we feel very encouraged.

"The best way to have a good idea is to have a lot of ideas"
-Linus Pauling-   (Nobel Laureate)

THE LEADER AS A FACILITATOR

LEADING VERSUS FACILITATING

Facilitating has sometimes been described as a form of indirect of soft leadership. The core concept of facilitation means: 'To make easy' or 'To help'. It is the coordination and orchestration aspects of Leading, rather than the directing component. While a facilitator uses structure, it is more loose and flexible, so it enables people to be more participative. The structure uses non-directive, humanistic and team oriented processes. The facilitator is essentially an 'enabler' and is more process oriented. Knowledge focus is on processes and group dynamics, more than facts.

TEAM LEARNING

A facilitator places high priority on team learning and creating a climate for experiential learning. Communication is two-way and team member motivation is by overt encouragement. Assumptions underlying facilitation are that team members like to learn and grow, and are mature enough to be responsible for self leadership and self directed learning.

Based on the forgoing, leader-facilitators tend to share their power base, rather than retain it. They see group members as inter-dependent and their knowledge base is more 'inter-disciplinary'. They equally believe in shared learning and feedback and their own learning is experiential. It comes from the process of learning and growing with their team members or client.

TEAM TASK VERSUS RELATIONS

What a team has to achieve, must be clearly understood. The leader-facilitator ensures such understanding is clear, and shared by all. However, the knowledge of customer expectations – such as quality, price acceptance or delivery dates – comes often from team members, rather than the leader.

TEAM EMPOWERMENT

The leader needs to ensure that members are empowered to access critical information, and that avenues for this and all resources are open and accessible.

Finally, the clarifying of role perceptions, responsibilities, authority and autonomy must be a process that the leader can facilitate. Knowing the maturity level, personality traits and competencies of the team members and of oneself, are additional leader-facilitator accountabilities.

TASK VERSUS PROCESS

Just as management consultants can be either 'resource' focused (a content expert) or 'process' oriented, leaders can be either. The leader as a facilitator is more process oriented. Task demands come more from the client or customer, whereas processes focus on how the tasks will be achieved. Facilitators need also to strive for a balance between task, process and team relations. The process oriented leaders may also find themselves in the role of coach, trainer or mentor. These roles can help members or the team understand key processes needed to achieve the task.

"Great leadership is offering people opportunities - not obligations or rules. With freedom goes responsibility and reciprocity to those who give you freedom"   - Thoughts of Tao

GROUP DYNAMICS

GROUP DYNAMICS DEFINDED

The term dynamics means energetic movement. The study of group dynamics infers that we analyze the interactive behaviours of people within a group. We study whether they are positive, productive and energizing or negative, less productive and de-energizing. Three areas for this study are:

1) Leader – Member Interaction
2) Member – Member Interaction
3) Team to Team Interaction

While behaviour may be productive within a team, due to shared values and norms and effective leadership, there's no guarantee the same effectiveness exists in inter – team dynamics. Conflict or tensions can often occur between teams – or individual members of different teams. Usually here the leaders of each team need to use a teambuilding model to clarify perception differences and align interdepartmental values and norms.

INTERACTION PROCESS ANALYSIS (IPA)

This is used to evaluate the levels of productive behaviours between team members. Its design is based on the premise that we can observe and document behavioural interactions. Often this is done by a process consultant, but the team leader as a facilitator could do this. The difficulty may be in the ability to remain objective and impartial, as the leader can sometimes be tied up in the knots of interaction. Also, does the leader have behavioural observation skills? (Bales, 2014)

GROUP DYNAMICS TRAINING

Training in group dynamics may be necessary. Observers track the frequency and types of behaviour. These include: Questioning, Listening, Contributing, Interrupting, Agreeing, Disagreeing and Conflict. Laughter, Humour, Tension, Silence, Awkwardness, Embarrassment, Loss of Face etc. and can all be observed. Frequency of these behaviours by individual team members is documented.

CATEGORIES OF INTERACTION

When team members are jointly analyzing problems, making decisions, or planning projects, interaction and tensions can be high. This is a good time to 'stand or sit back' and record behaviours. The chart below can be useful as a check list for the type of interactions. This model consists of 12 factors, divided into two sets of orientations. A task orientation and a socio-emotional orientation.

- Task orientation Behaviours
  - Asks for: 1- Suggestions 2- Opinions 3- Information
  - Gives: 4- Suggestions 5- Opinions 6- Information
- Socio-Emotional Behaviours
  - Shows: 1- Solidarity 2- Tension Release 3- Agreement
  - Shows: 4-Antagonism 5- Tension 6- Disagreement

"Leadership is a process not a position, but principle precedes and influences processes"
Warren Bennis

WHOLE BRAIN TEAM WORK COMPETENCE

WHERE OUR BRAIN FITS IN

All behaviour is directed or controlled by our brain. One Whole Brain model shows groups thinking and feeling preferences in four modes. These are: Left or Right and Cerebral (Thinking) or Limbic (Feeling). If we study these, we can see how all the processes and competencies of teamwork are grouped according to how we prefer to think and feel.

Remember, these are merely natural preferences or learned competencies. Although our natural or innate preferences drive our behaviours, we can learn to stretch ourselves situationally. By assessing how we prefer to behave in each of the four areas, we can see where we need to develop strengths.

COMPETENCE VERSUS PREFERENCE

While the two are not the same, there is a close correlation. If we naturally prefer, or have habitually learned, to behave in a particular way, this comes to us more easily. In fact these behavioural preferences often operate at a non-conscious level. The more we do something, the faster and easier it becomes – providing we either like it – or have a strong motivation to do it. And as we do things better, we see positive consequences or results, and we may receive praise and rewards. Thus this cycle is reinforced, and our competence level increases. Where we have a lower preference or dislike for a type of behaviour, we tend to find ways to avoid this. However, we may still need to learn to apply some of the related competencies.

WHOLE BRAIN TEAM WORK

By exercising all the practises and competencies from both brain hemispheres of the whole brain model – we are developing 'Whole Brained' team work. Equally, each member or team may have a strong preference in some areas, and perhaps weaker preferences in others. By knowing members preferred styles and skills, we can help develop a high performing team, by synergising these practices and competencies.

When team members are able to apply skills and use practises they prefer, they will be more motivated and satisfied. The challenge for the leader, is not only knowing these, but ensuring the team composition is whole brain. Such teams out perform homogeneous teams, once their diversity is valued.

WHOLE BRAINED TEAMS

Organizations of more than 100 members are likely to be a more balanced composite of both hemispheres and therefore are an ideal pool from which to select homogenous and heterogeneous teams. Homogenous teams can quickly achieve a consensus of opinion and will typically respond in ways predictably consistent with their preference. Heterogeneous teams behave in entirely different ways. They experience difficulty in reaching consensus, but through synergising their diversity they are ideal for creative/innovative assignments. High-performing teams share common characteristics of key functions, such as: visualization, intensity, focus and imagination and tend to be more diverse.   *- Adapted from Ned Herrmann (1996) –*

"I used not only the brains I have, but all I can borrow" - Woodrow Wilson -

SUMMARY OF KEY POINTS

- A team has been defined as a group of committed, motivated and supportive people, working in harmony and synergy to achieve shared goals and standards.

- Effective teams have a shared mission, with goals and roles being clear. Leadership is enabling and facilitative, with high levels of communication. Dysfunctional conflict is minimal.

- The concept of socio-technical system implies a need for balance between people and technology and research shows that participative design brings about higher team effectiveness.

- Task structure, boundaries and behavioural norms are clear and accepted. Members have a wide scope of authority and feel empowered management, yet with a balance between self and external controls.

- High Performance Teams (HPT's) would be exemplified by such examples as an Astronaut crew, a Heart surgery team, a Formula one 'pit-stop' crew or a Rowing eight.

- Team building models can be divided or combined. Typically they may include: clarifying values, vision, mission, strategy, goals, roles and role negotiation. Also, interpersonal relationship and trust building, as well as team work competency development.

- Often teams need to produce higher levels of creativity and innovation. Creativity doesn't come naturally to all individuals or teams. It has to be nurtured and developed. Facilitating team creativity by the leader takes time and skill.

- Adequate resources are needed and a climate and culture of trust has to exist. Leaders need to be creative and highly participative. Structure must have both loose and tight properties and specific incentives may be useful.

- The team leader as a facilitator calls for a particular style that is more process oriented. Achieving a balance between team task and relationships, assumes members can exert a high level of self-directed learning and self-control (autonomy).

- Interaction Process Analysis (IPA) is a useful technique. It helps the team leader understand how to balance socio-emotional and task orientations. Skills in asking questions as well as in conflict management are helpful. Leaders should be familiar with group dynamics theory and dangers of "group think".

- A 'whole brained' approach to teams is very useful. High Performance Teams are likely to be more diverse and 'whole brained', more creative, but harder for the leader to 'synergise' member's talents and efforts. But once achieved, they perform better.

- Preference for use of either our left or right brain hemisphere is more natural, but not the same as competence. Leaders must develop teamwork competencies, based on both hemispheres.

"I am always ready to learn, although I do not always like to be taught"
-Sir Winston Churchill-

A Lesson from Geese

When you see geese flying along in "V" formation, you might consider what science has discovered as to why they fly that way. As each bird flaps its wings, it creates an uplift for the bird immediately following. By flying in "V" formation, the whole flock adds at least 71 percent greater flying range than if each bird flew on its own. People who share a common direction and sense of community can get where they are going more quickly and easily because they are traveling on the thrust of one another.

When a goose falls out of formation, it suddenly feels the drag and resistance of trying to go it alone — and quickly gets back into formation to take advantage of the lifting power of the bird in front. If we have as much sense as a goose, we will stay in formation with those people who are headed the same way we are.

When the head goose gets tired, it rotates back in the wing and another goose flies point. It is sensible to take turns doing demanding jobs, whether with people or with geese flying south. Geese honk from behind to encourage those up front to keep up their speed.

What messages do we give when we honk from behind? Finally — and this is important — when a goose gets sick or is wounded by gunshot, and falls out of formation, two other geese fall out with that goose and follow it down to lend help and protection. They stay with the fallen goose until it is able to fly or until it dies, and only then do they launch out on their own, or with another formation to catch up with their group.

If we have the sense of a goose, we will stand by each other, like that.

REFERENCES

Bales, R.F. (2014). *Interaction Process Analysis.* Retrieved March 5, 2014, from Bales Interaction Analyis: http://www.csudh.edu/dearhabermas/cnipa.htm

Bennis, W. (1993). *An Invented Life: Reflections on Leadership and Change.* Mass: Addison Wesley.

Emery, F., & Trist, E. (1981). *Participative Design: Evolution of Socio Technical Systems.* New York: Wiley.

Emery, F. (1969). *Systems Thinking.* UK: Penguin.

Emery, M., & Devane, T. (2010). Search Conference. In P. Holman, T. Devane, S. Cady, & Associates, *The Change Handbook: The Definitive Resource on Today's Best Methods for Engaging Whole System* (pp. 347 - 387). California: Berrett-Koehlar.

Ginnet, R.S. (1993). *Leadership : Enhancing Lessons of Experience.* New York: Richand D.Irwin.

Hackman, J.A. (1980). *Work Redesign.* Mass: Addison Wesley.

Pauling, L. (2010). *How To Live Longer and Feel Better.* Oregon: Oregon State of University.

Senge, P. (1990). *The Fifth Discipline.* New York: Double Day.

CHAPTER NINE

LEADING CHANGE

LEARNING OBJECTIVES FOR THIS CHAPTER

By the end of this chapter, you will be able to:

- Identify how different parts of the brain respond to change, so that leading change can be more 'whole brained' (Transformational)

- Assess the nature of change and some key dimensions of change.

- Recognise how levels of change can move from simple knowledge change to attitudinal, behavioural, group and more difficult organizational or societal change.

- Identify some main reasons why people resist change and examine various ways to reduce the resistance.

- Differentiate between systems versus culture change and the challenges for leaders

- Apply value based change leadership by using a systematic, step by step model.

- Contrast some classic and contemporary models of change leadership.

TABLE OF CONTENTS

WHOLE BRAIN LEADERSHIP

OUR CEREBRAL SELF
From the model of the brain in an earlier chapter, we know the brain comprises different parts. The two hemispheres of our cerebral cortex – or our 'thinking' self – include our cognitive view on change. Our left cerebral self is concerned with the 'facts' of change. This is our profit driven self, and needs proof of the benefits of change. **Here we think in terms of rational analysis.** We ask what change is needed and seek evidence to support this.

OUR RIGHT CEREBRAL SELF
Our right cerebral hemisphere is more open to change. It is curious, experimenting and risk taking. **Here we seek novelty and variety and approach change as a creative** alternative to where we are now. We ask 'why' or 'why not'? We are driven more by creating a new and exciting vision of change. This is the leader's visionary self.

OUR LIMBIC (EMOTIONAL) SELF
The lower two halves of our limbic system, house the centre for the direction and control of our emotions and plays a critical role in change. Our left limbic brain needs structure and form and tends to resist change. It is that part of us that values stability and predictability. **Here we prefer to maintain the status quo and like systems that keep us 'on track'.** It is the cautious and conservative part of management that provides support for such change that may be needed. The left side of our limbic system, which Ned Herrmann (1993) calls our 'safekeeping' self, acts as a control to the expressive and adventurous right.

OUR RIGHT LIMBIC SELF
This represents our expressed emotions and will embrace change, providing it 'feels' good. If morale is not adversely affected and we can inter-act happily with people, then change is welcome. Providing we have adequate peer support and can spend time with our family and friends, change is fine.

Here, we are value driven, and if change is aligned to our deeply felt values, we will strongly support it. Our support will be expressed emotionally. This is a key for the change leader, who must articulate the need and value of change in a sincere and emotionally strong way. Here, integrity and spirit is woven together to provide an intensity of passion for the value and need for change. This is exemplified by the magnetic style of people like Martin Luther King, John F. Kennedy or Nelson Mandela. Thus a whole brained approach to leading change will be more effective.

The right brain (especially the right cerebral hemisphere is the only part of our brain that deals effectively with change. As essential as left brain models are to business success, they spell slow death for a company when used without the right-brain modes. If change is a constant, in order to compete effectively in a world characterized by change, business managers must function in all four of the brain's different modes, right as well as left, cerebral as well as limbic. This needs to happen at all levels of management, not just at the top

(Ned Herrmann in, The Creative Brain)

"You see things, and you say 'Why?' But I dream of things that never were, and I say: Why not?" - George Bernard Shaw -

THE NATURE OF CHANGE

WHAT IS CHANGE

Webster's dictionary defines change as something: - different, altered, modified, transformed or converted – as something that is not the same as before. Living organisms go through a process of change. The cells in our body are constantly changing. Mostly these changes are positive, keeping the body healthy, fit and free of disease. Sometimes, however the changes are not for the best. We may find our immune system is weakened or attacked, and we succumb to negative and unhealthy changes. These can range from minor ailments like a cold or saw throat, to a major and potentially lethal change, like cancer.

CHANGE IS NORMAL

What is important here is that change is a normal phenomenon. Nothing remains more constant – or as the ol.d quotation goes, 'There is nothing as permanent as change' (Heraclitus: 540-475 BC). If a living organism is growing, developing and maturing, we say this is positive change. All organisms go through a natural process from birth, growth, maturation, decay and eventual death. That is the nature of the human cell, or body, but need not be the nature of a social organization. Spirit can live on and energize a social entity. Many organizations may come and go. Some become bankrupt, some are acquired or merged, but some live on for centuries and go from strength to strength. **It is their ability to adapt to their changing environment that ensures their future success**.

PERCEPTIONS ON CHANGE

Change is also a perception; we may see it as positive or negative, as too fast, slow or about right. We perceive it as great, small, simple, and complex or in between. It is subjective. As we say "One man's meat is another man's poison". One thing is certain however. It's here to stay and won't go away.

CHANGE: RAPID AND COMPLEX

What is different today is that much of the change we experience in working in an organization, is that it seems to have increased in rate and scope. Dr. Parikh (1991), a leading proponent on change leadership, coined the wonderful phrase 'Raplexity' which combines the concept of 'Rapid' and 'Complex'. We feel the impact of change daily, and it's sometimes magnified due to the media. The world is shrinking, as telecommunications and travel bring us closer together, to bring globalized change.

FUTURE SHOCK & KNOWLEDGE MANAGEMENT

Letters that once took weeks to travel by sea mail, now take only seconds by e-mail. Yet this leads to the 'future shock' syndrome or our sometimes feeling overwhelmed by, and even drowned in information. Managing change to some extent is the changing of information into knowledge. It is the digesting of only what we need, turning it into nutritious knowledge. Knowledge that is useful, value added and applied. This process has become known as Knowledge Management (KM). The leading of change must be based on sound Knowledge Management.

"Nobody can force change on anyone else. It has to be experienced. Unless we invent ways where paradigm shifts can be experienced by a critical mass, then change will be a myth "
Adapted from: Emery and Trist,
The Evolution of Socio Technical Systems

LEVELS OF CHANGE

AT THE INDIVIDUAL LEVEL

All social systems, such as work organizations, comprise individual employees as the basic building blocks. Change can be from bottom up, which starts with each of us, as an individual. Here, our cerebral or cognitive self operates at a knowledge or awareness level, knowing what change is needed and why. We need to be aware of the nature, causes and outcomes of change. Knowing the benefits of change maybe critical. On the other hand, change can be from top down also.

OUR EMOTIONAL SELF

Another level – still individual – is in our emotional self, and in the limbic system. Here, our attitudes, values, motives and drives come into play. **How strongly we believe and feel about the changes is fundamental to whether we are willing to change.** This level is more complex and difficult when it comes to change. The leader needs to gain commitment to, or ownership of, the need to change. Typically, high involvement and participation help.

THE GROUP OR TEAM LEVEL

As we move towards the next level, we would appreciate that most employees work as members of a work group or in a team. Peer pressure maybe effective where the majority are in favour of change, but this can depend upon the degree of resolve among the group minority. Even if the minority feel strongly, and resolutely opposed, or have a stro.ng personality, peer pressure may not work. In fact, sometimes such pressure produces a more stubborn resistance. **The leader must understand their team members motivations, values and attitudes towards change.**

THE ORGANIZATION LEVEL

Organizations comprise teams and individuals. A social system by itself only changes when the majority of its stake holders support the change. Leading team change is only one step. Aligning all the teams is another step. Organizational values and vision can be applied, as well as the policies, systems or structures, to support the change needed. (See 'McKinsey's 7-S model, Chapter 4).

A WHOLEBRAINED APPROACH (TRANSFORMATIONAL)

Aligning top down, with bottom up initiatives is ideal. A holistic or whole brained approach is likely to be more effective in achieving total organizational change, although it may be far more difficult and take longer. This is another major competency of the whole brained leader.

PRO-ACTIVE OR REACTIVE

There are different reactions to change. Some people are more 'pro-active', willing to change and even initiate change. Others maybe more reactive and merely waiting for or resisting change. We need to integrate both the cerebral and limbic reactions to bring about individual behavioural change. Teams may comprise a diverse mix of individuals, some wanting change and falling into the positive and 'proactive' type. Others maybe indifferent towards or even opposed to change and more the 'reactive' type.

"True freedom is not the absence of structure....but rather a clear structure that enables people to work within established boundaries in an autonomous and creative way." Rosabeth Moss Kanter, in The Change Masters.

CHANGING BEHAVIOUR

IDENTIFYING INDIVIDUAL TRAITS

If we agree that the individual building blocks of organizational change are employees, we need to further understand their make-up. Traits are predisposed to accepting or initiating change, and some traits may predispose to resistance. We have already explored some, such as whether people are optimistic and open to change, or more pessimistic and closed to change. **Knowing what the main 'resistors' are, is essential for the change leader.**

WHY WE RESIST CHANGE

Looking at reasons or common causes of resistance to change is helpful. They fall into two groups. Those that are merely due to ignorance and those that are more attitudinal. There is of course an interdependency between these, as our attitudes may actually stem from ignorance.

For example, the 'fear' of change may be as a result of a feeling of insecurity or a fear of the 'unknown' or unfamiliar. On the other hand, we may experience a psychopathic fear – such as a phobia – like fear of heights or vertigo. No amount of education will overcome this. It is as much biological as psychological. When we look down from a height – we may feel nausea or dizziness – and then panic. Usually, only treatments like hypnotherapy can cure such phobias.

COMMON CAUSES OF RESISTANCE

Other than pure ignorance, or psychological phobias, we find some resistance to organizational change relates to either personality traits or social programming. A naturally quiet, shy or introverted person may not be comfortable having to perform tasks that require a high level of social interaction. Equally, a highly social and extroverted person will not be stimulated by a job that requires them to work all alone for long periods of time. **People's tolerance for ambiguity, which is a personality trait, can help us** determine who will find the uncertainty of change acceptable or not.

SOCIAL PROGRAMMING

Where there are cultural patterns and norms, or strongly held shared values, it may be difficult to get people to shift a belief system. Just try to get people to give up white bread or rice, and we can see how difficult it can be. These are culturally entrenched habits that have become an unconscious way of life and extremely hard to change.

A STRONG MOTIVATION TO CHANGE HELPS

Try getting people to give up something they like. Even if we convince people that a plate of refined carbohydrates lack nutritional qualities and that it may contribute to obesity, diabetes and ill health, they may still find it difficult to change. Even more difficult, would be trying to get a smoker to give up cigarettes, or a religious person to renounce their faith. Some changes may seem almost impossible to bring about. Motivation to change has to be incredibly strong. Without a fundamental value shift, we may just as well give up trying to change others. Yet they are all learned beliefs or habits, which can be unlearned.

"Organizations don't change, people change. If you want your organization to do something differently, then you'll have to figure out how to get people to change their behaviour" - David B. Peterson -

SYSTEMS VERSUS CULTURE CHANGE

THE PARADOX PARADIGM

Systems, as they currently exist, may create the culture that fits, yet a culture that is driven by the system. Cultures are dynamic and not static, and changes according to the demands of internal and external environments. As those demands change, especially after crises, new policies, strategies, structure and systems are introduced.

As these new systems are imposed on an existing culture, there may be either acceptance or resistance. If the culture is open to change, the new initiatives can quickly become the norm and we evolve a new culture. They in turn become institutionalized and habitualised, further strengthening the culture. And so change continues to evolve in both systems and culture.

CHANGING THE SYSTEMS

This is more a 'management' process, and 'leadership' is not essential. Systems change is left-brained and mechanistic. There is a logic of efficiency, where controls and measures are easily established. Diagnosis involves discovering any non-alignments
between sub-systems. The non-alignments or weaknesses in the meta-system are addressed. Process re-engineering may be one example, and given the budget, expertise and time, they can be continuously introduced as a consequence of new technologies, and may be installed by outside experts.

CHANGING THE CULTURE

As culture is dynamic and organic in nature, it is less easily managed. Changes occur due to external demands, whether we want them or not. The key is to bring about the desired change. It requires the diagnosis of the values and their underlying core assumptions. Once we know these assumptions, and their sources and strengths, we can do something to channel this energy for progressive change. Here, leadership has to be value oriented. It involves transforming the core assumptions where needed.

Unless we have developed a culture of shared learning, the change process won't be competitive. Strategic planning for change is where continuous learning, skill development and systems modification are inter-dependent. Hofstede, (1986) developed a 'Theory T', which posits the adding (+) of new norms to old ones, without forcing people to give up the old. (T+) Finally, all actions need to be value driven. (Expanded on below).

HOFSTEDE'S THEORY T

Hofstede (1986) developed an interesting model of change which he called 'Theory T+'. Its basis is that: T=Tradition, and that people may resist giving up valued traditions. Instead of trying to change tradition, he suggested merely adding new values that were more productive. This he called 'T+'. We can add new ones to our repertoire, without insisting that traditional ones be given up. Once people see that new more 'productive' ways bring benefits, they will incorporate these new ways. Eventually the old ways may slowly slide down the value scale. As we do not force people to give them up, they do not stubbornly resist. When people do not see the new 'plus' values as forced upon them or as a threat to their revered ways, culture change emerges. It is evolutionary and not revolutionary.

"First, be the change that you want to see......in others." -Mahatma Gandhi-

VALUE BASED CHANGE PROCESS

VALUES BEFORE VISION

If we agree that values are at the heart of any motivation to behave, then directing any behavioural change must start with values. We need first to be aware of the degree that employee values are in alignment with those of other stakeholders. Values clarification, for all stakeholders is the first step. **Stakeholders might include: shareholders/owners, managers, union representatives or other employees and even customers or suppliers.**

The next step is to look at paradigm options that align these stakeholders. Quantum thinking uses the 'and-both' approach. Shareholders usually want profits, but long-term profits can only occur if there is also a reasonable investment in physical and human capital, not merely financial capital. **The leaders challenge is to bring about a 'win-win' paradigm that aligns individual, team and organizational values.**

A SHARED VISION

Once there is a consensus on core values and a paradigm consensus, we can move to the building of a shared vision. Again, this can only be based by consensus seeking. **Leadership needs, styles and competencies must be aligned with internal system needs**. Again, this is a type of 'Socio-Technical Systems' (STS) alignment. For example, striking a balance between the 'E-face' and 'face to face'. E-face means the Electronic-interface, such as E-Mail and talking to a computer, versus talking face to face.

VALUE ALIGNED COMPETENCIES

Value gaps must be continuously addressed to underpin the newly required competencies and behaviours. For example, if 'Integrity' is a core value, competencies or skills and appropriate behaviours must support this core value. Leaders must support this core value. **Leaders must be seen to be both 'walking their talk', as well as 'talking their walk'**. A sincerity and consistency must exist, otherwise no trust and sound relationships can be developed.

SYSTEMS/PROCESSES ALIGNMENT

Systems, structures and processes will also need to be reviewed. Gaps in internal systems must be aligned with structures. An airline system is only as good as the airports' structure or air traffic control processes. All must be well aligned. The ongoing change process can include the simple tried and tested PDCA model (Plan-Do-Check-Act), Imai (1986).

E-FACE vs FACE TO FACE
While there are obvious advantages to Electronic communication they cannot replace the biology and chemistry of human interaction. Human communication may in fact be more 'non-verbal' than verbal, more emotionally based than cerebral. A computer does not have a 'heart' (a limbic system). Values are in the limbic part of us – not our laptop and modem. Even a telephone call is preferable to an email, as it is instant two way communication, where the vocal tone and pathos can be sensed, and we get immediate feedback.

"What we need is to be able to do, is to come together with a constantly increasing mindset of wanting to do the right thing,......even though we know very well that we don't know how or where to start-". Malidoma P. Some

APPRECIATIVE INQUIRY AS A CHANGE MODEL

OVERVIEW OF APPRECIATIVE INQUIRY (AI)

Appreciative Inquiry (AI) is an Organization Development (OD) tool that was first proposed by Cooperrider and Srivasta(1998) and eventually developed by Cooperrider and Whitney with the Taos Institute. (1998) In British English, the word ' Inquiry', starts with an 'E' (Enquiry). However, here we will use 'Inquiry'. Whitney says that AI is based on the philosophy that an organization changes in the direction of study. **It is based on enhancing organizational effectiveness by focusing on what one wants more of**, rather than on what one wants less of. Hence it approaches organizations from the point of what works rather than scrutinizing what is broken and needs to be fixed. Cooperrider and Whitney (Ibid) state that AI involves asking questions that strengthen an organization's capacity to apprehend, anticipate and heighten its positive potential. It is a 'positive change' technology. **The leader becomes a positive catalyst.**

AI AS AN ADVENTURE

AI is an organization change process that can include hundreds and thousands of an organization's members to bring about change. AI is an adventure, as claimed by Cooperrider and Whitney that because organizations are centres of human relationships and connections, such relationships can only thrive when people see the best in each other and/or in the organization and affirm these rather than playing the blame game, as typical OD techniques are often accused of. **Therefore, AI from a pragmatic perspective is a data based technique, for developing and practicing the collective will of an organization.**

TRACKING AND FANNING

As a change technique the appreciative process involves tracking and fanning. Tracking is when one is constantly looking for what one wants more of and fanning is any action that stimulates, enhances and assists in obtaining what we want. Since AI is a paradigm shift in OD, it needs a change of attitude from the default mode of being critical and providing corrective feedback. In order to implement AI, we need to be mindful that AI must be seen from a radical point of view, instead of a conventional OD technique, or it will not be transformational.

Bushe and Kassam (2005) report that since 2001. AI has undergone significant research The number of companies employing this technique has increased exponentially. An examination of one AI consultant's website in the US, indicates that the industries that have used AI fall into the following categories; restaurants, NGO's, health clinics and centres, universities and colleges, government institutions, automotive suppliers, information and technology and nursing homes.

AN 8 STEP LEADING CHANGE MODEL (Cotter, 1996)

S T E P S	1 Establish a Sense of Urgency	2 Form a Powerful Guiding Coalition	3 Develop a Compelling Vision and Strategy	4 Communicate Vision Widely	5 Empower Employees to Act on Vision	6 Generate Short-Term Wins	7 Keep-up the Urgency. Tackle Problems	8 Make the Changes

SOME SITUATIONS OF AI EFFECTIVENESS:

- Reducing sick leave, reducing work errors and improving interpersonal relationships at a hospital, thus being useful as a tool for mentoring, appraisals and personal development.
- Accelerating the professional development of a large sales force at a consumer goods company working together as a cohesive team to meet or exceed their sales targets.
- Developing collaboration between a university and a high school that improved the examination scores of the high school's students.
- Improving morale of a homogeneous Arab Muslim organization in a Middle East oil refinery
- Strategically managing first line managers to be more effective in their leadership.

A POSITIVE MODEL FOR VISIONARY CHANGE

The positive model focuses on what the organization is doing right. It helps members understand their **organization when it is working at its best** and builds on those capabilities for even better results. This positive approach to change is consistent with a growing movement in the social sciences called 'positive organizational scholarships'. Considerable research on expectation effects also supports this model of planned change.

It shows that people tend to act in ways that make their expectations occur. Thus, positive expectations about the organization can create an anticipation that energizes and directs behaviour toward making those beliefs happen.

AI encourages a positive orientation to how change is conceived and managed. It promotes broad member involvement in creating a shared vision about guiding the organization's positive potential. **That shared appreciation provides a powerful and guiding image on what the organization could be.**

THE FIVE PHASES OF AI

Drawing heavily on AI, the positive model of planned change involves five phases as follows: -

1. **Initiate the Inquiry**. The first phase determines the subject of change. It emphasizes member involvement to identify the organizational issue they have the most energy to address. For example, members can choose to look for successful male-female collaboration (as opposed to sexual discrimination). Instances of customer satisfaction, particularly effective work teams, or product development processes that brought new ideas to market especially fast. If the focus of inquiry is real and vital to the organization's members, the change process itself will take on these positive attributes.

THE A1 SIMPLE 4 STAGE PROCESS

1. DISCOVERY   2. DREAM/ IMAGINE   3. DESIGN   4. DESTINY

2. **Inquiry into Best Practices**. This phase involves gathering information about the 'best of what is' in the organization. If the topic is organizational innovation, then members help to develop an interview protocol that collects stories of new ideas from the organization's members. They interview each other and tell stories of innovation in which they have personally been involved. **These stories are pulled together to create a pool of information describing the organization as an innovative system.**

3. **Discover The Themes**. In this third phase, members examine the stories, both large and small, to identify a set of themes representing the common dimensions of people's experiences. For example, the stories of innovation may contain themes about how managers gave people the freedom to explore a new idea, the support organization's members received from their co-workers, or how the exposure to customers sparked creative thinking. **No theme is too small to be represented**; it is important that all underlying mechanisms that helped to generate and support the themes be described. The themes represent the basis for moving from 'what is' to 'what could be'.

4. **Envision a Preferred Future**. Members then examine the identified themes, challenge the status quo, and describe a compelling future. Based on the organization's successful past, members collectively visualize the organization's future and develop 'possibilities propositions' – statements that bridge the organization's current best practices with ideal possibilities for future organizing. **These propositions should present a truly exciting, provocative and possible picture of the future**. Based on these possibilities, members identify the relevant stakeholders and critical organization processes that must be aligned to support the emergence of the envisioned future. **The vision becomes a statement of 'what should be'.**

5. **Design and Deliver Ways to Create the Future**. The final phase involves the design and delivery of ways to create the future. It describes the activities and creates the plans necessary to bring about the vision. It proceeds to action and assessment phases similar to those of action research. **(Act. Reflect. Modify. Act) Members make changes, assess the results, make necessary adjustments**, and so on as they move the organization toward the vision and **sustain 'what will be'**. The process is continued by renewing the conversations about the best of what is.

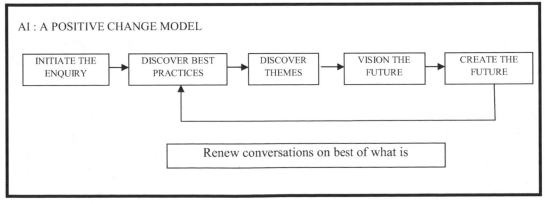

AI : A POSITIVE CHANGE MODEL

| INITIATE THE ENQUIRY | DISCOVER BEST PRACTICES | DISCOVER THEMES | VISION THE FUTURE | CREATE THE FUTURE |

Renew conversations on best of what is

SOME USEFUL DIAGNOSTIC MODELS

As change is a permanent phenomenon, using various models can always help. And as the speed and complexity of change are growing, such models can be even more useful. From classic works like the 'Change Masters' by Rosabeth Moss Kanter (1983) to 'Blur', by Davis & Meyer (1998) with the concept of 'speed of change in the connected economy, or 'Blink' by Malcolm Gladwell (2005). All put forward profound ideas on the challenges for those who lead change today. Such leaders, many of whom are too busy to read such brilliant works, perhaps can benefit from a short overview of some change models. **There can be three basic types, diagnostic, and curative or preventative.**

FORCE FIELD ANALYSIS (FFA)

Kurt Lewin (1974) was a pioneer in behavioural change and developed on effective diagnostic model called 'Force Field Analysis' (FFA). Simply, one identifies the change goal(s) and then, often though brainstorming, comes up with a list of those forces that are **restraining and inhibiting** the organization from change. Opposing or positive forces that are **driving change** are then identified. It is assumed there is disequilibrium, but as long as the forces 'for' are stronger – or greater in number – change can be made. **The strategy is to minimize the restraining forces and maximize the enabling forces (mini-max).**

In Kanter's (Ibid) Change Masters book, she identified five forces that can increase an organizations capacity to deal with change. These were: **A) Departures from Tradition, B) When an event, like a crisis, galvanizes change. C) Strategic Decisions to Change. D) Identify the 'Prime Movers'** (those with the power) who are often in a leadership position. **E) Action Vehicles**. Like strategy maps, that ensure the change is 'Institutionalized'.

Kurt Lewin (Ibid) also puts forward a model called '**Unfreezing-Changing-Refreezing**', just like if we want to change the shape of an 'ice cube' to an 'iceball'. We remove cubes from the fridge, melt the water, pour into a mold of ball shapes and refreeze. However, it then poses the question – who will do this**? Lewin found the participative process worked best, when all the stakeholders 'buy-in' to the change processes.** However, many current change agents believe 'speed of change' now is too fast for this model to be as useful as it was. But it can still be a useful model.

KAIZEN (Ky'zen)

During the quality revolution of the 80's, the Japanese evolved a series of techniques to continuously improve processes. Kaizen literally means 'improvement' with emphasis on continuing improvement everywhere, in personal life as well as work life. It is actually a total philosophy, rather than a model and the word was trademarked by the Kaizen Institute, (Imai, 1986). Kaizen incorporates a wide range of change techniques, especially in the use of Statistical Quality Control (SQC). The more widely used include: Cross Functional Management, The Kamban System (often called 'Just-In-Time, or JIT). The Deming Cycle or Wheel and SDCA Cycle (Standardize, Do, Check, Act) or its 'sister', the PDCA Cycle (Plan, Do, Check, Act). TPM (Total Preventative Maintenance), QC & QA and TQC (Total Quality Control). Many of the techniques were used by Quality Control Circles (QCC) which later evolved into Quality Assurance (QA) and Quality Improvement Teams (QIT). They are still in wide use today for Change Improvement, especially in Manufacturing.

LEADERSHIP IMPLICATIONS FROM O.D.

In French, et al (2005) in their writings on Organization Development and Transformation (ODT), Marvin Weisbord states how important this early work of Emery and Trist became, as historically the turning points, and new building blocks for enlightened change leadership. He says "The leaders he has learned most from seem to have a knack. They focus attention on worthy aspiration and mobilize energy by involving others. (Weisbord, 1992).

Alvin Toffler (1980) the pioneer futurist, who wrote 'Future Shock', in 1980, also produced a book called the 'Third Wave' as well as 'The Adaptive Organisation'. From his writings, as well as Weisbord (1992), came the conditions required for 3rd Wave" change. **Condition 1, is 'Committed Leadership' and Condition 2, 'Energised People'**. Useful practices also includes 'getting the whole system' together which teaches leaders to view both 'inside' and 'outside' pictures of the Socio-Technical and Economic Systems. Then focus on the future. This gave rise to the positive power of 'futuring' and the role of visioning. This is why, even today, great leadership recognizes the importance of visioning as an inspirational and motivational tool. Charles Garfield, author of Peak Performers (1986) introduced the power of 'imaging the possible' and 'feeding forward', rather than 'feedback'. That is why the technique of 'Appreciative Inquiry' (AI) has been introduced into this chapter.

STRATEGIES FOR DELIBERATE CHANGE

Views of enlightenment and many findings from social research, can be summed up as a 'Rational-Empirical' approach and include: **1) Universal Educational Opportunities, 2) Applied Research and its Diffusion**. Further strategies developed from early therapists, like Freud, would include **'Normative Re-educative'** approaches. Here, techniques like, non rational, psycho-social or Industrial Psychology, now usually called 'Organizational Behaviour'(OB), are applied. A third approach would include the **'Power-Coercive' model**, which involves political strategies, where those with a strong power base, might institutionalize the changes.

From a perspective of the earlier behavioural and participative techniques, such as FFA, STS, KAIZEN and AI, **the Normative Re-educative** approaches probably work best when related to human motivation.

THE PDCA CYCLE

PLAN ⟶ **DO** ⟶ **CHECK** ⟶ **ACT**

"A leader is one who knows the way, goes the way and shows the way"
John Maxwell

BALANCED SCORED CARD: A CHANGE OF SYSTEM

One of the more holistic or total systems change strategies, is called the 'Balanced Score Card' (BSC). While it is an effective system for measuring specific important criteria, it has been found to be very tedious and quantitative, thus highly resistant to many leaders and managers. It maybe thought of as a 'quick' fix, but in reality it requires a **lot of measurement, in 4 areas, that ideally should balance**. BSC has been used in strategic leadership on either the whole organisation or in Human Resource Management (HRM). It can also be conveniently divided into our 'Whole Brain'
Model (See below).

Essentially there are 4 dimensions on a grid, and each should balance. Picture it as a 4 point compass. The **'North'** point represents financial performance or an internal business perspective. High scores here would indicate profits and financial performance. This is where shareholders returns or overall ROI would be measured. The other end, the **'South'** point – represents external factors like how customers see the organisation, such as customer loyalty and satisfaction. On the **'East'** point would be where innovation, learning and development are measured. Opposite to this would be the **'West'** point, representing business processes and decisions made on customer satisfaction processes – such as quality or meeting delivery of products or services.

This system was the content of books and articles by Kaplan and Norton (2000). To view it **from the Whole Brain perspective, North and West points would require left brain thinking**. (Finance, ROI and Business Processes). **The East and South would require right brain thinking** (and feeling), where innovating learning and development, and employee satisfaction, would be assessed. These series of metrics become a 'score card' with an ideal of all being balanced. When data is audited and provided to management, it becomes a very objective technology for change.

The Balanced Score Card "Compass"

A balance in all four dimensions produces a Whole Brain Perspective.

INNOVATION AS A COMPETITIVE FORCE

CREATIVE THINKING

In changing the organisation, to not only meet the future, but create it, leaders need to facilitate creative thinking and innovation. Innovation in both processes, products or services give leaders, the competitive edge. **Creative thinking is an 'input'**, variably associated with 'lateral thinking' (De Bono, 1992) or 'thinking outside of the box' (Parnes, 1957). **It is a right brain process** and requires a leadership style that promotes a climate that fosters experimentation, risk taking, tinkering and even, making mistakes. Not all leaders are comfortable with such behaviour or with leading a very open culture and climate, but entrepreneurial leaders usually are.

Innovation on the other hand is the production of something new, not the idea, but something tangible that adds value to the organization. If it is a product, it must still be manufactured at a cost that customers are willing to pay. The term **'open innovation'** has been used for those who include customers, strategic partners or alliances, suppliers or others who can contribute to the innovation effort. Leaders of innovation must still balance the creative input processes, with the **innovation output.** This calls for a certain amount of optimism, tempered with patience. It really calls for a 'Whole Brain' approach of approximately **40% left and 60% right brain thinking.**

There can be exceptions, if one is a **'Technopreneur'**, then a lot of teamwork will be more technical or technological, but the leader need not be so technical .
(see: www.credotrust.org for an entrepreneurial leadership traits assessment).

BENCHMARKING INNOVATION

Benchmarking requires measuring the quantum of innovation from competitors, which can be very difficult when their new products may not be revealed until they reach market. So one area to win a competitive edge is **in marketing, advertising, selling** and customer service. This is another form of innovative leadership of change. Continuously changing to get a competitive edge with consumers. This is where open innovation and closeness to customers plays a role.

LEADING CREATIVITY

Another change leadership edge, will be the leadership and motivation of creative people. As they tend to be very open, curious, imaginative, confident, independent, intuitive and spontaneous, it calls for a very special leadership approach. Leaders will of course need to be open, receptive and patient, and they cannot take their eye off the end mission. In many ways, **leaders who are competent in facilitation, will find they can excel with highly creative people**. While they don't need to be so creative themselves, they must facilitate a climate and culture that allows for high creativity. This implies that hierarchy or too much structure, bureaucratic red tape or rules must either be minimized or the employees be protected from such inhibitory forces. This is where 'parallel' structures can be useful, such as putting together a separate task force or project team, often with members from across the organization (a diagonal slice). They may also have a different leader, perhaps on a rotational basis – or a 'champion' who becomes the leader.

SPEED OF CHANGE IN THINKING

How do we keep up with the speed of change? Can we actually think faster? Of course the answer is YES! In Malcolm Gladwell's book 'Blink: The Power of Thinking Without Thinking, - he talks about choices that appear to be made in an instant – in the 'Blink of an Eye'(2005). He maintains that **great decision makers are those that have perfected the art of "thin slicing",** or knowing the very few things that matter. It is relying on a balance between deliberate left brain thinking and trusting our right brain intuitive or instinctive thoughts. Such fast thoughts, as Daniel Kahneman (2010) says, are not 'empty' thoughts. **Our non conscious right brain is a store house of all our memories and experiences.** When challenged with new clues, especially non verbal clues like a facial expression, body movement or posture or another person's eyes blinking or avoidance of eye contact, it searches instantly for patterns and actually makes 'well informed' decisions. That is the power of intuition, which is, 'knowing' something, without recognizing why.

Neither 'fast or slow' thinking is right or wrong, it is more situationally how we choose one or the other .When we don't have a lot of information, or the time for analysis, we are forced to make snap judgements and trust our instincts.(Fast – Right BrainedThinking).

There is some neuroscientific evidence for the power of the connectivity of information (new stimuli, past memories and emotions). Antonio Damasio (1994) a famous neurologist discovered that a part of our brain, the ventro medial pre-frontal cortex plays a critical role in decision making. This part of the brain is like a giant clearing house for all types of clues, observations, perceptions and both rational and emotional data. **But when that part is damaged, it can't make full and meaningful connections** between our conscious and non conscious brain. This actually slows thinking and can prevent a 'whole brain' approach to making instant, fast or even ponderous decisions.

So, in coping with the speed of change or thinking faster than the change, we need to be aware that we are constantly searching, observing and processing information. Thousands of bits of information, often subliminally, is entering our brain every second. (sights, smells, sounds especially) and our non conscious brain is storing and classifying it. **And a good night's sleep helps consolidate this data** and that's why we often go to sleep with a problem on our mind, and wake up with a perfect answer. Or even, when we can't remember a name, and we switch our attention to something else, only to find the name 'pops up' when we 'least expect it!.'

SLOW THINKING
(Left Brain Hemisphere)
- Conscious, Alert and Awake
- Analytic, Detailed
- Quantitative
- Verbal
- Deliberational

FAST THINKING
(Right Brain Hemisphere)
- Non Conscious
- Whole Picture/Synthesis
- Qualitative
- Non-Verbal
- Instant/Intuitive

SUMMARY OF KEY POINTS

- Change can be led by using the 'Whole Brain' model. Here we can apply right brained leadership, using vision and values to excite people. Left brain techniques have to do with cost-benefits, rational analysis, systems and structural support.
- Change has been defined as newness, transition, transformation or how things are different than before. Change is a natural organic process. All living things change.
- The speed and complexity of such change is what makes the leadership of this more challenging. Change can be mixed in continuous or discontinuous parallel modes. It can be simple or complex, slow or fast, small or big, welcome or resisted.
- People welcome or resist change based on their perception of the change and possible consequences. People's perceptions can also differ, depending on their personality, gender, age, values needs/wants or culture.
- Change can be divided into a number of levels, from a lower simple, to a higher more difficult level. At the lower level, we have knowledge and awareness, followed by feelings or emotions. Then at less simple levels, individuals and group behaviour, and finally at the more difficult higher level, organizational/societal change.
- We resist change for a number of reasons. These may include lack of knowledge or skill: values and attitudes; psycho-social factors, such as phobias or social programming and; personality factors like low tolerance for ambiguity or high safety-security needs.
- Change can be analyzed from either a 'systems', or a 'culture' perspective. Systems change is more easily introduced and sustained. Culture change is harder and here leadership is crucial.
- Leading change requires that shared values, vision and competencies must all be aligned. The benefits of change must be collectively perceived by all stakeholders. Leadership styles, systems, structure and processes must also be aligned.
- The positive change model of Appreciative Inquiry (AI) is one visionary approach, where shared effective practices can be used.
- Some models for diagnosing the need for, or types of, change, include Force Field Analysis, Kaizen and the Balanced Score Card.
- There are leadership implications for Organization Development (OD) change interventions , like deliberate change strategies such as innovation and creativity.
- Speed of change requires a balanced whole brain approach in terms of 'fast and slow' thinking as well as between rational and emotional factors.

REFERENCES

Bushe, G.R. & Kassam, A.F. (2005). When is Appreciative Inquiry Transformational. San Fransisco: Berrett & Koehlar.

Cooperrider, D.L. & Srivista. (1987). Appreciative in Enquiry : Organisation in Life. San Fransisco: Berrett & Koehlar.

Cooperrider, D.L.& Whitney, D. (1998). Appreciative Inquiry : A Positive Revolution In Change. San Francisco: Berrett & Koehlar.

Cotter, J. (1996). Leading Change. Boston: HBR Press.

Damasio, A. (1994). Descartes Error : Emototion,Reason,and the Human Brain. NY: Putnam, New York.

Davis, S. and Meyer, C. (1998). Blur-The speed of change in the connected economy. USA: Warner Books, Reading.

De Bono, E. (1992). Serious Creativity: Using The Power of Lateral Thinking. NY: Harper Business.

Devane, T. (1999). The Change Handbook . San Francisco: Berrett-Koehlar.

Emery, F. & Trist E. (1981). Evolution of Socio-Technical System. Toronto : Ontario QWL Centre.

French, W. (2005). Organization Development and Transformation. NY: McGraw Hill.

Garfield, C. (1986). Peak Performers. NY: William Morrow and Co.

Gladwell, M. (2005). Blink:The Power of Thinking Without Thinking. NY: Time Warner Books.

Herrmann, N. (1993). The Creative Brain. USA: Herrmann Group.

Hofstede, G. (1986). Culture Consequences. Beverly Hills: CA:Sage.

Imai, M. (1986). Kaizen. NY: McGraw-Hill.

Kahneman, D. (2011). Thinking, Fast and Slow. London: Penguin Books.

Kanter, R. (1983). The Change Masters. NY: Simon and Schuster.

Kaplan, R.S. and Norton, D.P. (2000). Having Trouble with Your Strategy? Map it. Boston: Harvard Business Review.

Lewin, K. (1951). Field Theory in Social Science. NY: Harper & Row.

Parikh, J. (1991). Managing Yourself. London: Blackwell Publishers

Parnes, S. (1957). Creative Problem Solving. NY: Buffalo.

Schon, D. (1971). Beyond The Stable State. NY: Random House.

Toffler, A. (1980). The Third Wave. London: Bantam Books.

Weisbord, M. (1980). Discovering Common Ground. San Fransisco: Berrett & Koehlar.

TABLE OF CONTENTS

CHAPTER TEN

LEADING A LEARNING ORGANIZATION

LEARNING OBJECTIVES FOR THIS CHAPTER

By the end of this chapter, you will be able to:

- Describe more about the nature of a learning organization.

- Identify the key values, norms, policies and strategies for developing a learning culture.

- Contrast between group dynamics and team learning.

- Differentiate between some earlier and more recent theories of organizational learning.

- Clarify some key ways to ensure learning is shared.

- Recognize the characteristics of a learning organization, a learning society and the role of Knowledge Management.

- Evaluate a range of individual learning principles that are helpful in becoming a "Learning Leader".

THE ORGANIZATION AS A LEARNING CULTURE

LEARNING ORGANIZATIONS DEFINED.
"Organizations where people continually expand their capacity to create results they desire. Where new and expansive patterns of thinking are nurtured, where collective aspiration is set free, and where people are continually learning how to learn together" (Peter Senge, 1990) and "The ability to learn faster than your competitors" (Arie De Geus: Royal Dutch Shell)

Two important points – First is empowerment, where every individual has decision-making power within an organization. The second aspect is, that everyone shares knowledge of, and concern for the organization in its entirety

Each employee has to understand the whole organization and to share a vision of where it's going. **In a learning organization, everyone takes responsibility for helping the organization achieve its vision.**

INDIVIDUALS AND ORGANIZATIONS
Individual learning occurs as people acquire knowledge through education, training, experience or experimentation. Organizational learning occurs as the systems and the culture in the organization retain learning and transfer ideas to individuals. This learning is shared throughout the organization and survives the turnover of staff.

Senge (1990) lists 3 levels, with level 3 being the ideal;

Three Levels:
1) **First level – an organization has a kind of memory**. It learns processes, then puts them into procedures and keeps them going i.e. phenomenon of bureaucracy. Any organization that achieves that performance has learnt at least to remember a procedure and to be able to repeat it.
2) **Second level – organizations are adapting systems**. They manage to change and adapt to meet the changing demands of markets, economics, etc. which determine their survival. They are "self-interested" and the outcome of their learning is their survival. This can lead to exploitation of customers, clients, employees, suppliers, resources, etc.
3) **Third level – organizations develop their contexts** and make their own world better for them to live in and contribute to. They assist the development and enrichment of the organization's stakeholders, resources, trading partners etc.

DOUBLE LOOP LEARNING
Double loop learning re-evaluates the nature of objectives and values and beliefs underlying them and involves changing the culture. This occurs when there is a double feedback loop which connects the detection of error not only to strategies and assumptions for effective performance, but also to the very norms which define effective performance. It is when alignment takes place between incompatible organizational norms and new priorities and weightings of norms. It may include restricting the norms themselves together with associated strategies and assumptions.

"Learning Organizations discover how to tap people's commitment and capacity to learn - at all levels in the organization". - Adapted from Peter Senge - The 5th Discipline

CHALLENGES FOR A LEARNING ORGANIZATION

CAPACITY FOR CHANGE AND COMPETITIVENESS

- Globalization, higher customer expectations, greater competitive pressures, shorter cycle times – each signal **a need to work differently.**
- With a more rapid pace of change, **organizations that cannot adapt** in technology and service may fall behind become bound by tradition and fail. There are many examples of organizations firms that have not changed or adapted.
- The ability to adapt quickly stems from **an ability to learn,** i.e. the ability to assimilate new ideas and to transfer those ideas to action faster than a competitor.

Without mental and physical dexterity, a company will fail to recognize changing customer expectations, remain with existing product lines and remain unresponsive to their competitor's initiatives.

ORGANIZATIONAL LEARNING

In order for organizational learning to occur, we need to ask the following questions:

- Do individuals detect an outcome which matches or mismatches the expectations derived from their images and maps of organizational theory-in-use? (Argyris and Schon, 1978)
- Do they carry out an enquiry which yields discoveries, inventions and evaluations pertaining to organizational strategies and assumptions?
- Do these results become embodied in the symbols and practices employed for purposes such as policies and control systems?
- Do employees subsequently act from these symbols so as to carry out new organizational practices?
- Can employees change symbols and organizational practices so they're aligned and systematized and remain unaffected by employee turnover?
- Do employees know how they each learn best, learn continuously and share their wisdom? (Implicit or Tacit knowledge)
- Do new employees view these features of their organization's 'theory- in-use' as part of their socialization to the organization?

If the answers to all these questions are "Yes", then both double loop and deutero learning are occurring.

DEUTRO-LEARNING
There is also a 2nd order learning, which is about learning how to learn. When an organization engages in deutro-learning, its members learn about organizational learning, i.e. how to carry out single and double loop learning. Learning how to learn focuses on learning styles, use of multiple intelligences and multi-sensory, whole-brained and accelerative learning strategies. Due to today's time and cost competitiveness, reducing the learning cycle time has become an important strategy.
-Argyis and Schon, 1978-

"When there is a genuine vision, people excel and learn, not because they are told to, but because they want to". - Peter Senge -

SENGE'S FIVE DISCIPLINES

In relation to one's responsibility to help the organization achieve its vision, let's review Senge's five disciplines of a learning organization.(Senge,1990)

WHAT ARE THE DISCIPLINES
There are five core disciplines to a learning organization. They are:

- Personal mastery
- Systems thinking
- Team learning
- Shared vision
- Mental models

Personal mastery is the discipline of continually clarifying and deepening our **personal vision** of focusing our energies, of developing patience, and of seeing reality objectively.

The second discipline of a learning organization is **systems thinking**. It is a conceptual framework, a body of knowledge and tools to make the full patterns clearer, and to help us see how to change them effectively.

The third discipline of a learning organization is **team learning**. This discipline of team learning starts with dialogue. The practice of dialogue has been preserved in many "primitive" cultures.

Team learning is vital because teams, and individuals, are the fundamental learning units in modern organizations. The organization cannot learn, unless teams can learn.

Fourth, the practise of **shared vision** involves the skills of sharing a 'picture of the future'. There is a need for genuine commitment of all members in organizations. But many leaders have personal visions that never get translated into shared visions that galvanize an organization.

What had been lacking, is a discipline for translating individual vision into shared vision, which are a set of principles and guiding practices. To master this discipline, leaders need to learn the counter productiveness of trying to dictate a vision.

Fifth are **Mental models**. These are deeply held assumptions, generalizations, or even symbols or images that influence how we understand the world and how we take action. Very often, we are not consciously aware of our mental models or their effects on our behaviour. Unless the value and importance of shared learning is reinforced and rewarded – it is at best likely to be haphazard, erratic and inconsistent.

Argyris and Schon (1978), early pioneers in the concept of a learning organization, put forward this idea, which is as true today as it was then. They stress the paradoxical nature of the relationship between individual and organizational learning. Individual learning is an important, necessary condition of organizational learning. On the other hand, the organization is capable of learning independently of each, though not of all individuals. Evidently, an organization learns through its individual members and is therefore somehow influenced by individual and team learning.

"A learning organization is an organization that is skilled in creating, acquiring and transferring knowledge and at modifying its behaviour to reflect knowledge and insight"   - Garvin, 1993 -

GROUP AND TEAM LEARNING

ROLES AND RESPONSIBILTIES

A group is like a mini society. In a society people take on roles of shopkeeper, homemarker, teacher, manager or leader, etc. and these roles have different effects on different people in terms of learning. Responsibilities will include both those of group members or leader. In a group, the responsibilities may develop and change over time but they all contribute to the functioning of the group learning. The responsibilities of the leader include:

- **Providing a shared cognitive set of information between group members.**
- **Motivating group members to learn and share their learning.**
- **Ensuring that group members also construct their own knowledge.**
- **Providing formative feedback**
- **Developing social and group skills necessary for success in the group.**
- **Promoting positive interaction between members of different cultural and socio-economic groups. Ensuring other group member's diversity is understood and managed, including ethnic, gender, age and personality differences.**

Group roles are not static and permanent. The length of time members spend in the group allows them to develop their talents in different ways. Therefore, they may rotate their roles depending on the circumstances.

This not only provides a relief for one person playing one role (which may not always be played effectively) it enhances the multi skilling of members.

GROUP versus TEAM LEARNING

Group learning has become an important element in Organization Development (O.D) where it is organized according to the group size and its own structure and roles.
The transfer of learning experiences **between the group members (intra-group) and between other groups (inter-group)** is a key ingredient here. Creating the ideal environment for effective learning in a group and team is as important as ensuring that individual learning takes place.

What must be clarified here, is **that a group is not the same as a team**. A group can be individuals working together, but not interdependently. A team is when members know each other's roles, responsibilities, personalities and competence, and need to work synergistically. They depend upon each other for both individual and group results.

THE MYTH OF THE MANAGEMENT TEAM

Most of the time, teams in business tend to spend their time fighting for 'territory' (power or influence) and avoiding anything that will make them look bad personally. To keep up the image, they seek to squelch disagreement. People with serious reservations avoid stating them publicly, and joint decisions are compromises that everyone can live with. If there is a disagreement, it's usually expressed in a way that lays blame, polarizes opinion, and hides the underlying differences in assumptions in a way that the whole team could learn. This prevents people from learning.

"A mistake is evidence that a person tried to do something".–Anon-

DESCRIBING A KNOWLEDGE SOCIETY

Let's start by clarifying there is a hierarchy, from data, information, understamding, knowledge (from experience and learning), to finally wisdom. But a never-ending activity in human life. The process to wisdom begins with a compilation of data and information. The output of this process is called knowledge. **One will only achieve wisdom through knowledge**. However the knowledge needs to be accurate, relevant and timely.

A KNOWLEDGE SOCIETY
A knowledge society is a continuously developing society, building on the foundation of the information society in a never-ending **iterative** manner.

Basically, the knowledge society will resemble a **kaleidoscopic** environment as the different sources of information are integrated into the society as a whole. Individuals are recognized as the major sources of the knowledge society. **It is they who translate data into information and then into knowledge.**

AN ONGOING PROCESS
This process will never stop, as people will always identify new ideas or information to learn and analyze. Since the resources are available everywhere, what is needed is **the credibility of people to identify the usefulness of the resources**. Then the next process will be the selection of the right information required for the support and implementation of the knowledge society.

Let's further examine the relationship between knowledge and a knowledge society. Individuals are recognized as being knowledgeable in certain fields when they have achieved a concrete foundation in the **subject**, and at the same time maintain an understanding of the leading developments and improvements in that field.

COLLECTIVITY OF KNOWLEDGE
A knowledge socicty, therefore only exists when this **collectivity of individual knowledge is shared**, so that **society learns**. We then also have a **learning society** (This is the basis for a learning organization where employee knowledge is shared).

Let's move on to the basic thought relating to knowledge. Information alone does not provide knowledge or **wisdom**. Attaining wisdom implies more than learning facts and scoring well on multiple-choice exams! It is applied knowledge in action.

Drucker, in his describing the Post-Capitalist Society asserts that knowledge is always embodied in a person; carried by a person; created, augmented, or improved by a person; applied by a person; taught and passed on by a person; used or misused by a person. He believes that the shift to the knowledge society puts the person in the centre. The computer or library is merely a source for accessing the information or data. Only when people process, understand and use the information can we say they have acquired knowledge.

THE HIERACHY: From Data → Information → Understanding → Knowledge → Wisdom

"Real knowledge is to know the extent of one's ignorance". -Confucious-

DESCRIBING A KNOWLEDGE ECONOMY

KNOWLEDGE ECONOMY DEFINED

According to the UK Department of Trade and Industry (1998), a knowledge economy is one in which the generation and exploitation of knowledge play a **predominant** part in the creation of wealth. In this context, the two important elements involved are **people and knowledge**. People are responsible for generating and exploiting the knowledge for a creation of a knowledge society.

A knowledge economy is often related to high-technology industries such as financial services and telecommunications. Contrary to popular beliefs, it actually covers all aspects of human resource management (HRM) and development (HRD), the work environment, and knowledge management. As a result, the **synergy between human intelligence and technology,** has produced better outcomes in human wealth and economic development.

TYPES OF KNOWLEDGE

These include:

- **Know-what**, or knowledge about facts.
- **Know-why** is knowledge about the natural world, society, and the human mind.
- **Know-who** refers to the world of social relations and is knowledge of who knows what and who can do what. (Here, social networking, helps)
- **Know-where and know-when** are becoming increasingly important in a flexible and dynamic economy, especially with globalization.
- **Know-how** refers to skills, the ability to do things on a practical level.

There is no alternative way to prosperity except to make *learning and knowledge-creation* of prime importance.

KNOWLEDGE CREATION

Wars have been won or lost on correct and timely knowledge. In a 'marketing war' – we need knowledge of how a competitor operates, or when they will launch a new product, or pricing strategy. All are useful in making commercial or marketing decisions.

The knowledge industry will build on the **integration of selected resources of the other industries** that support the information society. This effort can be seen through the creation of the knowledge economy tools such as computers, tablets, smart phones, TV, telephone and the influx of the entertainment industry into the information society arena. These tools then, witness the knowledge economy existence by bringing many efforts and moulding them into true knowledge development.

*Neo-classical economics has recognized two factors of production in economics; labour and capital. However, Romer (1990) proposed a change to this model by seeing technology and knowledge as an **intrinsic** part of the economic system. According to Romer, knowledge has become the third factor of production in leading economies after labour and capital. While Knowledge is the basic form of capital, Romer, adds new technology as a platform for economic growth and a factor for investment. Investment is also a key for economic growth, especially in R&D.*

"Knowledge Management is common sense, but not common practice". - Rob van der Spek, m CIBIT

A LEARNING AND LEARNED SOCIETY

There are two types of societies: 'Learning' society and 'Learned' society.
- A **'learning' society** - is one that is oriented with processes to ensure **continuous learning** of knowledge, skills and productive values.
- A **'learned' society** - while it still involves learning also includes its **educated, skilled and wise members** sharing their learning, experience and wisdom, widely.

A LEARNING SOCIETY

A learning society is one in which learners adopt a learning approach to life, drawing on a wide range of resources to enable them to support their lifestyle practices. The usefulness of education and training becomes a guiding criterion.

While many of the drives to learn are needed for existence, and for individualistic egoism and self-fulfillment, the emphasis is on the self and short term. It includes "self mastery", but the values may not be so noble or long-term, in relation to society's well being.

CHARACTERISTICS OF A LEARNING SOCIETY

- **Commitment to support learning**
- **Learning for living and work**
- **Equitable access to learning**
- **Learning mobility**
- **Commitment to update knowledge**

A LEARNED SOCIETY

Next, let's study the second type of learning societies, a 'learned' society. A large number of learned societies were founded between World War 1 and World War II. Founded during this period were (among others) virtually all of those in the disciplines included among standard humanities and social science departments of colleges and universities.

People in this society **gain knowledge and wisdom through experience**. The learning activities continuously take part even when people are retired. The learning activities will never stop until the end of their life. These activities include intellectual readings, attending seminars, forums, and discussions.

CHARACTERISTICS OF A LEARNED SOCIETY

Can be grouped into two historical eras.
1. Before the first world war (Pre 1914).
2. Modern learned society (1919 onwards).

In the pre-world war era, mobility of people was less and slower (no jets and limited migration.) Communication technology was also in its infancy, with no satellites, internet of wireless application protocol WAP, etc. Historically - the great era and early civilizations of China, Egypt, Greece, Rome and the Islamic world could only transfer and share knowledge in a very limited way. Most of the world's population was still largely uneducated and illiterate. Only the few wealthy elite could expect to be well read, well travelled or obtain a university education.

"The education of a man is never complete until he dies".- Robert E. Lee -

ROLE OF KNOWLEDGE MANAGEMENT

Lifelong learning is a deliberate progression throughout the life of an individual, where the initial acquisition of knowledge and skills is reviewed and upgraded continuously, to meet challenges set by an ever-changing society. This is where knowledge must be managed.

For a 'learned' society, nationally and globally, people need to share their learning and experience. **World-wide break through's, in science, medicine and even business, are now instantly shared globally**. The G-Nome project where the mapping of the human genetic code, would probably be the most significant learning.

However, that wouldn't have been possible without the invention of the computer. So, perhaps, indirectly, the advent of the computer micro-chip, started what some call **'post-modernization'**.

KNOWLEDGE MANAGEMENT

Currently, there is a growing awareness of the need for individuals to **take responsibility for their learning**, not just at school, college or university level, but throughout their lives, and to constantly review and update their knowledge and skills.

Organizational policies and systems must ensure that **relevant knowledge must be classified, stored and shared**. Such policies and systems constitute knowledge management.

LIFE-LONG LEARNING

The **purpose of life-long learning** in view of a learning and learned society is to contribute to the **whole quality of life**, which covers the development of people, society and economy as a central vision. **Knowledge and skills** must be **continuously updated,** especially as people face job loss through downsizing. We cannot afford to have the skilled, unemployed**! Knowledge capital is in employed human capital**.

Education and training has been a tool for continuous learning in traditional society as well as modern society. Even with the constant change in our modern society, especially in political, economic, environmental, technological or social changes, the role of education and training are still the same; to develop human capital.

However, due to the nature of change being more rapid and complex, especially in technological areas, every indication, is that **learning needs to become a lifelong and accelerated function**.

If knowledge, skills and learning abilities are not renewed, the capacity of individuals and by extension, of communities or nations to adapt to a new environment will be considerably reduced, if not cut off entirely. Even when people retire, they still have to learn to adjust to a new life-style and learn new skills in terms of retirement hobbies, sports or other activities. The importance for persons to continue learning throughout their active working life and even beyond, will increasingly move to the top of individual, national and international agendas in the future. This is purposeful as well as life-long.

"The only knowledge that matters is knowledge in action"
Tom Brailsford- Knowledge Leadership Department.
Hallmark Cards

THE LEARNING LEADER

HOW FAST CAN YOU LEARN

So far we have talked about the 'speed of change', so the challenge for leaders, not just change leaders, but all, is can we learn faster than our competitors? Can we indeed learn faster than our team members? If we are to gain a competitive advantage that as we discussed earlier in this chapter, learning 'how to learn', and deutero learning where we use the ongoing 'double loop' learning can be a start. Here however, we must move from Organisational to Individual Learning. The concept of Accelerative Learning (AL) can be largely attributed to Georgi Lozanov (1978), a Bulgarian psychologist. He initially developed a technique called 'Suggestapaedia' to help KGB spies, master a foreign language in a couple of weeks.

Fast forward a few decades, with the innovation of functional Magnetic Resonance Imaging (FMRI) techniques, we can now actually understand how learning in the brain, can be accelerated. Essentially it can be summed up as using our 'Whole Brain', as many senses as possible and our multiple intelligences (Gardner, 1995). It involves ways of improving the use of our attention, perceptions and emotional reinforcement. It involves motivation, repetition and reinforcement, and especially understanding the role of both sides of the brain, and how they each learn differently, yet in complimentary modes.

Whole Brain Learning (Shephard, 2007) has been well documented, tried and tested, yet still largely resisted by formal educational institutions, except in a few enlightened countries like Finland and New Zealand. Some equally enlightened large multinationals have introduced many Accelerated Learning techniques, with astounding results, but traditional modes of learning still persist. Much of the effectiveness of AL, is tapping into the brain, when it is an 'alert-relaxed' mode, or what is called 'Alpha' Learning. Our brain waves emit at between .5 up to 25 cycles per second (CPS). When we are wide awake, consciously alert, we are operating at the Beta Level or 13 to 25 CPS. Due to this high level of consciousness, our mind can easily be distracted, until we pass that and enter our alpha level of 8 to 12 CPS.

BRAIN RULES FOR INDIVIDUAL LEARNING

Professor John Medina (2007) has developed a number of principles for more 'whole brained' learning. He has given lectures, made videos and appeared in TED talks that form that elite list of world class speakers. To end this chapter, as well as this book, which after all the reader studies to learn, I have adapted some of John Medina's, as well as other eminent learning specialists ideas, to 'speed' up our learning and hopefully help you digest better, much of this book. (Lozanov, Gardner, Rose, Ibid). There are also some myths that we can expel.

Learning Principle #1: Sleep Well, Learn Well.

The brain itself doesn't sleep, but the brain works differently, yet still hard, while we sleep. Those who get around 8 hrs ± per night have been found to out perform others on cognitive tests (including exams) by 3 to 1, especially procedural tasks. During sleep we process much of our memories, consolidating what we learned that day. **Loss of sleep interferes with attention, judgment, working memory, logical reasoning, movement dexterity** and even mood. In fact, we need to sleep in order to learn. Sleep loss means mind loss or brain drain! Sleep deprivation also weakens our immune system, and over many years, our brains are more likely to succumb to dementia (memory loss). You hear people say "I'm getting old, so I'm losing my memory," but this need not be so, as there are many 80 and 90 year olds who still have excellent memory. They should say, "I'll get enough sleep so my memory will be good".

Learning Principle #2: Exercise: A learning brain needs to move.
Exercise increases blood circulation and blood brings oxygen and glucose to the brain. It stimulates the release of proteins that keep neurons firing and connecting. Aerobic exercise for 20 minutes, 3 times a week is optimal, but some movement, like walking, throughout the learning day helps. Some experts say 10,000 steps a day is ideal! Others advocate some brain movement every 20 minutes together with some stretching and deep breathing to boost oxygen to the brain" (Dennison, and Dennison, 1986). Those who exercise outperform others in, attention, reasoning, problem solving and improved long term memory. More recently the best form of aerobic exercise is HITT (High Intensity Interval Training). Eg: Run as fast as you can for 1 minute, then walk for 2 minutes. Repeat this for 5 times. Sitting still too much can shorten your life!

Learning Principle #3: Attention and Focus
We earlier discussed the role of dopamine, the excitement stimulus hormone, which is produced in the amygdala, a part of our emotional brain. **Dopamine greatly aids information processing and memory, but needs some emotional stimuli**. Learning that can be attached or associated with strong emotions will invariably be remembered, stronger and longer! However, emotional arousal focuses attention more on the 'gist' of the learning, rather than the detail. So 'meaning' comes before detail, which is actually important. Memory is enhanced when we connect concepts and related associations to emotions logically, not randomly. We will understand up to 40% more when each concept is logical. Then the details can be filled in more meaningfully. An emotional connection further strengthens recall.

One myth concerns multi-tasking. The brain cannot multi task, if it is to be very efficient. Think of sitting at your computer/smart phone and an alert comes up "You've got mail". Your attention is stimulated. Now providing you read and answer it, without interruption, you will complete the task 50% faster. Once any other part of the brain gets distracted or tries to do something else, your full attention on what you are doing is dissipated. Eg: answering your email. It is not that you cannot answer the phone, but your mind wanders and when it returns, you will say "now where was I?"

That's why, when our right brain listens to baroque type music, it is not bored, and allows our conscious left to focus attention. This music induces 'Alpha' Learning.

Even when we are aroused and absorbed, our brain can usually only focus for around 10 minutes. It's the right non conscious self that is easily distracted, and the conscious self has to be the prompted. It needs to be constantly brought back on track.Anything that keeps emotional arousal high, will help keep you on track. And that's where the appropriate type of music can be played.

"I do not teach my students. I create a climate which us conducive to learning"

Albert Einstein

Learning Principle #4: Repetition and Memory
Our brain has several types of memory systems. Short term or working memory is when we encode incoming information. It then immediately sends this information to various parts of the brain to 'connect', relate, act or store. Sounds, sights, smell, taste and touch all use different parts of the brain to encode, connect or relate. The sight, sound and smell of sizzling steak on the barbecue and later the taste are good examples of our brain as a multi-sensory and parallel processing system, with each 'experience' being laid down as chemical 'pathways and strengthened when' emotionally reinforced!

When we want to recall the total barbeque experience, we only need one trigger, perhaps the smell of smoke or sight of a flame, and then the whole experience comes flooding back. If we explain this experience to someone else, within minutes, that is repetition. Tell it a few more times, or show a video clip of cooking or eating the steak, and the memory sticks. Don't repeat, or get distracted, and the memory, especially details, can get 'lost'. For example, leaders who teach something, is a great way to reinforce their own learning. Each time they teach, the easier it is.

The more elaborately we encode, and consider the context or surrounding environment, early as possible, and repeat the experience, the stronger our recall will be. Also, the more senses we use, the easier will be our 'total recall'. Trying to integrate the use of as many senses, intelligences and emotions as possible, helps.

Learning Principle #5: Learning Styles – Vital To Know.
This is a classic of nature and nurture! We are born with certain preset circuits hard wired into our body and others 'soft' wired, which therefore we can change. However, genetics, culture and environment kick in. While we are hardwired to learn and speak, what we learn and how we learn differs individually and culturally. Smaller classes, or even home based schooling are better than large classrooms. **Students of the same age show a lot of intellectual variability**. IQ varies enormously with genetics playing a major role. But the style of teaching may not vary!

Even gender differences affect our learning abilities and style preferences. More strongly still our diversity of personality traits. **Left brain learners learn differently from right brainers**. Science, logic, words versus art and philosophy are examples.

Our brain's 'soft' wiring changes constantly as we grow and develop, not only through growing up in a different culture or environment, but also from how we genetically differ in our talents and preferred ways of processing information. Some of us are more precocious, extroverted and curious, asking lots of questions, while others are are more introverted, reflective, quiet and passive. **Some respond to words (auditory), some to pictures (visual), some to movement and touch (kinesthetic) and some to computer aided learning (digital),** where touch and sight are combined. Millenials and the very young are increasingly becoming addicted to tablets and smartphones and most of their schooling and learning will be dependent on technology. Sadly, many will not learn naturally through interpersonal interaction and physical play. Computer games can take centre stage at home, to the detriment of the development of social skills, unless time at the computer is regulated.

What is important here for leaders, is for them to know their own dominant learning style preferences (Active versus passive, logical versus creative, visual or artistic or more balanced (whole brained). Then they must also know the differing styles of their team members. We each learn differently.

Learning Principle #6: Use all Senses – Especially Visual

Remember the expression **"Seeing is Believing"**. Even if we are highly auditory (like I am), where I can 'listen' to TV, but do occasionally need to glance up at the TV, to check out visually, what really is happening. And if I am listening to something I really want to remember, I will usually 'Mind Map' the key points. So the visual is still important. I can listen to long lectures, and love to read with relaxing 60 beat music. Another learner maybe less auditory and more visual or kinesthetic!

The visual cortex is in the largest lobe in the brain, the occipital. We not only see in movement, colour, 3D, but actually it is the brain that 'sees' not the eyes. You may have heard the phrase, the "eyes are the mirror to the soul". The reason why vision is so dominant is probably evolutionary, as most dangers to our existence can be 'seen'. Whether it is a speeding car, the edge of the cliff or the food we eat. **When information is presented to us verbally, we remember only around 10% after 72 hours. But when the information is pictorial, we recall 65% after the same time**. If we want people to recall some facts, numbers or words, link them each to a picture. An effective power point slide should be more pictorial with less text.

Lastly, the other senses of taste and smell are also important, but less so here, where we are talking about leadership. These senses of visual, auditory and touch are similar to the learning styles highlighted in Learning Principle #5 and are each interrelated.

Learning Principle #7: Nutrition for the Brain

There is a saying **"we are what we eat"**, but I would rather say "we become what we eat". As research shows, it can be 10 – 20 years of inadequate nutrients or a poor diet that can lead to brain deterioration and memory loss. Longevity of life, brain health and memory can all be enhanced with the right type nutrition. Of course, sleep and exercise and low stress are other factors, which we cover under other learning principles.

So what nutrients should we include in our diet? We know that glucose is critical to brain energy, as the brain utilizes more glucose than, any other part of the body. But glucose is converted from the sugars we consume and fructose (fruit sugar) is more efficient. Best sources for this are fruits like bananas, (also high potassium) apples, dates, raisins, berries, papaya – **but not too much** – as it might overwork the liver which metabolizes fructose. Glucose also comes from sucrose or starchy sugars, which comes from carbohydrates. The complex carbohydrates in corn, potatoes, or whole grains are slower in conversion to glucose, but also important, yet too much can produce a sugar 'high' and then a sudden 'low', leading to faintness.

Other 'micronutrients' important for the learning brain, are: mono-unsaturated fatty acids – like Omega 3, EFA's, DHA/EPA – from fish or krill oils, tree nuts (almonds and walnuts), some seeds, like sunflower seeds, and primrose oil. Potassium (Bananas, Pistachio nuts) carries oxygen to the brain, whereas Magnesium (Pumpkin and Sesame seeds) helps prevent dementia, as also does Vitamin E (Almonds and Hazelnuts). Also, micronutrients, like lutein, (spinach, eggs, citrus fruits) or flavenols (tea, wine, broccoli) are helpful. Caffeine (20mg or 2 strong coffees) is not only a stimulant, but also enhances memory. However, we need to drink our coffee about one hour after our learning, and not at night time, if we want a good night's sleep!

Various minerals and trace elements are also critical. These include: Calcium, Iodine, Thyroid hormone, Iron, Zinc, Magnesium, Selenium and anti-oxidants. Sources for some of these include potatoes, spinach, orange, apricots and prunes and cashew nuts.Thus, if we consume some of these nutrients, regularly, we will improve our memory, well into old age. However this all reads serious dietary planning!

Learning Principle #8: Gender-Male/Female Brains Differ
As we have already mentioned earlier, brains differ genetically, with 10-12 % more connective fibres between the two hemispheres of the female brain. They also differ biologically and hormonally. Females will use both the left and right language cortices more, producing superior verbal capacity with better verbal speed and memory.

Male brains on the other hand are superior in visual-spatial skills (movement objects in space) from activating the right amygdala, but also from testosterone. Men remembering the 'gist' of things, with the female brain recalling details better. Here, women and men react to stress differently. Women activate their left amygdala, remembering emotional details better than men. Genetically, there is also the difference in the 'X' chromosome, which males only have one, and females having two, with a larger percentage of genes involved in brain development as a result. Men's 'Y' chromosome carries less than 100 genes, whereas the X chromosome has about 1500 genes, giving an advantage to woman and their female offspring.

Biochemically and structurally, men have larger amygdalas, producing serotonin faster (the 'calming' hormone) which results in lower anxiety, more sociability, conscientiousness and a religious / spiritual orientation. Most women produce more of the female sex hormone, estrogen, and oxytocin, which result in stronger introspection and empathy. Women seem to be more drawn to those who are similar. Women are also more prone to depression. And most men produce more testosterone – the male sex hormone – making them more prone to dominance, competitiveness and aggressiveness. This also involves their right amygdala, enhancing visual-spatial capacity. Equally, men seem more drawn to similar types, which perhaps can also lead to 'male' bonding (Fisher, 2014).

BRAINWAVES: Beta,13-15 CPS. Alpha, 8-12 CPS. Theta, 4-7 CPS. Delta, 5-3 CPS

"We hear and forget! We see and remember! We do and understand"
Confuscious

Learning Principle #9: Stress Kills Learning and Memory.
Brains that are stressed don't learn as well! When chronically stressed, surplus
adrenaline (a hormone) triggers the release of another hormone, cortisol. This is

in turn can damage cells in the hippocampus – essential for processing memory. Under an acute stress attack the brain produces chemicals called 'Beta Blockers', which may temporarily close down our 'executive' brain, **preventing us from thinking clearly and logically**. Avoid making important decisions when feeling stressed, other than trying to manage the stress at that moment. Stop, deep breathe, count to 10 slowly, lie down for 1 or 2 minutes and get the heart rate back to normal.

While we do need some positive stress (eustress) in our lives, to get us moving, too much can lead to 'distress'. **Personality types do differ in the amount of stress absorption or tolerance.** However, there is the type 'A' personality (the hare) and the type 'B' (the tortoise). Know your type, and ensure you design a life-style that matches. Some jobs do have a higher level of stress than others. **Leadership, can present a lot of stress,** so generally leaders need a personality that can tolerate more stress. When we slow down, our heart rate lowers and brain waves go into **alpha** and that's what happens during meditation, prayer or even when taking 'power' naps.

COMBINING ALL PRINCIPLES

Ultimate learning is to integrate all 9 Principles into the actual doing of what you are learning. Unless you can do something well, you may not really know what you have learnt. Simulation is safe, but still not full reality. Here we have been talking about the **Individual Learning Leader**. Unless leaders are fully engaged active and life long learners, they cannot be role models. Also, unless each employee is also emotionally motivated to learn, learn by trial and error, share their learning insights, it cannot be called a 'Learning Organisation'. These principles also embody what we call **'Action Learning'**, or now in schools, **'Project Based Learning'** real learning through doing, but reflecting on its success or failure and relearning on all successive attempts. It's **'Kaizen Learning'** and reviewing how each of the 9 principles can become habitual.

SUMMARY OF LEARNING PRINCIPLES

Learning Principle #4, states that we must repeat to remember, so we will repeat all principles, but using two acronyms - another memory technique - **'SEAR'** (to burn into our memory) and **'LUNGS'** (needed for oxygenated blood in our brain)

S – Sleep Well – Learn Well
E – Exercise - A learning Brain Needs To Move
A – Attention and Focus
R – Repetition and Memory – Repeat To Remember
L – Learning styles – Vital To Know Our Preferred Style
U – Use all Senses – Especially Visual
N – Nutrition for the Brain – Eat and Drink for Memory and Brain Longevity
G – Gender Differences in Learning – Men and Women Learn Differently.
S – Stress Kills Learning and Memory – So Manage your Stress

SO! ABOUT LEADERSHIP

There are many qualities, traits, skills or processes. Here are 30 that are covered in this book:

LEADERSHIP IS:
1.   Achieving Goals/Objectives
2.   Being a Role Model
3.   Building High Performance Teamwork
4.   Building Trust
5.   Coaching and Development
6.   Having Courage
7.   Cultural Sensitivity and Respect
8.   Discipline of Self with Others
9.   Empowering Others
10. Encouraging, Praising and Rewarding Effort
11. Engagement of Self with Others
12. Giving Constructive Feedback
13. Having Integrity
14. Helping others grow
15. Influencing Others
16. Innovation and Risk Taking
17. Inspiring Team Members
18. Learning Continuously
19. Leaving a Legacy
20. Listening with Empathy
21. Managing Conflict and Diversity
22. Motivating Self and Others
23. Openness to New Ideas
24. Being Optimistic
25. Questioning for Understanding
26. Right Brained Thinking
27. Showing Enthusiasm
28. Speaking/Writing with Clarity
29. Values Driven/Sharing Values
30. Being Visionary

Some are included as Concepts, Models, Theories or merely as Adjectives

THE COMMON DENOMINATORS ARE:
BEHAVIOUR, PERFORMANCE AND RESULTS

SUMMARY OF KEY POINTS

- Key values and norms of a learning culture include curiosity, innovation, experimenting, risk-taking and sharing.

- Strategy and policy can help create a learning culture. They must promote openness and participation, empowerment and teamwork.

- Organizational learning requires that all individuals are continuously learning, and sharing this learning throughout the organization. For this, we need systems.

- There are 3 levels in the process of organizational learning.
  1) Organizational memory.
  2) Adaptive systems to fulfil self-interests like survival.
  3) Context development and enrichment of own environment and that of all stakeholders, with the leaders, taking ultimate responsibility.

- As much of our learning comes through mistakes, people may not be willing to share this learning, as having to admit mistakes might result in "loss of face". Equally, in order to save face of others and maintain harmony, we may not want to criticize others. This can be a major challenge for leaders!

- A way of promoting learning, and its sharing, is having policies and strategies that allows for and rewards this.

- Challenges for a learning organization include its capacity to adapt quickly to changes brought about by globalization, the rapid pace of change, new technologies, competitiveness and customer expectations.

- There are 2 orders/levels of learning. One is called 'double loop' where you get feedback about problems so you can fix them. The other is about the learning itself. How and why we learn, so we can improve or accelerate our learning.

- Employees do need to understand the culture of their organization. What the symbols, rituals, norms or practices are. These need to be well-aligned and strong, so new employees can be quickly socialized into the culture and that it remains strong, even with employee turnover.

- Strategies that encourage and ensure shared learning occurs, when we include dialogue, meetings, reviews, debriefings and evaluation of learning & training.

- There is a hierarchy of Data, Information, Knowledge and Wisdom. Wisdom in turn helps us select relevant data and turn information into useful knowledge.

- A knowledge society is one that is intrinsically linked to the Knowledge.

- Economy (K-economy). Its context is the creation of wealth so as to improve society's quality of life.

- Knowledge is not - just knowing - it is more, understanding. There is know-what, know-why, know-who, know-where, know-when and know-how.

- A society that seeks to become learned requires that it becomes and continuously stays a learning society. This necessitates that learning is supported and available to all members of that society. Such enabling comes primarily from governments, but can also be from employers and other.

- For organizational learning, the leader needs to be able to learn more and faster. Understanding how we can each accelerate our learning becomes critical. There are 9 principles of individual learning, which when all integrated, provided on ideal receipe for 'Whole Brain' accelerated learning, better memory and brain longevity.

SPECIFIC GOALS FOR KM
The conference board did a survey of 158 organizations on their KM goals. This was the ranking of goals.

1. Share Practices/ Increase Collaboration	*41%*
2. Increase productivity/Use of Knowledge	*18%*
3. Transfer Employee Knowledge	*8%*
4. Increase Innovation	*7%*
5. Improve Decision- Making	*7%*
6. Transfer Knowledge from Customer	*4%*
7. No Specific Goals	*15%*

Gaining Insight
IBM invests systematically in communities of practice. Each has a competency leader and a core team of practitioners. They manage intellectual capital and organizational knowledge through these communities.

GROUP LEARNING
Group learning involves the social aspects of learning. It involves pooling knowledge, understanding the limits to the team's knowledge in each situation and sharing of possible solutions. It respects minority views as these help the team to view as these help the team to view alternatives perspectives and options to achieve 'win-win' outcomes. Unconscious behaviours need to be recognized and understood as well as 'hidden' agendas. Shared learning occurs when any of these processes involve group members.

- *Goals & role clarification*
- *Action learning projects*
- *Cross-functional meetings*
- *Multi-disciplinary teamwork*
- *Benchmarking meetings*
- *Interaction Process Analysis*
- *Computer conferencing*

"Wise people may know what they know, but more importantly they are willing to admit to what they don't know." -Anon-

REFERENCES

A Survey of specific goals of Knowledge Management. (2000). NY: Conference Board Reports.

Argyris, C and Schon, D. (1978). *Organizational Learning : A Theory of Action Perspective.* Mass: Addison, Wesley.

Davenport, T.H. and Prusak, L. (1998). *Working Knowledge:How Organizations Manage What the Know.* Boston: HBS Press.

Davenport,T.H. and Prusak, L. (1998). *Harvard Business Review on Knowledge Management.* Boston: HBR Press.

Denisson, P.E. and Denison G.E. (1986). *Edukinesthetics In Depth, Ventura As Educational Kinesiology Foundation.*

Dryden, G. and Vos. J. (2008). *Unlimited , The New.* Auckland: The learning Web.

Fisher, H. (2014). *Rutgers University Research Paper.* NY: Rutgers University Press.

Gavin, D. (1993). Building a Learning Organization. *Harvard Business Review* , Jul-Aug,Boston.

Gardner, H. (1995). *Reflections on Multiple Intelligence Myths and Messages.* Mass: Phi Delta Kappan,Cambridge.

Kline, P. (1988). *The Everyday Genius. Great Ocean Printers.* Arlington: V.A.

Lozarnov.G. (1978). *Suggestology and Outlines of Suggestopedy.* NY: Gordon and Breach.

Medina, J. (2007). *Brain Rules.* Seattle: Pear Press.

Ornstein, R. (1991). *The Evolution of Consciousness.* NY: Touchstone.

Perkins, D. (1996). *Outsmarting IQ.* NY: Free Press.

Romer, D. (2011). *Advanced Macroeconomies.* McGraw-Hill: NY.

Rose, C. and Nichol, M.J. (1997). *Accelerated Learning for the 21st Century.* NY: Dell Books.

Schumacher, E. (1993). *Small is Beautiful.* London: Random House.

Senge, P. (1990). *The Fifth Discipline.* NY: Doubleday.

Shephard, P. C. (2007). *Personality Matters: A Whole Brain approach to why we Learn, Think and Behave.* Kuala Lumpur: Brainworks Media.

Sternberg, R. (1988). *The Triachic Mind.* NY: Viking.

(1998). *UK Department of Trade and Industry. A report on the Knowledge Economy.* London: UK Government Printers.

GLOSSARY OF TERMS

Ability
The power to perform a physical or mental act. Includes knowledge or skill which is learnable. Natural ability, however, like an aptitude or talent, is more inborn or genetic than learned.

Accountability
From an accounting term – to keep account of - it refers to a responsibility to report back (or up). Managers are (answerable) to their superiors or other stakeholders. To report fully on their efforts / results.

Action Research
Action Research is a set of activities in which a group of people work toward an agreed goal, based on a process of deliberate planning, acting, observing and reflecting on their work.

Adrenalin
A hormone that is secreted by the adrenal medulla in response to stress and increases heart rate , pulse rate and blood pressure and raises the blood levels of glucose and lipids. It can help boost our energy for short period to fight or flee.

Aerobic(s)
The the effect produced when we increase our heart rate to around 2 1/2 times our normal resting heart rate. The effect speeds up breathing and oxygen intake, as well as metabolism. It stimulates the production of the positive hormones called endorphins. These relax us, produce euphoria, and boost our immune system as well as brain health.

Affective
From the word 'affect' .Used to refer to the learning domain that relates to emotions or feelings about a topic. Opposite would be 'Objective'. Rational or raid of emotion.

Affirmative Action
A form of action in policy, strategy and decisions to enhance the status – usually of minorities – such as women in senior position or of ethic groups.

Alpha
The band of EEG Brain wave patterns in the range of 8 13 cycles per second (Hz), usually taken to indicate the absence of arousal, and therefore, a more relaxed state.

Ambiguos/ity
Where situations or outcomes are uncertain or unsure, as in risk taking. Where messages are unclear or mixed.

Amygdala
An organ or section of tissue in the limbic system and is involved in the processing and expressing of emotion, especially anger and fear.

Anatomy (eg Left and Right Brain Hemispheres)
The science of the structure or composition of organisms.

Analysis
To break down elements of a situation (eg a problem) into measurable elements. It requires logical and critical thinking. (left brain) Opposite to this is synthesis or putting elements together (right brain).

Aptitude
A capacity or natural talent or giftedness. More inborn rather than learned. It includes all the intelligences

Astrocytes
One of the large number of micro nerve cells (glia) that enhance and protect the functions of neuronal networks, especially the synapses.

Attitude
A person's disposition or outlook towards something. It stems from values, needs and feelings.

Authority
The right to influence other individuals or groups.

Autocratic
The leadership style, sometimes called authoritarian, where the leader dictates the planning and execution of tasks with little or no participation from subordinates.

Autonomy
The extent to which an individual is given freedom on the job.

Axon

A long fibre extending from a neuron, which transmits messages to other neurons.

Baby Boomer(s):

Refers to a generation of people born between 1946 and 1960. Comes from the large number of young service personnel returning after World War 2 – and the result - an immense increase in babies born during that era.

Baroque

A period of history from around early 1600 to 1800 AD., when a certain style of music and art were produced. The music has a 60 beat tempo which is close too, resting heart rate and in synchronicity with alpha brains waves of relaxed alertness.

Beta

A band of EEG brain wave patterns in the range of 13 - 30 cycles per second (Hz), indicating an aroused state such as when actively thinking.

Behaviour

To act or react in a specified way. Sometimes instinctive, non-conscious or influenced by thinking and/or emotions.

Benchmarking

To assess whether products, services, practices and performances are of a certain standard and quality, comparing them against a standard or benchmark. Such benchmarks are usually other organizations who are known to excel in producing these products and services.

Biology

The science or study of living organisms and how they function, includes genetics and physiology.

Birth Weight

When babies are born below average weight their body and brains maybe under developed, resulting sometimes in lower intelligence or other handicaps in brain or body.

Brain Waves

Electro-magnetic impulses, rather like radio-waves. When we are alert (BETA) the electrical activity operates at a higher frequency of hertz or cycles per second. The lower frequency rates are called Alpha, Theta & Delta.

Career

A career can be a sequence of related working experiences over a period of time, sometimes they are very similar, with little variety or change. Other times we may experience more variety or change when we change career direction.

Cerebral Cortex

The thinking brain is an eighth of inch thick, intricately folded layer of nerve cells that covers each brain hemisphere. The outlayer comprises tightly packed neurons, call 'grey matter' the neurons have longer white nerve fibres that reach out in a complex network to all parts of the brain. This is the 'White Matter'. If this cortex is unfolded, it would spread out like a thick mat (1/8th inch thick) of about 30 x 42 cm.

Cerebrum

The largest past of the brain, divided into two halves, or hemispheres, which are connected by 300 million nerve cell fibres, called the Corpus Collosum. It is covered by the cerebral cortex.

Ceremonies

The formal activities conducted on some important occasions by organizations which tend to become recognizable aspects of their culture. (eg: an anniversary or annual awards dinner)

Character

Values and traits that form the individual <u>nature</u> of personality. The values can be changed through experience.

Charisma/tic

A special personal quality or magnetic energy of leaders making them capable of influencing or inspiring people.

Chaos Theory

A theory, applied in various branches of science, where apparently random phenomena have underlying order

Coalitional

The forming of a 'partnership' between the leader and his team, or other groups, that together can produce a greater output. From word 'coalition' or coalescence (to gell) .

Collectivism

The degree that people behave that strongly reflects, or adheres to, the collective values and norms of a group or culture.

Competence

A broad term that includes the ability, capability or skill to perform well some tasks or functions. May include appropriate attitudes, knowledge or skills (loosely applies to individual, team, task, job or an organization).

Cognition (Thinking)
The mental process of knowing about something through perception, reasoning or intuition. (Thinking). Sometimes called thinking

Cognitive Map
A personal mind map or a mapping of the thoughts an individual has about a particular situation or problem of interest.

Conceptual Thinking
Is the ability to identify patterns or connections between situations that are not obviously related, and to identify key or underlying issues in situations. Ability to conceive thoughts and ideas.

Conscious
Aware of one's own existence, sensations, thoughts, surroundings, etc. A state of Beta brain waves and left brain activity in learning. When we are aware or alert.

Context High/Low
High context is that which is close to, or in harmony with, natural laws and nature (flow). Low context is the opposite and is more contrived for 'man-made'. Sometimes applied to cultures or behavior.

Contingency Leadership
Dependence on chance or on the fulfillment of a condition. In leadership, it is a style of behavior that is situationaly determined.

Convergent
One of two or more lines, paths, etc moving towards or meeting at some common point or two forces or ideas tending toward the same result of merging. Use of logic and analysis in left brain thinking.

Corpus Callosum
A dense body of fibres that joins the two cerebral cortices of the brain. (Part of White Matter).

Cortex
The outer layer of the brain, such as the grey matter in the brain that cover the cerebrum.

Cortisol
Often referred to as the primary stress hormone. When we experience stress, the hypothalamus secretes another hormone that stimulates the pituitaries to produce ACTH, which in-turn stimulates the adrenals to secrete cortisol, which can suppress our immune response leading to higher susceptability to descease.

Creativity
The ability to transcend traditional ideas, rules, patterns, relationships, to create meaningful ideas, forms, methods, interpretations

Critical Thinking
Identifying and challenging assumptions that underlie ideas, beliefs, values and actions.

Cronyism
The word 'crony is slang for close friends or even relatives (Nepotism) to whom leaders may extend favours.

Culture
The characteristics of a group of people that include those values, norms, symbols, rituals, artifacts or taboos that represent that group. (Can be of a team, class, organization, ethnic group, tribe or nation).

Culture Mapping
A way of mapping or profiling a culture according to various criteria. Such as in brain dominance and collective thinking styles. Eg: if a group is more cerebrally left in their thinking preferences, this gives an indicator of their preferred behavioural patterns.

Data
Individual facts, statistics, or items of information, which represent the results of data analyses.

Delta
A band of EEG brain wave patterns in the range of .05 - 4 cycles per second (Hz) indicating deep, dreamless sleep.

Demographics
This refers to the measurable aspects of demography, which is the study of human populations in terms of size, density, location, age, sex, race, occupation.

Dendrites
Short fine branches from neurons that receive impulses (messages) from other neurons through their synapses.

Dissonance
A term often used in psychology to denote opposing internal forces or values, as in 'cognitive' dissonance, when we want to do two opposing things equally as much at the same time

Dimentia

A brain disease where decline in mental ability progresses slowly often caused by a stroke, whereby memory, thinking, judgment and the ability to pay attention and learn deteriorate. Alzheimers is a common type of dementia.

Divergent

Separate and to go in different directions An aspect of creative thinking where we open up to new and unusual ideas.

Diversity

In terms of people, organizations or even cultures, language/dialects, it includes differences in any or all of; age, gender, ethnicity, personality traits, culture or religious beliefs, occupations, professions language/dialects and sexual preferences. (Not acceptable in some cultures).

DNA

Deoxyribonucleic acid. A molecule containing hereditary information to be passed on to the next generation.

Dominance

The condition where one member of a paired organ is principally used, often naturally and unconsciously (e.g. eye, hand or brain hemisphere)

Double loop learning.

Occurs when mismatches or errors are corrected by first examining and altering the governing variables and then taking action.

Drive

An extension of Temperament, strongly chemical and rooted in the Limbic System. It is that which energises us, a force or need felt within that we feel to achieve, be with people (affiliation) or influence others (power).

DueteroLearning

A form of '2nd order' learning, which is about 'learning how we learn'. It includes organizational and individual learning. Understanding and evaluating the learning processes and preferred learning styles.

Dyad/Dyadic

A Dyad means two (a duet). Dyadic linkage, is the vertical relationship between leaders and each team member. basis.

Effectiveness

The 'effect' or impact or outcome that is desired. "Doing the right thing."

Efficiency

A positive ratio of output to input. "Doing things the right way". (Reducing input of costs, energy, time etc).

Empowerment

Is the act of putting employees in charge of what they are do. Delegating more authority or power.

Emotions

The production of brain chemicals in the limbic system, that produces a feeling. Maybe consciously felt and expressed or non-consciously, like instincts. These in turn can also produce chemicals.

Emotional Intelligence

Skill in perceiving, understanding, and managing emotions and feelings in self and ability to empathize and read emotions in others.

Empathy

Ability to see things from another's perspective. To literally put one self in another persons shoes. To understand how others think and feel.

Empowerment

To give power or authority to; authorize, especially by legal or official means. In leadership if denotes trust and delegating authority and autonomy.

Engagament

The relationship between an organization and employees and their team members. A high level of engagement infers there is frequent two-way communication and might include coaching, training, regular dialogue on employee performance, feedback, development needs and plans etc.

Ergonomics

The study of body movement and shape. Is utilized in the design of machines, machine systems, production methods and the physical environment, especially chair or car seat design.

Endorphins
A type of hormone or endocrine produced in the brain that reduces stress, pain and enhances relaxation and learning.

Endrocrines
An internal secretion; one of a type of hormone.

Equity
In the simplest form, this term generally means fairness, with neither party having an unfair advantage over another. In organizations, it includes non discrimination among employees.

Equity Theory
This is a motivational theory attributed to the social psychologist, J. Stacy Adams.

Ethnic/ity
The more specific subsets of people within racial, geographic or cultural groups, who's DNA is closely related. Sometimes referring to Tribal or Clan similarities.

Estrogen
The female sex hormone, a chemical messenger that determines some female characteristics and may help neuro-transmitter function. In leadership, it can influence behaviourial differences.

Ethics / Ethical
The conduct of human behaviour that may include moral or legal standards, often guided by values or codes of professionalism, such as in business or leadership behavior.

Entrepreneur
A person who displays the interests and drives to initiate new ventures. More often they are commercial in nature. The entrepeneur possesses strong right cerebral brain dominance, displaying, creativity, imagination innovation and risk taking.

Explicit Knowledge
Knowledge that is documented and widely available to be used and shared. (The term is used in Knowledge Management) The opposite is 'Tacit', or only known by employees.

Extrinsic Motivation
Motivation resulting from factors external to the individual.

Extrovert
A personality trait, under temperament, that needs an external frame of reference of people or objects. Quickly and easily exposes thoughts, reactions, feelings, etc. to others)

Facilitator / Elicitor
A person who pays constant attention to group processes, the roles of individuals in the group, and the business of drawing out knowledge and insights from the group. Ensures everyone's ideas get heard.

Feng Shui
The Chinese art or practice of creating harmonious surroundings that enhance the balance of yin and yang, as in arranging, doors, windows for the flow and direction of positive energy from wind, water and sun.

Flow
A term to describe a feeling we have when energy is aligned and our life- force or 'chi' flows positively through our body, free of mental or physical blocks. When we are performing well, we can say we experience a "flow" state. It is both psychological and physiological in nature.

Force-field Analysis
A theory by Kurt Lewin, which states that every behavior is the result of a balance between driving and restraining forces. The concept is to analyze the forces 'for' and 'against' and developing strategies to maximize the 'fors' and minimize the inhibitators.

Frontal Cortex
A section (lobe), of the brain towards the front and includes the 'Pre Frontal' lobe. This area is associated with logical, analytic and judgmental thinking. Sometimes called our 'executive' brain, where decision analysis takes place.

Generational Eras
Baby Boomers (born between 1946 - 1960) and a series of generations, born before 1945 that has come to be labelled as Traditionalists. Gen X refers to these born between 1961 – 1980, Gen Y, those born between 1981 and 2000 and Millennials, those born after the new millennium (2000)

Genetics/Genes

Pertaining to or from genes, the coded inherited material in every living cell, which determines a predisposition for all the characteristics of an organism and much of its 6ehavior, including talent, intelligence, temperament and many other personality traits.

Genius (IQ)

A high level of any of several intelligences (Artistic, Intellectual, Musical etc). Originally referred to as Intellectual intelligence rated above 140 on a quotient (IQ), (average is 100). Now we recognize that Picasso was an art genius or Mozart, a musical genius.

Gen Y

Refer generational eras

Gen X

Refer generational eras

Glass Ceiling

The invisible barrier in organizations that prevents many women from achieving top level management positions.

Globalization

Where trade, money, information, business, products or services freely move across borders or when companies having production facilities away from their home base.

Glocal

A form of hybrid thinking.Thinking 'global' while respecting and acting 'locally'. Attributed to a frenchman-Andre Laurent.

Goal Setting

Agreeing on (and writing down) desired targets or end results.

Grey Matter

The cell bodies of neurons in the brain, close to its surface, but also exists inside the spinal cord.

Group Dynamics

Processes of interaction (synergy) among group members which facilitate a groups operation.

Groupthink

A strong concurrence-seeking tendency that interferes with effective group decision making, due to members seeking harmony and avoiding conflict or disagreement. Includes an illusion that group is invulnerable.

Hard-Wired/Wiring:

Where our neural networks are are strongly genetic and difficult to change. Those instincts, traits or behaviours are said to be 'Hard-wired'.(opposite is 'soft-wiring' – see neurogenesis).

Heart-Math

The concept that there are neural connections between the brain and heart (as also with many others organs, like the stomach). When stressed for example, chemical messages direct the heart to pump more blood to the brain.

Hemisphericity

The tendency of one brain hemisphere (left and right) to be dominant, independent of the task.

Hippocampus

An organ or piece of tissue in the limbic system. Plays a critical role in learning and memory

Holistic/Wholistic

Viewing things as inter-dependent and related. Looks at the whole or total picture, rather than only its parts

Homeostasis

The processes that ensure a physiological and psychological balance, or the production of a state that is normal and stable. When stressed it is returning to a normal state.

Hormones

Sometimes called endocrines. They are a chemical substance produced in the brain and body. They influence emotions as well as behaviourral activity. Some are positive and healthy, others can be negative and stressful. They are controlled by the endocrine system.

Human Resource Management (HRM)

In broad terms, HRM embodies all the important decisions and practices that have a direct impact or influences on the employees (or human resources), includes HRD, L & D or Talent Management (see abbreviation).

Hybrid

The result of mixing two or more phenomena such as in genetics, where the cross breeding results in a new breed. May also refer to ideas, policies, practices or mixing cultures. Some times the result in superior and is called 'Hybrid Vigour'.

Hypothalamus

A part of the limbic system. About the size of a pea, it regulates eating, drinking, sleeping, waking, body temperature, some balance and directs the pituitary gland to produce or pump out some hormones.

Incentives

Normally used to label those benefits used to induce or reward behavior or motivation. Relates to extrinsic motivation, and might include financial or non financial factors.

Individualism

The degree that people are free to express themselves or behave as themselves individually, rather than by adhering to the collective values or norms of a group or culture.

Immune System

This is the body's natural defense mechanism that prevents or fights disease. It can be boosted by exercise, diet or sleep. Lack of these, or stress, can reduce our capacity to ward of infections, illness and many diseases.

Innovation

The result of creative thinking to produce new products or processes. Innovation is an output, whereas creative thinking is the input.

Intrinsic Motivation

Motivation resulting from inner feelings of satisfaction (eg: from having achieved a challenging goal or a high level of competence).

Intelligence

The ability to think, reason, solve problems, learn or adapt to the environment. There are many types of intelligence. Intellectual intelligences is only one of many types of intelligence. (Refer Gardner, 1999).

Introvert

A personality trait, under temperament that needs an internal frame of reference directed more towards inward reflection and understanding than toward people and things outside of self. Slow to expose reactions, feelings and thoughts to others.

Intuition

Knowing something without thinking it out - having an instant understanding without need for facts or proof. It can be a gut feel (limbic) or a hunch (cerebral), but only in the right brain.

Job Design

The structuring of a job in terms of duties, responsibilities, scope of authority, conditions and grade. Job redesign is a restructuring to suit better the job holder.

Just-In-Time (JIT)

The concept of JIT was originated by the Toyota company of Japan. Its main objectives are to eliminate waste, including excess raw materials, work-in-process, worker time or machine capacity. EG: The delivery of parts just-in-time, thus saving storage space or cost.

Kaizen

A Japanese word that means improvement. It also means continuing improvement in work, personal, home and working life.

Kinesthetic

Refers to touch or body movement. Gardner (1999) describes one type of intelligence as 'Body-Kinesthetic', where sports people, dancers or gymnasts are strong in this. A learning style where learning comes more easily through touching, movement or actually doing something physical is called kinesthetic learning.

Knowledge

Knowing or familiarity gained by experience. It builds on data, and information. It exists only in human minds. The next level is understanding and application (knowledge in action).

Leadership

The process of inspiring people through a shared vision, mission & goals and aligning their values and energy to motivate them to achieve the goals. The process may also use influence or power to persuade others.

Learning

Occurs when an people in a problem situation invent, then produce solutions. It can include the transformation of knowledge into understanding.

Learning Organisation

An organization that develops its people to be proactive and able to adapt and change. They should all share the learning that is relevant. Shared understanding and solutions.

Learning Styles

The preferred way that we find we can learn more, better and faster- including how we process information and produce recall. For example, some learn better from visual, auditory, or touch (kinesthetic) and digital stimuli.

Legitimate Power

It is the power a person is given because of their position in an organization. It is also known as formal authority or position power.

Limbic System

Mammalian Brain/Mid -Brain. The centre for instincts and emotions. Also where short term memory is processed. Includes the Amgydala and Hippocampus.

Locus of control (Internal vs External)

This refers to the degree people think or believe they are in charge of their own fate. (Internal) or that influence is controlled by external forces.

Mammalian Brain

Also referred to as the 'Mid-Brain' or Limbic system, or emotional brain (See limbic system)

Management

It has variously been described as an art or science. It is both. Some say it is getting things done through and with people. Some describe it as the process of setting and achieving goals and objectives through the five management functions of planning, organizing, staffing, leading and controlling. It can be differentiated from leadings, as most, management processes are more 'left brained' and leading more 'right' brained.

Mentor

This refers to an experienced and usually senior person in the organization, who would have acquired enough wisdom and trust to be an advisor, helper or councellor.

Mental Model

Refers to both the semi-permanent 'tacit maps' of the world which people hold in their long-term memory, and the short-term perceptions which people build up as part of their everyday reasoning processes

Metacognition

Seeing inside our own thought processes: the process of meta cognition means thinking about thinking.

Millenials

Those born in the new millennium (year 2000 or after) some may use the term generation 'Z'. Some people in the USA call Millenials what is also Generation 'Y' (Gen Y). Refer also to generation eras.

Mind

That which the brain does, as in thinking, reasoning, understanding and intellectual powers, including memory. There is a conscious mind (left brain) and non-conscious (right brain).

Mind/ful/ness

The mind is what the brain does. If the brain is the hardware then the mind is the software. There is the aware or conscious mind (left hemisphere) when brain waves are in Beta mode (15-30 CPS). Mindfulness is when we are fully conscious and behaving from a fully aware state. (eg: Mindful of the consequences) Opposite is 'Mindless' or not 'Thinking'/ a non-conscious state.

Mission /Mission Statement

A statement of why the organization exists and its purpose of being, or its main functional purpose and what it hopes to achieve broadly.

Monochronic

A term derived from the Greek word mono, meaning one, and chronos meaning time. It refers to people or cultures who prefer to do things one-at-time, in a linear or sequential mode.

Motive/Motivation

The reasons or purposes for our behaviour. The felt needs that produce our motivational drives to behave.

Mutation (Genes)

The alteration or change in the function of some genes in a person. We only inherit around 50% from our parents, the remainder changing, due sometimes to changes in environment, after conception, and some inherited from earlier generations, where gene function remained dormant for one or more generations. A genius like Einstein was probably due to a mutation, but some mutations may be 'negative', such as body deformities or brain abnormalities (Downes Syndrome. Autism etc).

Need/s

A deficiency experienced at any point in time, the perception of which can be a precursor to drives. Maybe instinctive and physiological or psycho-social. Can be conscious or non-conscious.

Nepotism

Normally refers to the giving of special favours and privileges, to the employing of one's kin, who may argue their case from the viewpoint of loyalty. (kinship)

Neuron

The basic unit of the nervous system (also called a nerve cell), consisting of a cell body, axon and threadlike projections (dendrites) that conduct electrical impulses.

Neural Networks

Also referred to as neural circuits. This is a network of linkages of various neurons, where connectivity is responsible for types of brain function. For example, the connectivity between neurons in the left and right hemispheres, or between neurons in the prefrontal lobes (logic/judgement) and the limbic system (emotions).

Neurogenesis

The growth of new genes or gene functions. When genes are damaged or destroyed, perhaps through brain injury, like stroke. New genes can grow, replacing the damaged or lost genes. Some Neuro Scientists claim a form or neurogenesis occurs as we develop new behaviours or change habits (Unlearning and relearning) or changes in the brains 'soft-wiring'.

Neuro-Physiology

The study of the bio-chemical effects on the brain and behavior, which includes hormones and neurotransmitters. Thus can include effects of food and drink on behavior, such as caffeine, camomile, tryptophan, sugars or alcohol, or nutrients like flavenols, vitamins or essential fatty acids (Omega 3+6). It also includes the study of the chemistry of sleep, stress or exercise.

Neuro- Transmitter

One of approximately thirty messenger molecules that transmit impulses between neurons to neurons. Stored in axon terminals, this substance is released into the synaptic gap when a neuron fires and locks onto a receiving cell's dendrites. They are aided by astrocytes (clumps of micro calls around dendrites).

Non-Conscious

This term used more widely is 'sub-conscious', but there is also 'unconscious'. It is the opposite to conscious and is a preferred term to differentiate these states. Unconscious relates more to not being conscious (like being knocked unconscious). Whereas our 'non-conscious' brain is our enormous reservoir of memories that reside in our right hemisphere of which we are unaware while consciously thinking.

Objectives / Goals

Broad, general or specific statements of what an organization, department, group or individual plans to achieve. Usually measurable in terms of quality, quantity, cost or time.

Optimism/tic

A type of positive attitude that people display. It has a strong genetic predisposition, as we often use the terms 'born optimist". Statistically, optimists tend to achieve more, are healthier and live longer. It is considered an important trait for entrepreneurs and leaders. (The opposite is pessimism).

Organisational culture

Refers to a set of common values, belief, attitudes and norms that are shared by all members of an organization.

Organisational Context

Includes the way the organisation is structured and how it operates, but also its 'culture'.

Oxytocin

A hormone that plays a role in human bonding, empathy and expression of love or affection. One party who displays empathy or affection can also boost the flow of oxytocin in the other party. We often use the term that there is a good 'chemistry' between people.

Participatory Management

The involvement of stakeholders at all levels in analysis of problems, development of strategies and implementation. It implies asking, listening and sharing in information and decision making.

Perception(s)

The act of sensing anything from our environment, through our six senses, and interpreting or placing a meaning on them. The core of perception is this interpretation. Perception may trigger drives and behaviour.

Performance

The outcome of ability, motivation and behavior of individuals at any activity (work, sports etc).

Personality

The total make-up of a person's mental, emotional, social and physical characteristics - especially drives, talents and temperament. A combination of strongly genetic traits (Nature) as well as learned or shaped by the environment (Nurture).

Philosophy / Values
The philosophy of an organization is its "belief system", based on the thinking and values of its leaders, governors and / or employees. This guides its mission, purpose, ethics and policies. Leaders themselves also have values.

Physiology
The science of dealing with the functioning of living matter. May include components of physics, and chemistry and is a sub-set of Biology. (See also Neuro Physiology)

Plan/Planning
The setting out of a course of action steps that, when carned out, produce results. We can have short-term or tactical plans, ongoing operational plans, or longer-term strategic plans. (See also goals/objectives).

Plasticity
Refers to the degree that parts of the brain's soft-wiring (some neural networking) is malleable and can we rewired.(See also neuro genesis)

Polychronic
A perception or application of activity in time, where more than one thought or task can be done together. A type of parallel processing often at random or in no specific order or sequence.

Policy/cies
A guiding rule(s) applied to a point in a system. A guideline for an entire range of functions (like pricing) or behaviours.

Power/Influence
The capability of A to exercise influence over the attitudes or behavior of B. The influence can be 'authority'.

Power Distance
Refers the extent to which the less powerful members of the organization or family accept and expect power to be distributed unequally. The distance between the leader and subordinates show the extent of the distance (eg. Large Power Distance in a tall hierarchy or small power distance in a flatter hierarchy. (Hofstede, 1976).

Pre-Frontal Cortex (See also Frontal Cortex)
The area of the brain in front of the Frontal Cortex.

Pro-Active
Thinking or behavior that anticipates or is ahead of, events.

Problem
A deviation from what is normal. When our normal pace or progress is blocked or slowed by an obstacle.This obstacle may be called the problem, which can be physical or behaviourial).

Productivity
The ratio of output to input - ideally, so output exceeds input and produces desired results and standards. Ratio of output to input also determines efficiency.

Professional
Often refers to a way of thinking and behaving, but is derived from the word profession. This is typified by work of a highly skilled nature, such as law or medicine, for which people are paid well and often enjoy a higher status. Professional behaviour would include working to high standards of competence, reliability and with honesty and integrity.

Psychology
The study of the mind and behavior of individuals. There can be normal or abnormal psychology. Or the study of groups (Social Psychology/ Sociology). Organizational or Industrial psychology (Now more commonly called Organizational Behaviour, (OB) and relates more to leadership.

Psychiatry
Psychiatry relates to the medical profession, where psychiatrists must be a medically qualified and can prescribe drugs for mental diseases, as counseling the mentally ill.

Psychomotor
Literally it means 'mind and movement.' 'Psycho' is the function of the mind, 'motor' refers to the motor cortex of the brain, which governs all movement of all parts of the body including the coordination, synergy or control of mind and movement. Learning in this mode is about learning through touch, movement and related skills (eg: kicking a football) and requires eye, brain and body coordination.

Psychopath
A psychological term used to describe a person with serious abnormal obsession or types of behavior or mental disorders. Psycho means 'mind' and pathic comes from pathology or diagnosis of disease.

Purpose
Similar to Mission, it is the "reason" for existing, for being, for doing. The purpose is guided by the philosophy, values and vision of the organization, or by an individual.

Quantum Physics
A study of the subatomic particles, such as electronics, as a theory of uncertainty in how they would behave. (Chaos Theory). They could however be predictable based on probability. In leadership it is used to analyse patterns of energy and motion in peoples especially as part of motivation and spiritual energy.

Quality Control Circles (QCC)
Groups or teams of employees who voluntarily participate to improve quality and productivity. Sometimes called Quality Circles (QC's) or Quality Improvement Teams (QIT's).

Racial
A race is a broad term that relates to people from the same geographic region such as African, Arab, Caucasian or Native American etc. (Also refer to 'Ethnic').

Raplexity
A word coined by Dr. Jagdish Parikh, that is a hybrid of 'Rapid' and 'Complex', such as in 'change'.

Rapport
The degree of emotional closeness or 'wave length' between people, especially when communicating. When we 'think alike; or empathize of feel we understand each other well, we can say we have close or good rapport. It is a french word that denotes harmony or connectivity between people's mental and emotional states. Used in communication and NLP.

Rational
The use of reason or logic, (eg: Rational Thinking). The opposite would be emotional, but the emotional brain is more powerful than the rational brain. Strongly felt emotions can override logical or rational thinking.

Re-active:
(Refer also to 'Pro-Active) Is when we re-act to something without having thought it out. Our temperament is displayed when we 'react' to situations-such as being angry or remaining calm.

Referent Power
This is fifth category of power referred to by French and Raven and refers to an individual's desirable traits of resources that attract others to him or her (similar to 'conferred').

Relational
Refers to a style of leadership that focuses on employee relations, such as in Leader Members Exchange (LMX) or as in high levels of employee engagement.

Religiosity
Sometimes called 'Religiousness'. Thought to be strongly shaped by genetics, rather than learned or culturally shaped. No matter how strictly we maybe indoctrinated into a religious belief, there will always be digress of strength versus weakness, or even absence of the belief. (Eg: A family of three children, brought up with the same religious beliefs, once mature, one maybe a strict and strong believer, an extremist the second, may become more more open, liberal or moderate and the third may not be a believer at all. (Note- where there is a strong cultural peer pressure to comform, the disbeliever maynot publicly admit it)

Reptilian
Pertaining to an ancient part of the brain at the beginning of the brain stem (adjoining the limbic or mammalian brain). It is responsible, for primitive and instinctive functions such as basic survival, territorial protection of personal space, grooming and breeding.

Rites/Rituals
With regard to organisatonal culture, these are the regular practices that are representative – and perhaps unique – to that culture. They may include ways of greeting people, communicating, conducting meetings.

Role ambiguity
Uncertainty surrounding the requirements of a particular role, either by the organization or by the individual.

Secular
A term used to describe where state and religion are separated. A culture, society or country often includes a statement, ruling or guideline that maybe in the constitution. The opposite to secular is 'religious', which maintains that a particular religion dominates the affairs of state and government.

Semi Autonomous Work Groups (SAWG)

Associated with the socio-technical systems school of thought, where groups of workers are given considerable autonomy and control over a complete unit of work which enables them to be responsible for planning, organizing, coordinating, executing and evaluating their work.

Seratonin

A brain chemical or hormone that acts as a neurotransmitter. It is responsible for producing positive, calm or relaxed mood changes. It regulates awake-sleep modes. Also effects heart rates and blood pressure.

Skill/s

A demonstrable and learned proficiency or technique, using the brain and/or body. Such as movement of hands or body (motor skills) or thinking (cognitive skills). It includes a feedback loop.

Single loop learning

Single loop learning is a term borrowed from electrical engineering or cybernetics where, for example, a thermostat is defined as a single-loop learner. In learning at work, it is a single feedback loop. It includes a feedback loop.

Socio-Technical Systems Approach (STS)

An approach which views behavior in organizations as a function of both social and technological factors which are independent but also interdependent.

Soft skills

Usually refers to human or interpersonal relations skills, such as communication and leadership motivation. Includes some thinking and emotional behavioural skills, and especially relates to emotional intelligence. Tends to be more 'right' brained , contrasted to its opposite, left brain skills which are quantitative, analytic or physical-such as in accounting, carpentry or engineering. ('Hard' Skills)

Spatial

The perception and undestanding of the relative position of objects in space and to manipulate them into a desired relationship. (see also 'Visual-Spatial').

Spiritual

An emotional feeling we have, when we experience phenomena that makes us feel at one or in harmony with the world around us. It maybe a natural or religious phenomena. For religious people, the act of worship or feeling the presence of God may also be described as religious spirituality. For non religious people, they may experience the feeling of harmony and energy (spirit) when by a waterfall, inspiring vision or by an example.

Spiritual Intelligence

Refers to a situation where one is connected with one's self, others and the entire universe and fully understand the feeling of spirituality.

Split-Brain

A term used to describe the two hemispheres or values of the Brain, that are separated or "Split." A Break through understanding occurred when Nobel Prize winner Dr Roger Sperry and his team in the 1960's, conducted experiments with brain damaged and epileptic patients. The two cerebral hemispheres were surgically separated and studies revealed the different behaviours dominant in each hemisphere.

Stakeholder

A person involved in, or affected by, the process of developing any organisational change or strategic intervention, or the outcomes of that intervention.

Strategy / Strategies

General programs of action toward the attainment of comprehensive objectives, with commitment to resource utilization, and the direction on how they will be applied. They give plans their details for implementation. It involves positioning the organization to provide a competitive advantage.

Stress/ Stressor

A physiological response of the body to an external event, or perception of the event's consequences, It produces heightened or reduced change with physical and later, psychological effects. This response is stress, which may be positive (eustress) or negative (distress). The causes of these are called stressors.

Structure

In organizations, it is a framework of how people or roles report or relate to each other, usually in a hierarchy. It includes the lines of authority, responsibilities and accountabilities. There are tall hierarchies with many levels, or flat, matrix, centralized or decentralized in terms of authority.

Style

Usually associated with behaviours, such as communication or leadership. Can be natural or preferred, such as an innate part of personality, but can also be learned, such as cultural, or modeled on the behavior of others.

Suggestapedia/ Suggestology
Originally conceived by a Bulgarian Psychologist, as a learning technology, used to 'accelerate' the learning of languages by 'Russian Spies' (KGB). Later, it become widely used in many areas other than language ; and is know variously called 'Accelerated' or Quantum or Whole Brained Learning. It uses multi-sensory and 'alpha' brain wave learning techniques.

Symbols
In culture, especially organizational culture, symbols are the things we can see the represent that culture. They are like the tip of the iceberg or outlayers of an onion.

Synapse
The microscopic gap between two adjacent nerve cells. Chemical neuro transmitters carry nerve impulses across the synapses.

Synergy
The interaction of elements that when combined produce a total effect that is greater than the sumof the individual elements, contributions. Whole brain thinking is synergy between both sides.

Synthesis
Literally the opposite to Analysis. It is the process of synergized (whole brain) thinking where ideas or concepts are put together. (see also Synthesizing)

Systems Thinking. A type of thinking is based upon the ideas of emergence, hierarchy, communication and control as characteristics of system. It links the parts with the whole information.

Tactics
The action plans through which strategies are executed. They are the 'nuts and bolts' and may change rapidly, depending upon the situation of environment.

Tacit (Knowledge)
A form of knowledge , only known to an individual, which may include knowledge and skills unique to their a persons experience. It is unknown to others, so is not documented. The opposite is 'explicit' knowledge.

Talents
Genetically endowed 'gifts' or natural aptitudes or intelligences.

Technopreneur
A type of entrepreneur, who has skill and experience in areas of technology and is entrepreneurial in nature.

Thalamus
Two contiguous egg shaped masses of grey matter at the base of the brain. Both of these masses are considered as one functional unit.

Theta
The band of EEG brain wave patterns in the range of 5 - 8 cycles per second (Hz). A barely conscious level associated with creativity and a free flow of ideas and images. A state of deep relaxation. May include day dreaming or even light sleep.

Temperament
The tendency to think, learn and act in certain ways. An inborn biological pre-disposition to behave in predictable and unique ways. A key compoment of personality. It is also why we react in certain ways.

Testosterone
The male sex hormone, or chemical messenger, responsible for many male characteristics and behaviour, especially aggressiveness.

Time
The measure of the duration or passing of activity, usually man-made, and described by seconds, minutes, hours, days, months or even years. It is also a feeling or a perception, when we talk about time 'flies', 'drags' or even 'stands-still'. There is also natural time, like biorythms, menstrual cycles, seasons, daytime or night time, sunrise/set, higher or low tide, or the luna calendar (moon).

Traditionalist
Refers to the age or generation of people, born before the end of worldwar 2 (1945). That means aged 69 years or more.

Traits
A distinguishing characteristic or quality, especially of one's personal nature. It is enduring and generally remains stable after age 25 – 30. Often described as consistent as predictable patterns of the characteristic.

Transformational Leadership

A style of leadership where whole systems are changed/improved through highly participative involvement of employees leading to strong commitment to change.

Transactional

Refers to a style of leadership, where we state – or negotiate- that certain tasks should be done according to the leaders direction. In return, the employees will be compensated (a transaction).

Transformation process

Refers to how organization transforms inputs (labour, money, equipment, supplies etc) into outputs (goods or service).

Triune Brain

The separation of the brain into three component layers. Described by Dr Paul Maclean as evolutionary in sequence from Reptilian to limbic to cerebral.

Uncertainty

Stems from unpredictable chains of events and from excessive complexity. The reduction of uncertainty is the major objective of organizations in the information processing perspective. It is partly reduced by structuring activities inside the organization, and enhancing control over the environment.

Values

A strongly held principle or belief of what is right or important, which strongly influences behaviour

Vision

Based on the belief, values, dreams and hopes of the organization – and its leadership – it shapes the mission and goals. Its what we hope to become.

Visualization

To recall or form mental images or pictures (See also 'spatial').

Visual-Spatial

One of our many intelligences, where we coordinate what we see (visual) with the size, shape, movement, speed or direction of objects in space.For example driving a formula one car, landing a fighter aircraft on an aircraft carrier or hitting a tennis ball accurately. These are all visual-spatial skills, but can also be at the micro-level, like threading a needle.

Vocation

A description for a type of work, job, or profession which we feel strongly attracted to. A type of 'calling' in which we are drawn or feel 'destined' to follow.

White Matter

Connective fibres of brain cells, consisting of axons and their whitish coating called myelin. They transmit messages deeper into the brain and connect both hemispeheres through the corpus callosum.

Whole Brained

Using our 'Whole' Brain, which rarely happens at the same time, as the many parts of our brain are used for specific functions (Hearing, Seeing, Touching and Movement, Smelling and Tasting). We may use The parts separately (Close eyes, sit still and smell) or simultaneously, as we combine other senses. We may think and reflect on how we feel. (The Cerebral combined with the limbic parts). Then we may analyse the meaning or cost (Our left cerebral) and admire the colour, shape or texture (our right cerebral). Thus using the many parts, almost instantly can be said to be ' whole brained'. Here, when we use all our senses together, we can say whole brain learning and thinking occurs.

X and Y Chromosomes

There are 46 chromosomes, each carrying the DNA and genetic information that makes us who we are. 23 chromosomes, some from our mother, and 23 from father. At least one has to be an 'X'. Females have two X chromosomes, and men have an X and Y. The Y carries less than 100 genes, and the X about 1500 genes. Many of these govern how we think, some types of intelligence and social behaviours and verbal skills. They also strongly determine a lot of gender differences in cognition, emotions and behavior.

GLOSSARY OF ABBREVIATION

AA	Affirmative Action
AI	Appreciative Inquiry (A positive OD and change intervention)
AL	Accelerated Learning/Action Learning
BCG	Boston Consulting Group
BSC	Balanced Score Card
CPS	Cycles per second (Hertz) Brain Waves Speed
DHA	Docosallexaenic Acid. An essential Fatty Acid in Nutrition
DNA	Deoxyribonucleic acid
EEG	Electro Encephalographic (Brain Imaging)
EEO	Equal Employment Opportunities
EFA	Essential Fatty Acids (Eg: Omega 3)
EPA	Eicocasa Pentagenoic Acid. An essential fatty acid in nutrition, such as Omega 3.
FFA	Force Field Analysis (Analysis of change enablers or inhibitors)
fmRI	Functional Magnetic Resonance Imaging
HITT	High Intensity Interval Training
HCM	Human Capital Management
HR D/M	Human Resources/Developmeny/Management
IR	Industrial/Labour Relations
IPA	Interaction Process Analysis (after Bales)
IT	Information Technology
JIT	Just-In-Time
KM	Knowledge Management
LMX	Leader-Member Exchange
MBO	Management by Objectives
MBWA	Managing By Walking Around
NLP	Neuro Linguistic Programming. The study of excellence in how people process information and use language in the brain.
OD/T	Organisation Development/Transformation
OB	Organisational Behaviour
PCDA	Plan, Check, Do and Act
PESTELIED	Political, Economic, Social, Technical, Environmental, Legal, International, Ethical/Ecological, Demographic
QA	Quality Assurance (Prevention ahead of control)
QC/C	Quality Control/Quality Circles/Quality Control/Quality Circles
QIT	Quality Improvement Teams (Builds on QCC)
ROAM	Return on Assets Managed
ROI	Return of Investment
SAWG	Semi Autonomous Work Groups
SDCA	Stabdardize, Do, Check Act
SQC	Statistical Quality Control
SWOT	Strengths, Weakness, Opportunities and Threats
SX	Social Exchange
T/T+	Theory T and T Plus (Hofstede)
TPM	Total Preventative Maintenance
WASP	White Anglo Saxon Protestant (their work ethic)